Principles
of
Sufism

by al-Qushayri

Translated from the Arabic by
B.R. VON SCHLEGELL
With an Introduction by
HAMID ALGAR

 Mizan Press, Berkeley

LIBRARY OF CONGRESS CATALOGING IN PUBLICATION DATA
Qushayri, 'Abd al-Karim ibn Hawazin, 986-1072.
   [Risalah al-Qushayriyah.   English   Selections.]
   The Principles of Sufism / by al-Qushayri; translated
from the Arabic by B.R. von Schlegell.
          p. cm.
   Includes bibliographical references and index.
   ISBN 0-933782-21-7 : $25.95
   ISBN 0-933782-20-9 (pbk): $14.95
   1. Sufism—Early works to 1800. I. von Schlegell, B.R.
II. Title
BP189.Q7313   1992
297' .4—dc20   92-82685
                                           CIP

CONTENTS

INTRODUCTION

Contrary to the frequent supposition of some Western scholars and numerous present-day Muslims, Sufism is neither an extraneous growth owing little to the authoritative sources of Islam nor a sectarian development that occurred at a given point in Islamic history. It had a hidden and implicit existence in the Islamic revelation from the very beginning, and even when it became an identifiable and, in some measure, autonomous mode of Islamic practice, its integration into the spiritual, intellectual, social, and even political life of the community remained unmistakable. This is apparent not only from the tone and content of al-Qushayri's great work on Sufism, the *Risala,* but also from the principal events of his life.[1]

Abu'l-Qasim 'Abd al-Karim b. Hawazin b. 'Abd al-Malik b. Talha al-Qushayri was born in the month of Rabi' al-Awwal 376/July 986 in the small town of Ustuwa in northeastern Iran. Like many other historical sites in Khurasan—the richest center of civilization in the eastern Islamic world down to the Mongol conquest of the seventh/thirteenth century—Ustuwa has disappeared without a trace, although it is thought to have been near the present-day city of Quchan, which may even have been constructed on its site. On his father's side, Abu'l-Qasim was descended from the Bani Qushayr, one of the Arab tribes that had settled in Khurasan in the course of the Muslim conquest. His mother too was of Arab descent, from the Bani Sulam. The family appears to have been both prosperous and learned. Al-Qushayri's maternal uncle, Abu 'Uqayl 'Abd ar-Rahman b. Muhammad, owned a number of villages in the Ustuwa area and was a renowned scholar of *hadith;* he was one of al-Qushayri's earliest instructors in that discipline. Al-Qushayri's father died when he was young; otherwise we know little of his earliest youth, except that he swiftly acquired a superior command of Arabic, primarily from a certain Abu'l-Qasim al-Yamani, and learned horsemanship and the use of weapons, skills not usually associated with a Sufi master.

At a date that cannot be established, al-Qushayri realized that a village his father had left him was being excessively taxed. Determined to prevent such abuses from recurring, he decided to go to Nishapur, study accounting and arithmetic, and join the fiscal administration. Nishapur was the greatest city of Khurasan, so large and populous that some of its quarters were big enough to be separate towns by the standards of the time. It was the political and administrative capital of Khurasan and a major center for trade and manufacturing, being particularly celebrated for its pottery and textiles. All the scholarly disciplines of traditional Islam—Qur'anic exegesis *(tafsir),* prophetic tradition *(hadith),* jurisprudence *(fiqh),* theology *(kalam),* Arabic grammar *(nahw),* and, not least, Sufism *(tasawwuf)*—were represented there, and it was most probably in Nishapur that the institution of the *madrasa* originated.

It is not surprising that al-Qushayri, already grounded in Arabic learning, was soon deflected from the study of accounting to the religious sciences. The change was occasioned by an encounter with a Sufi master, Abu 'Ali ad-Daqqaq, an initiatic descendant of Junayd al-Baghdadi (d. 297/910), the great exponent of "sober" Sufism.[2] Al-Qushayri relates that he so revered ad-Daqqaq that he would always fast and make a complete ablution *(ghusl)* on the days he went to see him; even then, he would tremble uncontrollably in his presence. Ad-Daqqaq rewarded his devotion by recognizing him as his foremost disciple and giving him his daughter, Kadbanu Fatima, in marriage. But at the same time, he directed al-Qushayri to pursue his studies with various prominent scholars in Nishapur. This was in itself an indication both of the interrelatedness of Sufism with the other religious sciences and of the collegial ties maintained by Sufis with specialists in other disciplines.

Most important for al-Qushayri was the study of *hadith*. In the course of his life, al-Qushayri studied *hadith* with at least 17 different authorities, and in turn transmitted *hadith* to as many as 66 students. From investigation and memorization of *hadith*, Qushayri derived not only a mastery of the *sunna* and its application to Sufism but also the methodology he used in compiling the *Risala,* his recording of sayings together with the chain of transmission *(isnad).*

The first teacher to whom ad-Daqqaq sent al-Qushayri was Abu Bakr Muhammad b. Bakr at-Tusi, the Shafi'i *mufti* of Nishapur; with him he studied not only *hadith,* but also the Shafi'i school of law, to which he remained devoted throughout his life. With Abu Bakr Muhammad b. al-Hasan

b. Furak (d. 406/1015), he studied both *hadith* and the Ash'ari school of theology. His formal education in the religious sciences seems to have been completed under the aegis of Abu Ishaq al-Isfara'ini (d. 418/1027), a scholar who administered his own *madrasa* in Nishapur. Al-Isfara'ini noted that unlike the other students, al-Qushayri did not take notes on his lectures, but questioning revealed that he had committed everything perfectly to memory. Accordingly al-Isfara'ini declared him free of need to attend his classes; it would be enough for him to read whatever he wished and consult al-Isfara'ini when necessary.

Ad-Daqqaq died in 412/1021, and al-Qushayri continued his Sufi training with another prominent figure of Nishapur, Abu 'Abd ar-Rahman as-Sulami. The period spent under his guidance must have been brief, however, for as-Sulami died later the same year, and al-Qushayri seems always to have regarded himself as the pupil of Abu 'Ali ad-Daqqaq. He also kept the company of Abu 'Abdallah Muhammad ash-Shirazi, a companion of Ibn Khafif (d. 372/982), the well-known Sufi master of Shiraz. But al-Qushayri's ties to Abu 'Abdallah were not those of a student to his teacher; he learned from him not the principles of Sufism but a number of the anecdotes concerning past Sufis that were incorporated in the *Risala*.

Tradition also associates al-Qushayri with another celebrated contemporary, Abu Sa'id b. Abi'l-Khayr (d. 441/1049). In many ways, al-Qushayri was the exact opposite of Abu Sa'id. The heir to the "sober" Sufism of al-Junayd, he was at all times concerned with demonstrating the congruity of Sufism with the *shari'a* and he was deeply involved in the cultivation of the formal religious sciences, above all *hadith*. By contrast, Abu Sa'id had swung from an extreme of asceticism and self-mortification to an extreme of suspicious ease and opulence at the *khanaqah* hospice where he resided in Nishapur; his was an ecstatic Sufism, given more to the recitation of poetry than to that of *hadith*. It might therefore be assumed that the two Sufis had hostile relations with each other, somewhat like those between al-Junayd and al-Hallaj in third/tenth-century Baghdad. However, the only evidence for contacts of any nature between the sober Sufi and his ecstatic counterpart is contained in the *Asrar at-Tawhid,* a biography of Abu Sa'id written by his grandson, Muhammad b. Munawwar b. Abi Sa'id.[4] In typical hagiographic fashion, the author is concerned to establish the absolute supremacy of his subject, and he would have us believe that al-Qushayri invariably came off the worst in his encounters with Abu Sa'id. This in itself casts doubt on the accuracy of his account. There were those in Nishapur who attended the circles of both Abu Sa'id and al-Qushayri, which suggests that the two men were not implacable enemies. Nonetheless, it is re-markable that the *Risala* contains no reference at all to Abu Sa'id; al-Qushayri must have regarded him at least with mild disfavor.

In 432/1040, at a time when al-Qushayri's prominence as a Sufi and scholar had become firmly established, the city of Nishapur passed definitively from the control of the Ghaznavids to that of the newly ascendant Saljuq dynasty. Whether al-Qushayri played any role in the events surround-ing this transfer of power or manifested any reaction to it is unknown. He appears to have had initially good relations with the first Saljuq ruler, Tughril (r. 429/1038–455/1063), obtaining from him the appointment of a protégé, Abu Sahl b. al-Muwaffaq, as leader *(ra'is)* of the Shafi'is of Nishapur.

Soon, however, the position of al-Qushayri was endangered by the religious policies of Tughril's minister, 'Amid al-Mulk al-Kunduri. An adherent of the Hanafi legal school and possibly a Mu'tazilite in theological persuasion, al-Kunduri gained permission from Tughril to initiate a campaign against the Shi'is *(ar-rawafid,* in the polemical language of the day) and against "innovators" *(ahl al-bid'a).* The latter is an imprecise term that seems to have indicated primarily, in this particular case, followers of the Ash'ari school of theology.[5] For reasons that are difficult to discern, there had taken place in Nishapur (as well as elsewhere in Khurasan) a near identification of the Ash'ari school of theology with the Shafi'i school of law, so that the assault on Ash'arism was in effect an attack on the Shafi'is as well.[6] The Shafi'is were the largest single community in Nishapur, but the city also contained a number of Shi'is, adherents of the Karamiya, and, most importantly, Hanafis. The history of pre-Mongol Iran is replete with bloody rivalries between Hanafis and Shafi'is, who often chose to be residentially segregated from each other, and when al-Kunduri showed himself hostile to the Ash'ari-Shafi'is, the Hanafis of Nishapur responded with delight. They prevented their opponents from teaching and preaching in the principal mosque of the city, and matters went so far that Abu'l-Hasan al-Ash'ari (d. 324/935), founder of the Ash'ari school, was cursed as an unbeliever from the pulpit.

Al-Qushayri did not remain indifferent to these developments. In 436/1044, he issued a *fatwa* (authoritative judgment) to the effect that the views of al-Ash'ari were fully in accord with the Sunni creed. Despite this challenge to al-Kunduri and his appointees in Nishapur, al-Qushayri was able to pursue his own activities in teaching Sufism and

hadith, although constantly harassed. Matters came to a
head in 446/1054 when al-Qushayri wrote an open letter to
the *'ulama'* of the Muslim world complaining of the vexa-
tions to which the Ash'ari-Shafi'is were exposed ("The
Complaint of the People of the Sunna Relating the Persecution that Has Befallen Them"). Thereupon al-Kunduri gave
orders for the arrest of al-Qushayri and other notables of Nishapur. Some, including the great Ash'ari theologian Imam
al-Haramayn al-Juwayni (d. 478/1085), succeeded in escap-
ing and making their way to Mecca, but al-Qushayri was
dragged from his house by a mob and imprisoned in the
citadel of Nishapur. His imprisonment did not last long; Abu
Sahl, the Shafi'i *ra'is,* gathered a force that stormed the citadel and released him. Somewhat unwisely, Abu Sahl made
his way to Tughril in Rayy, seeking to justify his actions, but
he was peremptorily imprisoned at the behest of al-Kunduri.
Al-Qushayri went to Baghdad, where he was well-received
by the Abbasid caliph, al-Qa'im bi Amri'llah, who had him
teach *hadith* at the palace, and by the *'ulama'* of the city.

Some accounts maintain that his sojourn in Baghdad was
preceded by a visit to Mecca, where he joined al-Juwayni
and other refugees from Nishapur. There he is said to have
intuitively perceived the disgrace and execution of al-Kunduri
and to have advised his fellow exiles that it would now be
safe to return to Nishapur. This is doubtful, and the story may
well be based on a confusion between this absence of al-
Qushayri from Nishapur and a performance of the *hajj* that
had taken place several years earlier. It is likely that al-
Qushayri's itinerary on this occasion took him from Nishapur
to Baghdad and then back to Nishapur, which he soon left
again for a brief sojourn in Tus.

On the death of Tughril in 455/1063 and the succession

of Alp Arslan to the Saljuq throne, al-Kunduri was indeed put to death and replaced in the vizierial office by Nizam al-Mulk. The new minister was himself a Shafi'i and sympathetic to Ash'ari theology, and it was not long before the Shafi'is recovered their lost privileges in Nishapur. Al-Qushayri accordingly returned to Nishapur from Tus, and the remainder of his life was spent there without apparent incident. He died on Rabi' al-Awwal 16, 465/December 31, 1072, almost a nonagenarian, and was buried next to his master, Abu 'Ali ad-Daqqaq.

Al-Qushayri's impact on his contemporaries was considerable. From 437/1045 onward, he was constantly engaged in the teaching *(imla')* of *hadith,* not neglecting this pursuit even during his two journeys outside Khurasan. Thousands are said to have "received" *(akhadha) hadith* from him in the traditional manner. He also maintained a *duwayra*—a kind of lesser *khanaqah*—in Nishapur where he trained his disciples in Sufism and gave instruction in his own books.[7] Apart from those who had such intimate contact with him, he attracted the townspeople of Nishapur to his sermons, which were renowned for their excellence in style and content.

He had a total of six sons: three by Kadbanu Fatima, herself a woman of scholarly accomplishment, and three by a second wife, the daughter of a certain Ahmad b. Muhammad al-Charkhi al-Baladi. Several of them became important scholars in their own right; a commentary on the Qur'an entitled *at-Taysir fi 'Ilm at-Tafsir* frequently attributed to Abu'l-Qasim al-Qushayri is in fact the work of his son, Abu'n-Nasr 'Abd ar-Rahim. The pattern of erudition persisted at least into the third generation, and included female as well as male descendants of the great master.[8] The Qushayris became in fact one of the four principal Shafi'i families of

Nishapur, and administered a *madrasa* that bore their name.

Al-Qushayri's greatest legacy, however, consisted of his writings.[9] He seems to have been conscious of their value himself, for he employed a number of scribes to copy them under his supervision and used them as texts in many of the classes he taught. Not all of the works attributed to him have survived, and by no means all of those have been printed. Apart from the *Risala,* there are six published works of al-Qushayri.

Lata'if al-Isharat bi Tafsir al-Qur'an is a complete Sufi commentary on the Qur'an, which al-Qushayri began writing in 437/1045.[10] The two significant words in the title— *lata'if* ("subtleties") and *isharat* ("indications")—were no doubt chosen by al-Qushayri in allusion to a celebrated dictum of Imam Ja'far as-Sadiq (d. 148/765). He had discerned four levels of meaning in the Qur'an: the *'ibara* (obvious verbal meaning), directed to the mass of believers; the *ishara* ("indication," which lies beyond the obvious verbal meaning), perceptible to the spiritual elect among the believers; the *lata'if* (further subtleties lying beyond the indications), addressed to the saints *(awliya'),* the elect among the elect; and the *haqa'iq* (ultimate truths), comprehensible only to the prophets.[11] In his commentary al-Qushayri does not discuss the *'ibara* of the Qur'an (having dealt with it, perhaps, in another *tafsir,* now lost); nor does he seek to unveil the *haqa'iq.* It is the second and third levels of meaning that he elucidates in a melodious prose of exemplary lucidity. He had been preceded in the Sufi exegesis of the Qur'an by Sahl at-Tustari (d. 283/897) and as-Sulami, and *Lata'if al-Isharat* shows particularly strong signs of influence by the latter. Al-Qushayri's work nonetheless stands out as an elegant summation of the first period in the evolution of Sufi *tafsir*.

Sharh Asma' Allah al-Husna is al-Qushayri's elucidation of the 99 names of God, together with the ethical and spiritual lessons to be drawn from their contemplation.[12]

At-Tahbir fi't-Tadhkir is a somewhat fuller work on the same theme.[13]

In *Kitab al-Mi'raj*, al-Qushayri examines the nature and meaning of the ascension of the Prophet (upon whom be peace) and also considers the claims of certain *awliya'* to have accomplished ascensions of their own.[14]

Ar-Rasa'il al-Qushayriya is a collection of three brief treatises of which the most interesting is *Tartib as-Suluk,* a description of al-Qushayri's own method of wayfaring—something not to be found in the *Risala,* for all its voluminousness.[15] Particularly significant is the recommendation that the initiate should gradually proceed from the cultivation of vocal *dhikr* (remembrance of God) to silent *dhikr,* the *dhikr* of the heart.

Four more short treatises are collected in *Arba'a Rasa'il fi't-Tasawwuf.*

The fame of al-Qushayri has always rested principally on his *Risala,* generally known as *ar-Risala al-Qushayriya.*[17] More fully, and perhaps more correctly, it is sometimes entitled *ar-Risala ila's-Sufiya,* "The Epistle to the Sufis," for despite its great length the book is intended, at least formally, as al-Qushayri's missive to the Sufis of his age. Like many of the early Sufis, al-Qushayri was filled with profound dismay at the apparently degenerate circumstances of the day. Shallow and deceitful men had emerged who, falsely invoking Sufism, claimed to have reached spiritual degrees that exempted them from the observance of the *shari'a*. It was al-Qushayri's aim to counteract their influence by providing an accurate and comprehensive record of the lives, teachings and practices of the earliest and most authoritative figures, those whom the Sufis of his own time should emulate. Sufis, however, were not the only intended audience of the book; al-Qushayri was also concerned to demonstrate to all the *shar'i* appropriateness of distinctive Sufi practices (such as *sama'*) and to show that the creed of the Sufis was identical to that of the *Ahl as-Sunna* (in its Ash'ari formulation).

Those twin purposes—reminding Sufis of authentic ancestral tradition and vindicating Sufism against those who doubted its legitimacy—had already inspired two earlier Arabic compendia on Sufism: the *Kitab al-Lum'a* by Abu Nasr as-Sarraj (d. 378/788) and *at-Ta'arruf li Madhhab Ahl at-Tasawwuf* by Abu Bakr al-Kalabadhi (d. 391/1000); later Sufi writers frequently invoked the same purposes as well. It can be said that Sufism has often been marked by a sense of historical pessimism, an awareness of spiritual decline that the Sufi must strive to arrest.

In the opening pages of the *Risala*, al-Qushayri explains his purpose in writing. In the first two chapters, he discusses the creed of the Sufis, laying particular stress on *tawhid* and the relation of the divine attributes to the divine Essence. Then comes the first main division of the book: a mention of 83 Sufis of the past. After tersely characterizing each of them, al-Qushayri provides a selection of his sayings, complete with *isnad*. It is noteworthy that a number of contemporary shaykhs are named at various points in the *Risala*, but none of them—not even Abu 'Ali ad-Daqqaq, al-Qushayri's own master—has a section devoted to him in the biographical part of the work. Al-Qushayri may have wished to observe a certain discretion with regard to the living.

Then follows a lengthy section on the terminology of the Sufis, each term being analyzed in terms first of its etymology and general usage and then of its particular Sufi application. Next comes a series of chapters on various stations and states that the Sufi traverses in his wayfaring. Each of these chapters is introduced by apposite quotations from the Qur'an and *hadith* and is built upon a reasoned succession of dicta by past authorities, always accompanied by full *isnad*. Finally, al-Qushayri deals with various aspects of Sufi practice and technique: the dealings of the *murid* with the shaykh and his fellows, the permissibility of *sama‘*, the meaning of saint-hood *(wilaya)*, the significance of dreams, and—above all—the permanent necessity of observing the *shari‘a* with all its minutiae.

Al-Qushayri himself gave instruction in the *Risala* to his pupils and associates, providing them with a license *(sanad* or *ijaza)* to teach it in turn to others. This was the customary mode of transmission for books of *hadith*, and it is one more indication of the close relation that existed between early Sufism and the science of prophetic tradition. He lectured on the *Risala* even while traveling outside of Nishapur; a copy of the work used by him for this purpose in Baghdad still exists.[18] After al-Qushayri's death, the transmission of the *Risala* seems to have become a widely established tradition in several cities, notably Ghazna. Najm ad-Din Kubra (d. 617/1220), the eponym of the Kubrawi order, is known to have studied the *Risala*, receiving an *ijaza* from a certain Abu'l-Fadl al-Hamadani,[19] and Mawlana Jalal ad-Din Rumi (d. 672/1273) alludes to it in the *Mathnawi* as a text commonly studied by Sufis.[20]

The attention continuously paid to the *Risala* is indicated also by the commentaries written on it and the translations made into different Muslim languages. In 893/1488, Zakariya al-Ansari, who had an *ijaza* for teaching the *Risala* that went back to Abu'l-Mahasin 'Abd al-Wahid ar-Ruyani, a pupil of al-Qushayri, wrote a commentary on difficult or obscure terms and passages of the *Risala* entitled *Ahkam ad-Dalala 'ala Tahrir ar-Risala.*[21] Al-Ansari's work was greatly expanded in 1271/1854 by Mustafa Muhammad al-'Arusi (an adherent of the 'Arusi branch of the Shadhili order) with his *Nata'ij al-Afkar fi Bayan Ma'ani Sharh ar-Risala al-Qushayriya.*[22] Two other commentaries in Arabic remain in manuscript: Sadid ad-Din Abu Muhammad al-Lakhmi's *ad-Dalala 'ala Fawa'id ar-Risala,* completed in 638/1240, and one by the celebrated Herati scholar, Mulla 'Ali al-Qari' (d. 1014/1605).[23] There is also a partial commentary in Persian by Sayyid Muhammad Gisudaraz (d. 825/1422), the well-known Indian Chishti; he criticizes al-Qushayri in several connections.[24]

A complete Persian translation of the *Risala* was made by a pupil of al-Qushayri, Abu 'Ali Hasan b. Ahmad al-'Uthmani, who was evidently an important *hadith* scholar in his own right.[25] There are two translations in Ottoman Turkish, one by Hoca Sadeddin Efendi (d. 1008/1599) and one by es-Seyyid Mehmed Tevfik; the latter was commissioned by Bezm-i Alem Sultan, the mother of Sultan Abdülmecid (r. 1255/1839–1277/1861).[26] Likewise, there are two translations in Modern Turkish: that of Tahsin Yazici *(Risale,* Istanbul, 1966, 2 vols.) and that of Süleyman Uludağ *(Doğuş Devrinde Tasavvuf,* Istanbul, 1978). An Urdu translation of the *Risala* by Pir Muhammad Husayn was published at Islamabad in 1970.

The influence exerted by the *Risala* on Sufi literature has been considerable. The *Kashf al-Mahjub* of Abu'l-Hasan 'Ali

Hujwiri (d. 464/1071?), the earliest complete treatise on Sufism in Persian, is indebted to the *Risala* for much of its contents. Al-Ghazali (d. 505/1111) can also be presumed to have drawn on the Risala when compiling his *magnum opus*, the *Ihya' 'Ulum ad-Din*; he had in common with al-Qushayri a threefold devotion to Sufism, Shafi'i *fiqh,* and Ash'ari theology. Much of the anecdotal material in the first part of the *Risala* is reproduced in the *Tadhkirat al-Awliya'* of Farid ad-Din 'Attar (d. 617/1220). Parts of the *Minhaj al-Fuqara'* of the Turkish Mevlevi master and commentator on the *Mathnawi,* Ismail Ankaravi (d. 1041/1631) read like a paraphrase of the *Risala*. Traces of the *Risala* in the literature of Sufism are, however, too numerous to be gauged even by an extended listing of specific titles.

The first attempt at translating at least a portion of the *Risala* into a European language was made by a certain Mme. Olga de Lébédew, whose *Traité sur le soufisme de l'imam érudit Abou 'l-Qasim* was published in Rome in 1911. This amateurish endeavor was followed by a much more scholarly work, Richard Hartmann's *al-Kuschairis Darstellung des Sufitums mit Übersetzungs-Beilage* (Berlin, 1914), consisting of a lengthy summary of the contents of the *Risala* together with extracts in translation. An English translation of the biographical section of the *Risala* was presented in 1935 by W.M. Hume as a doctoral dissertation to the Hartford Seminary in Connecticut. More than fifty years later, came a complete and meticulous translation of the entire text into German: Richard Gramlich's *Das Sendschreiben al-QusaYris über das Sufitum.* (Wiesbaden, 1989). With its extensive annotation bearing witness to the textual erudition of the translator, this version must count as one of the principal sources available in a European language for the study of Sufism.

The purpose and scope of the present volume — the first published attempt at presenting in English a significant portion of the *Risala* — are more modest. The sections chosen for translation relate to the stations and states of the Sufi path: 43 chapters beginning with repentance *(tawba)* and ending with longing *(shawq)*. This represents half the complete text. Sufism is a discipline notoriously difficult to define, but given the perennial centrality to Sufism of the topics discussed in the translation, the title *Principles of Sufism* seems justified.

It should finally be remarked that the chains of transmission given by al-Qushayri have generally been omitted; only the first source of each saying is identified.

Hamid Algar
Rajab, 1412/January 1992

1. Accounts of the life of al-Qushayri are to be found in: Ahmed Ates, "Kuseyri," *Islam Ansiklopedisi;* Badi' az-Zaman Furuzanfar, introduction to Abu 'Ali Hasan b. Ahmad al-'Uthmani, *Tarjuma-yi Risala-yi Qushayriya,* Tehran, 1345 Sh./1966, pp. 14-73; Heinz Halm, "al-Kushayri," *Encyclopaedia of Islam,* new ed.; and Qassim al-Samarrai, *The Theme of Ascension in Mystical Writings,* Baghdad, 1968, Vol. I, pp. 29-50. All these list the primary sources on which they have drawn. There is at present a single monograph devoted to al-Qushayri: Ibrahim Basyuni*, al-Imam al-Qushayri: Siratuhu, Atharuhu, Madhhabuhu fi't-Tasawwuf,* Cairo, 1392/1972.

2. The complete chain of descent of ad-Daqqaq is as follows: Abu'l-Qasim an-Nasrabadhi, from Abu Bakr ash-Shibli, from Junayd al-Baghdadi, from Sari as-Saqati, from Ma'ruf al-Karkhi, from Da'ud at-Ta'i, from Habib al-'Ajami, from Hasan al-Basri, from 'Ali b. Abi Talib, from the Prophet (upon whom be peace). See 'Abd al-Ghafir ash-Shirazi, *Kitab as-Siyaq,* f. 97a of the facsimile reproduced by Richard N. Frye, *The Histories of Nishapur,* Cambridge, Mass., 1965.

3. See Furuzanfar, *op. cit.,* pp. 22-25, 37-44.

4. See Muhammad b. Munawwar, *Asrar at-Tawhid,* ed. M.R. Shafi'i-Kadkani, Tehran, 1366 Sh./1983, index s.v. Qushayri. On the relations of al-Qushayri with Abu Sa'id, see also R.A. Nicholson, *Studies in Islamic Mysticism,* Cambridge, 1921, p. 33.

5. Concerning the persecution of the Ash'aris, see H. Halm, "Der Wesir al-Kunduri und die Fitna von Nishapur," *Die Welt des Orients,* VI:2 (1971), pp. 205-233.

6. See, on the assimilation of Ash'ari doctrine by the Shafi'is, H. Halm, *Die Ausbreitung der safi'itischen Rechtsschule von den Anfängen bis zum 8./14. Jahrhundert,* Wiesbaden, 1974, pp. 32-42.

7. Concerning the meaning of *duwayra,* see the explanation of Mujtaba Minuvi cited by Furuzanfar, *op. cit.,* p. 19, n. 1.

8. A genealogical tree of the Qushayri family is given by Halm in *Die Ausbreitung,* p. 61.

9. A list of all the writings attributed to al-Qushayri is given by Carl Brockelmann, *Geschichte der arabischen Litteratur, erster Supplementband,* Leiden, 1937, pp. 770-772.

10. Published Cairo, 1981 (2nd. ed.) by Ibrahim Basyuni in three volumes.

11. Paul Nwyia, *Exégèse Coranique et Langage Mystique,* Beirut, 1970, p. 167.

12. Ed. Ahmad 'Abd al-Mun'im 'Abd as-Salam al-Hilwani, Cairo, 1969.

13. Ed. Ibrahim Basyuni, Cairo, 1968.

14. Ed. 'Ali Hasan 'Abd al-Qadir, Cairo, 1384/1964.

15. *Ar-Rasa' il al-Qushayriya,* ed. Pir Muhammad Hasan, Karachi, 1964, contains, in addition to *Tartib as-Suluk, Shikaya Ahl as-Sunna bi ma Nalahum min al-Mihna* and *Kitab as-Sama'.* There are two other editions of *Tartib as-Suluk:* one by Fritz Meier in his article "Qushayri's Tartib as-Suluk," *Oriens,* XVI (1963) pp. 15-28, followed by a German translation on pp. 29-39, and the other by Qassim al-Samarrai, *The Theme of Ascension in Mystical Writings,* pp. 158-177, with an abridged English translation on pp. 179-182.

16. Ed. Qasim as-Samarra'i, Baghdad, 1389/1969. The four treatises are *Mukhtasar fi't-Tawba, 'Ibarat as-Sufiya wa Ma'aniha, Manthur al-Khitab fi Mashhur al-*

Abwab and *al-Qasida as-Sufiya*.

17. There are several editions of the *Risala*. That which has been used for the present translation, is the one prepared by 'Abd al-Halim Mahmud and Mahmud b. ash-Sharif and published in Cairo in 1385/1966 under the title *ar-Risala al-Qushayriya*. An earlier edition, frequently reprinted in Cairo and Beirut, includes Shaykh al-Islam Zakariya al-Ansari's commentary on the *Risala* in its margins; the original lithograph appeared in Cairo in 1330/1912. The commentary of al-Ansari gave rise to a super-commentary: Mustafa 'Arusi's *Nata'ij al-Afkar al-Qudsiyya fi Bayan Ma'ani Sharh ar-Risala al-Qushayriya* (Bulaq, 1290/1873); this includes in its margins the text of the *Risala* as given by al-Ansari. Both these earlier editions, as well as the Persian translation of al-'Uthmani, have been consulted.

18. Furuzanfar, *op cit*, p. 71.

19. *Ibid.*, p. 72.

20. *Mathnawi*, ed.R.A.Nicholson, Vol V, Leiden, 1933, p 423 (Book Six, l.2653).

21. Al-Ansari's commentary is printed in the margins of the 1367/1957 Cairo edition of the *Risala*.

22. Published in four volumes, Cairo, 1290/1873.

23. See Katib Celebi, *Kashf az-Zunun*, eds. Yaltkaya and Bilge, Istanbul, 1971, Vol. 1, col. 883.

24. According to Furuzanfar (*op. cit.*, pp. 72-73), part of this commentary has been printed in Hyderabad, Deccan.

25. See Furuzanfar's introduction to this Persian translation, p. 73.

26. See Tahsin Yazici's introduction to his Modern Turkish translation *(Risala,* Istanbul, 1966), pp. xv-xvii. He also mentions a partial translation that was published in 1307/1889.

TRANSLATOR'S NOTES

The selection from the *Risala* offered here forms the core of al-Qushayri's compendium of Sufi practice and knowledge. A manual on how to proceed on the Sufi path, the *Risala's* section on states and stations also provides a picture of individuals and groups of Sufis before the rise of formal Sufi institutions (6-7th/12-13th centuries). Al-Qushayri explains the theme of each chapter through quotations from the Qur'an, the sunna of the Prophet and by the lives of pious figures, great and small.

In an opening passage al-Qushayri outlines his plan, "We will now present chapters elucidating the stations [*maqamat*] which are the roads taken by those engaged in spiritual wayfaring. After that we will discuss chapters which detail the states [*ahwal*]." Although the author does not indicate the exact transition point from the stations to the states, the dividing line in the text seems to occur in Chapter 22 "Satisfaction" (*Rida*). In an earlier discussion of Sufi technical terms, al-Qushayri describes the stations as being the result of the seeker's effort. The states, on the other hand, come to the heart without any intention on the part of the recipient. "The states are given [by God], the stations are earned." *

In translating this portion of the *Risala*, four chapters not directly related to states and stations (including sections on travel and the manner of leaving the world at death) have

---

* *Ar-Risala al-Qushayriya*, ed. ʿAbd al-Halim Mahmud and Mahmud b. ash-Sharif, Cairo, 1966, p. 206.

been passed over. The translation, therefore, goes from "Correct Behavior" (40) directly to "Gnosis" (41). It should also be noted that Chapters 14 ("Envy") and 15 ("Backbiting") are not stations to which a Sufi aspires, but subheadings under the previous chapter on the failings of the self. Footnotes have been kept at a minimum. Explanations have on occasion been incorporated into the translation or, more often, explanatory words and phrases are given in brackets. What appears in brackets within a passage from the Qur'an is the completion of the verse alluded to by al-Qushayri.

Names in the translation and the index are given as written in the text. Cross-referencing in the index refers the reader to al-Qushayri's favored usage (e.g. from "at-Tustari" to 'Sahl b. 'Abdallah"; from " Abu Bakr ash-Shibli" to "ash-Shibli") but with some names, such as "Abu 'Uthman," the *nisba* has occasionally been omitted both in the text and translation. Historians of Sufism will want to consult the Arabic original to place the person in al-Qushayri's *silsilas*.

Work on this book began several years ago. Without the generous help of Hamid Algar, who has seen the translation through revisions and many delays, it never would have been published. I thank him for his skilled guidance, his encouragement, his good humor and for writing the introduction. I am also grateful to my family, to whom this book is dedicated.

B.R. von Schlegell is a doctoral candidate in the Department of Near Eastern Studies at the University of California, Berkeley. She has taught Islamic Studies and Arabic at Berkeley and elsewhere. Her dissertation is a study of the Naqshbandi Sufi scholar of Damascus, 'Abd al-Ghani an-Nabulusi (d. 1731).

1

Repentance

৯ Tawba

God says, "Turn all together toward God [in repentance], O Believers, that you may attain bliss" (24:31).

It is reported on the authority of Anas b. Malik that the Messenger of God (may God's blessing and peace be upon him and his family) said, "The one who repents from sin is like one without sin, and if God loves a servant, sin does not adhere to him." Then he recited, "Verily God loves those who turn unto Him [in repentance], and He loves those who purify themselves" (2:222). It was asked, "O Messenger of God, what is the sign of repentance?" He replied, "Remorse."

On the authority of Anas b. Malik, the Messenger of God (may God's blessing and peace be upon him and his family) is reported to have said, "There is nothing more loved by God than the youth who repents."

Therefore repentance is the first degree among the degrees of the wayfarers and the first station among the stations of the seekers. The inner meaning of repentance in Arabic is "return." It is said, "He repented," meaning, "He returned." So repentance is to return from what is blameworthy in the law of Islam to what is praiseworthy in it.

The Prophet (may God's blessing and peace be upon him) said, "Remorse is an act of repentance." Therefore, those well versed in the fundamentals of religion among the people of the Sunna have said, "There are three conditions of repentance [which must be present] in order that it be sound: remorse for the violations that have been committed, immediate abandonment of the lapse, and firm resolve not to return to similar acts of disobedience." One must apply these principles to make repentance effective.

Someone has stated, "By the saying 'Remorse is an act of repentance' he meant that the major portion of repentance is remorse, just as he (may God's blessing and peace be upon him) said, 'Pilgrimage is 'Arafat.'" That is, the greatest part of its elements is the standing at 'Arafat, not that there are no other elements in pilgrimage. So his saying, "Remorse is an act of repentance" means that the greatest part of the elements of repentance is remorse.

One among the people of realization has said, "Remorse is sufficient in fulfillment of that because it has as its consequence the other two conditions, for it is impossible one should be remorseful for an act in which he persists or the like of which he intends to commit." This is the meaning of repentance by way of summary definition.

By way of elucidation and explanation, we may say that repentance has causes, an order, an arrangement, and divisions. The first cause is the awakening of the heart from the slumber of heedlessness and the servant's becoming aware of his evil state. He attains this by means of the divine favor of attentiveness to the restraints imposed by God (may He be exalted) that come to his mind. This is by means of the audition of his heart, for it has come in the report, "The warner of God in the heart of every person is a Muslim." The tradition "There is a piece of flesh in the body which, if it be healthy, the whole body is healthy and if it be corrupt, the whole body is corrupt. Truly, it is the heart" also speaks to this matter. If his heart reflects on the evil of his deeds, he perceives the despicable actions he commits, and the desire for repentance comes to his heart, along with refraining from repugnant doings. Then God (may He be exalted) supports him in correcting his firm intention, in embarking on the path to a goodly return, and in becoming receptive to the means of repentance.

The first of these means is to part company with brothers in evil, for they prompt him to deny this goal and cause him to doubt the correctness of this firm intention. And that is not complete except by perseverance in witnessing, which increases his longing for repentance, and by the presence of motives impelling him to fulfill his resolve, from which he strengthens his fear and hope. Then the despicable actions that form a knot of insistence on his heart are loosened, he ceases the practice of forbidden things, and the rein of his self *(nafs)* is held back from pursuing passions. Then he immediately abandons his sin and concludes a firm resolve not to return to similar sins in the future. If he continues in accordance with his goal and acts in conformity with his firm will, this means that he has been granted true sincerity.

If repentance diminishes once or twice and his desire causes him to renew the lapse—which may happen quite frequently—one should continue to hope for the repentance of such a person, for "Verily, to each period is a decree established" (13:38).

Abu Sulayman ad-Darani said, "I frequented the gathering of a preacher, for his words made an impression on my heart. But when I departed, nothing remained in my heart of his words. So I returned a second time. That time there did remain a trace of his words in my heart until I returned to my house. Then I broke the instruments of sin and I adhered to the path." Yahya b. Mu'adh commented on this tale, "A sparrow catches a crane." By the sparrow he intended that preacher and, by the crane, Abu Sulayman ad-Darani.

Abu Hafs al-Haddad remarked, "I abandoned a certain [reprehensible] deed and returned to it. Then the deed abandoned me, and I did not return to it after that."

Abu 'Amr b. Nujayd, in the beginning of his wayfaring, frequented the gathering of Abu 'Uthman. His words made an impression on his heart, and he repented. Then a trial came upon him. Abu 'Amr began to flee Abu 'Uthman when he saw him, and he absented himself from his gathering. One day when Abu 'Uthman met him, Abu 'Amr turned away and went down another path. So Abu 'Uthman followed him. He continued with him, following his tracks until he overtook him and declared, "O my son, do not be a companion to one who does not love you unless it be one who is sinless. It is only Abu 'Uthman who will help you in your present condition." Then Abu 'Amr b. Nujayd repented and returned to muridship and remained faithful to it.*

Sheikh Abu 'Ali ad-Daqqaq (may God grant him mercy) said, "One of the *murid*s repented, and then there came upon him a trial. He was wondering, 'If I return to repentance, how will it be?'"

"Then an invisible caller said to him, 'You obeyed Us, so We thanked you; then you abandoned Us, so We granted you respite. If you return to Us, We will accept you.' So the youth returned to muridship and remained faithful to it."

When a man abandons major sin, loosens from his heart the bond of persistence, and firmly intends not to return to sin, at that moment true remorse comes to his heart. He regrets what he has done and reproaches himself for the repugnant acts he has committed. Then his repentance is complete, his striving is true, and he exchanges the comradeship of the evil companions he previously kept for isolation and for aversion to them. He works day and night in sorrow, and he embraces sincerity of regret in all of his states, erasing by the flood of his tears the traces of his stumbling and treats the wounds of his sin with the goodness of his repentance. He is known among his peers by his debility, and his emaciation testifies to the soundness of his state.

None of this will ever be complete except after satisfying the just grievances of his adversaries and

---

* Murid: the one who "wills," i.e., wills to attain the goal of the Path precisely by submitting his will to that of the spiritual guide.

putting right the acts of oppression in which he persisted. The first stage in repentance is satisfaction of adversaries as much as possible. If what he has is sufficient for restoring their rights or if they consent to abandon their claim and pronounce him innocent, so be it. If not, then he should firmly resolve in his heart to fulfill their claim whenever possible to God (may He be exalted) with sound supplication and prayer for them.

There are qualities and states for those who repent. They are characteristics of the penitent which belong to repentance without its being conditional upon them. This is indicated in the sayings of the masters on the meaning of repentance.

The master Abu 'Ali ad-Daqqaq (may God grant him mercy) said, "Repentance is divided into three parts. The first is *tawba* [repentance], the middle is *inaba* [to turn to God], and the last is *awba* [return]." He placed *tawba* at the beginning, *awba* at the end, and *inaba* between the two. Whoever repents out of desire for [divine] reward is in the state of *inaba*. Whoever repents for the sake of obeying the [divine] command, neither for the desire of reward nor for the fear of punishment, is in the state of *awba*.

It is also said, *"Tawba* is the quality of the Believers." As God Most High says, "Turn *[tubu]* all together toward God in repentance, O Believers" (24:31). *Inaba* is the quality of the saints and those drawn nigh unto God. God Most High says, "And those who brought a heart turned in devotion *[munib]* [to Him]" (50:33). *Awba* is the quality of the prophets and messengers. God Most High says, "How excellent a slave. Ever did he [Solomon] turn [*awwab*] [to Us]" (38:30 and 38:44).

Al-Junayd stated, "Repentance has three senses. The first is remorse; the second is the resolve to give up reverting to what God has forbidden; and the third is the righting of grievances."

Sahl b. 'Abdallah declared, "Repentance is giving up procrastination." Al-Harith asserted, "I never say, 'O God, I ask You for repentance.' I say, 'I ask You for the longing for repentance.'"

Al-Junayd went to see as-Sari one day and found him distraught. He asked, "What has happened to you?" As-Sari replied, "I encountered a youth, and he asked me about repentance. I told him, 'Repentance is that you not forget your sins.' Then he contradicted me, saying that repentance is that you *do* forget your sins." Al-Junayd said that in his opinion what the youth said was correct, and as-Sari asked him why he held that opinion. Al-Junayd replied, "Because if I were in a state of infidelity and then He delivered me into a state of fidelity, remembrance of infidelity in a state of purity would be infidelity." Then as-Sari fell silent.

Abu Nasr as-Sarraj is reported to have said that, when Sahl was asked about repentance, he answered, "It is that you not forget your sins." Al-Junayd was asked, and he said, "It is that you do forget your sins." Abu Nasr as-Sarraj related, "Sahl was indicating the states of the *murids* and the novices [*muta'arridun*], which are constantly changing. Al-Junayd alluded to the repentance of those who have attained the truth; for they do not remember their sins because of the majesty of God Most High, which has gained mastery over their hearts, and their constant remembrance of Him." He also observed that this is like what Ruwaym said about repentance: "It is repentance from repentance." Dhu'n-Nun al-Misri commented, "Repentance of the common people is from sin, and for the elect, it is from forgetfulness."

Abu'l-Husayn an-Nuri said, "Repentance is that you turn away from everything other than God [may He be exalted and glorified]." 'Abdallah b. 'Ali b. Muhammad at-Tamimi declared, "How great a difference there is between a repenter who repents from sins, one who repents from forgetfulness, and one who repents from the awareness of his own good deeds." Al-Wasiti said, "True repentance is that there not remain a single trace of sin, hidden or open. One whose repentance is true does not concern himself, morning and evening, with what state he is in."

Yahya b. Mu'adh stated, "O my Lord, I do not say, 'I have repented.' I do not return to You because of what I know to be my disposition, I do not swear that I will not sin again, for I know my own frailty. I do not say that I return [to You] because I might die before [truly] returning." Dhu'n-Nun noted, "The plea for forgiveness made without abstaining is the repentance of liars."

When Ibn Yazdanyar was asked about the principles underlying a servant's setting out toward God, he replied, "They are that he not return to that which he left behind, not heed anyone other than the One to Whom he goes, and preserve his innermost heart from perception of that from which he has dissociated himself." It was said to him, "This is the rule for one who has departed from existence. How will it be for one who has departed from non-existence?" He replied,

"The experience of sweetness in the future in exchange for bitterness in the past."

Al-Bushanji was asked about repentance, and he answered, "If you remember sin, and find no sweetness in it when remembering it, that is repentance." And Dhu'n-Nun observed, "The essence of repentance is that the earth be too confined for you, for all its spaciousness, so that there is no rest for you. Then your soul will be too confined for you as God Most High has told in His Book by His saying, 'And their souls seemed straightened to them, and they saw that there is no fleeing from God, except to Him. Then He turned to them that they might repent'" (9:118). Ibn 'Ata' declared, "Repentance is of two kinds: repentance of *inaba* [return] and repentance of *istijaba* [answering or fulfillment]. The repentance of *inaba* is that the servant repent out of fear for his punishment. Repentance of *istijaba* is that he repent out of shame due to His generosity."

Abu Hafs was asked, "Why does the repenter loathe the world?" He answered, "Because it is a dwelling where sins are pursued." And it was said to him, "But it is also a dwelling that God has honored with repentance." He said, "The sinner has certainty from his sin, but danger from acceptance of his repentance." Al-Wasiti stated, "The joy of David (peace be upon him) and the sweetness of submissiveness he enjoyed caused him to plunge into lifting breaths [lasting sorrow]. While he was in the second state [of sorrow] he was more complete than the time when the matter was hidden from him." One of them remarked, "The liars' repentance is on the tips of their tongues." That is, the saying,

"Astaghfiru'llah [I ask forgiveness of God]." Abu Hafs said, "The servant has nothing to do with repentance. Repentance comes to him (from God), not from him."

It is said that God (may He be exalted) revealed to Adam, "O Adam, I have bequeathed to your descendants burdens and hardship. I have also bequeathed to them repentance. I respond to the one among them who implores Me as you have implored Me [just] as I respond to you. O Adam, I will raise up the penitent from their graves cheerful and laughing, and their supplication will be answered."

A man asked Rabi'a, "I have sinned much and been exceedingly disobedient. But if I repent, will He forgive me?" She replied, "No. But if He forgives you, then you will repent."

Know that God Most High says, "Verily God loves those who turn unto Him [in repentance] and He loves those who purify themselves" (2:222). One who allows himself to yield to error is certain as to the slip. But if he repents, he is in doubt as to the acceptance of his repentance, particularly because God's love for him is a condition of that acceptance, and it will be some time before the sinner comes to a point where he find marks of God's love for him in his character. The duty of the servant, when he knows that he has committed an act calling for repentance, is that he be consistently contrite, persevering in renunciation and asking forgiveness, as in the saying "The awareness of dread until the time of death." And as it is said in God's words, "Say, if you love God, follow me, that God may love you" (3:31).

It was the practice of the Prophet (may God's blessing and peace be upon him) to ask for forgiveness constantly. He said, "My heart is clouded, so I ask forgiveness of God seventy times a day."

Yahya b. Mu'adh stated, "One single lapse after repentance is more dreadful than seventy before it." Abu 'Uthman observed, "As to the meaning of His saying 'Lo, unto Us is their return' (78:25), it indicates 'Unto Us is their return, even if they roam freely in the commission of sin.'"

'Ali b. 'Isa the vizier rode in a great procession, and strangers began asking, "Who is this? Who is this?" A woman who was standing by the side of the road inquired, "How long will you say, 'Who is this? Who is this?' This is a servant who has fallen from God's protection. So He has afflicted him in the way that you see." When 'Ali b. 'Isa heard her, he returned to his house, resigned from the vizierate, went to Mecca, and never left it again.

2

Striving

❧ Mujahada

God Most High says, "And those who strive for Our sake, We will certainly guide them to Our paths. God is with those who do right" (29:69).

On the authority of Abu Sa'id al-Khudri, it is reported that when the Messenger of God (may God's blessing and peace be upon him) was asked about the best kind of striving *[jihad]*, he answered, "It is a just word spoken to a tyrannical ruler." Tears flowed from Abu Sa'id's eyes when he heard this.

The master Abu 'Ali ad-Daqqaq (may God grant him mercy) declared, "God will beautify the inner faculties with contemplation for one who adorns his outer being with striving, for God Most High says, 'And those who strive in Us, We will certainly guide them to Our paths'" (29:69).

Know that anyone who does not exert effort at the beginning of his wayfaring will never attain the slightest benefit from the Path. Abu 'Uthman al-Maghribi stated, "It is a grave error for anyone to imagine he will attain anything or that anything will be revealed to him of the Path without persistent striving on his part." The master Abu 'Ali ad-Daqqaq (may God grant him mercy) asserted, "The one who makes no firm stand at the start of his wayfaring will not be allowed repose at its end." He also said, "[Their saying] 'Exertion is a blessing' means that exertion of one's outward abilities brings forth blessings in the inner faculties."

Abu Yazid al-Bistami related, "For twelve years I was the blacksmith of my soul. Then for five years I was the mirror of my heart. Then for one year I gazed at what was between the two, and I saw an infidel's girdle visibly around my middle. I worked at severing it for twelve years. I gazed once more, and I saw an infidel's girdle around my inward being. So I worked at severing it for five years, wondering how I could cut it. The answer was finally revealed to me. I looked upon mankind and saw that they were dead, so I pronounced *'Allahu akbar'* over them four times."

As-Sari said one time, "O young men! Strive earnestly before you reach my age, when you will become as negligent as I." Al-Junayd reported that, even though as-Sari said this, the young men at that time did not have as-Sari's fortitude in acts of worship. Al-Hasan al-Qazzaz explained, "This matter [Sufism] is based on three things: that you eat only when it is necessary, that you sleep only when overcome by drowsiness, and that you speak only in cases of urgent necessity."

Ibrahim b. Adham observed, "A man attains the rank of the righteous only after passing through these six steps: (1) He must close the door of bounty and open the door of hardship. (2) He must close the door of dignity and open the door of humility. (3) He must close the door of repose and open the door of striving. (4) He must close the door of sleep and open the door of vigilance. (5) He must close the door of wealth and open the door of poverty. (6) He must close the door of worldly expectation and open the door of preparedness for death." Abu 'Amr b. Nujayd declared, "Whoever holds his soul dear holds his religion in contempt."

Abu 'Ali ar-Rudhbari said, "If a Sufi says after five days [of deprivation], 'I am hungry,' then send him to the marketplace to earn something."

Striving is essentially weaning the soul of its habitual practices and compelling it to oppose its passions at all times. The soul has two traits that hold it back from attaining goodness: absorption in worshiping its passions and refusal to perform acts of obedience. When the soul bolts, like a horse, toward a desire, one must rein it in with the bridle of piety. When it stubbornly refuses to conform [with God's wishes], then one must steer it toward opposing its desires. When it rises up in a rage [at being opposed], then one must control this state. Nothing has a more excellent prospect than what arises in place of an anger whose power has been shattered by good moral character and whose fire has been put out by kind acts. When the soul finds sweetness in the wine of arrogance, then it will be dejected unless it can make a display of its feats and embellish [its deeds] to whoever looks at it. One must break it of this tendency and submit it to the penalty of the disgrace that will come when it is reminded of its paltry worth, its lowly origin, and its despicable actions.

The striving of the common people consists of

performing acts, and the goal of the elect [in striving] is to purify their spiritual states. Enduring hunger and sleeplessness is very easy, but cultivating moral characteristics and cleansing them of all lowly aspects are extremely difficult.

One of the harmful traits of the soul most difficult to perceive is its reliance on receiving acclaim. One who takes a drink from this cup bears the [weight of the] heavens and the earth on one of his eyelashes. A sign of this enormous burden is that, if that drink be [later] withheld from him, he will revert to indolence and cowardice in his striving.

For many years a certain sheikh prayed in the front row of worshipers in the mosque he frequented. One day something prevented him from arriving early at the mosque. He was forced to pray in the last row. After that he was not seen for some time. When someone asked him the reason for his absence, he answered, "I used to pray in the front row, and for a year now I thought I was sincere in doing this, for God's sake. But the day I was delayed, I felt ashamed to be seen praying in the back of the mosque. I knew from this that my lifelong zeal in prayer had been nothing but concern for the opinion men had of me, and so I had said my prayers."

It is related that Abu Muhammad al-Murta'ish said, "I used to go on the pilgrimage on foot without taking any provisions. I realized once that all my effort was defiled by my sense of pleasure in the way that I performed it. This came to me one day when my mother asked me to draw a jar of water for her. My soul found this burdensome. I knew then that what I thought was great obedience to God in my pilgrimages was nothing more than something pleasurable for me, coming from a flaw in my soul, for if my soul had been pure, I would never have found irksome something incumbent upon me."

There once was an old woman who was asked about her state. She responded, "When I was young, I had vigor and experienced many states. I thought they came from the real strength of my spiritual state. When I became older, these states faded away. I know now that what I thought were spiritual states was only the vigor of youth." Abu 'Ali ad-Daqqaq said, "Every sheikh who has told me this tale felt compassion for this old woman. Surely she was an honest woman."

Dhu'n-Nun al-Misri declared, "The greatest honor God can confer upon a servant is to show him the lowliness of his soul. The most degrading thing God can do to a servant is to conceal from him the lowliness of his soul." Ibrahim al-Khawwas asserted, "I have confronted all my fears straightforwardly."

Muhammad b. al-Fadl said, "Repose is being free of the desires of the soul." Mansur b. 'Abdallah related, "I heard Abu 'Ali ar-Rudhbari say, 'Harm comes upon mankind from three things: the weakness of natural disposition, clinging to habitual practices, and the keeping of corrupt company.' I asked him, 'What is the weakness of natural disposition?' He replied, 'Consuming forbidden things.' Then I asked, 'What is clinging to habitual practices?' He said, 'Viewing and listening to prohibited things and engaging in slander.' I inquired, 'What is the keeping of corrupt company?' He responded, 'That is when you follow whatever passion toward which men incite you.'"

An-Nasrabadhi said, "Your prison is your soul. If you escape from it, you will come into endless peace."

Abu'l-Husayn al-Warraq reported, "When we were starting out on the Path at the mosque of Abu 'Uthman al-Hiri, the finest practices we undertook were that when we were given charity, we gave generously of it to others; we never slept with anything left undistributed; we never retaliated against someone who offended us—we would excuse his offense and behave humbly toward him; and if we felt contempt in our hearts for a certain person, we would take it upon ourselves to serve him and behave toward him with kindness until the feelings of contempt ceased."

Abu Hafs said, "The self is complete darkness [of its own]. The lamp of the self is its secret. The light of this lamp is success [in striving]. One who is not granted success [in striving] by his Lord, in his secret he is darkness, all of him." In saying, "The lamp of the self is its secret," Abu Hafs means that the secret of the servant is what is between him and God Most High. It is the locus of his sincerity. By it the servant knows that all events are the work of God; they are neither the work of his self nor do they originate from him. When he knows this, he will be free, in all his states, of his own power and might. Then by the [light of] success [in striving], he will be protected from the evils of his self. One who achieves no success [in striving] will not gain any benefit from knowledge of his self or of his Lord. For this reason, the sheikhs have said, "One who has no secret will be insistent [on following his desires]." Abu 'Uthman declared, "As long as one finds anything good in his self, he will never be able to see its faults. Only one who accuses his self at all times will be able to see its faults."

Abu Hafs observed, "There is no faster way to ruin than that of one who does not know his faults, for surely disobedience to God is the path to unbelief." Abu Sulayman said, "I know there is no good to be found in a deed my self performs as long as I expect to be rewarded for it."

As-Sari commented, "Beware of the neighbors of the rich, the Qur'an reciters who frequent the marketplace, and the scholars attached to worldly rulers."

Dhu'n-Nun al-Misri stated, "Corruption enters men in six ways: (1) They have weak intention in performing deeds oriented to the hereafter. (2) Their bodies are held hostage by their lusts. (3) They remain full of hope for worldly gain in spite of the nearness of death. (4) They prefer to please created beings over pleasing the Creator. (5) They follow their own desires, without so much as a backward glance at the Sunna of their Prophet [may God's blessings and peace be upon him]. (6) They defend their failings by invoking a few slips of the early Muslims, while burying their many virtues."

3

Retreat and Seclusion

❧ Khalwa wa 'Uzla

It is related on the authority of Abu Hurayra that the Prophet (may God's blessing and peace be upon him) said, "Among the best ways of living for man are these: that he take rein of his horse in the way of God; if he hears sounds of panic or fear, he is on the back of his horse seeking death or killing in the most likely places; or that a man be with his sheep and goats on a mountain peak or in the depths of a riverbed and keep up his prayer, pay the *zakat,* and worship his Lord until death comes to him. All his dealings with men are based on the good."

Khalwa (retreat) is the attribute of the people of purity and *'uzla* (seclusion) is a token of the people of union.

Withdrawal from those of his own kind is indispensable for the *murid* in the beginning of his state, and then seclusion in the end, because of his attainment of intimacy with God. The proper attitude of the servant when he chooses seclusion is that he believe people will be preserved from his evil (by means of his retirement from mankind), not that he is preserving himself from their evil. The former is the result of thinking little of his own soul; the latter is supposing that he is superior to people. One who considers his soul to be of little worth is humble, and one who considers himself more worthy than another is vain.

Someone saw a monk and said, "You are a monk." He replied, "No, I am guarding a dog. My self is a dog that attacks mankind. I have removed it from them so they can be safe and sound."

A man passed one of the devout and that sheikh gathered in his garments from him. The man inquired, "Why do you pull away your cloak? My garments are not impure." So the sheikh said, "Your assumption is wrong. I gathered my garments away from yours because mine are impure and they would have soiled your garments, not to prevent my garments from being soiled."

To seclude himself properly, a man should acquire knowledge of the religious sciences to correct his conviction in God's Oneness so that Satan does not tempt him with his whisperings. He should also acquire knowledge from the legal sciences as to what is incumbent upon him so that the building of his affairs be on a firm foundation. Seclusion in truth is separation from reprehensible qualities and its effect is designed to change those characteristics, not to produce great distances from any given place. For this reason it was asked, "Who is the gnostic?" They replied, "One who is near and far at the same time." That is, being outwardly with men and distant from them inwardly. I heard the master Abu 'Ali ad-Daqqaq (may God grant him mercy) instruct, "Wear with mankind what they wear and eat what they eat. But be separate from them inwardly." I also heard him report, "A man came to me and said, 'I have come to you from a very distant place.' Then I said, 'This matter [attaining knowledge of the Path] has nothing to do with traversing great distances and undergoing journeys. Separate from yourself even by one single step, and your goal will be reached.'"

Yahya relates that Abu Yazid said, "I saw my Lord in my dreams and I asked, 'How am I to find You?' He replied, 'Leave yourself and come!'"

Abu 'Uthman al-Maghribi commented, "It is fitting for one who chooses retreat over keeping company with men to be free from all remembrances except remembrance of his Lord, devoid of all desires except the pleasure of his Lord, and free from the demands of the self for all things. If it is not done in this way, his retreat will only plunge him in trials or calamity."

It is said, "Being alone in seclusion is most apt to embrace occasions of solace." Yahya b. Mu'adh instructed, "Consider whether your intimacy is with retreat or with Him in retreat. If your intimacy is with retreat, it will vanish when you emerge from it. If your intimacy is with Him in retreat, everywhere will seem as one to you, whether the deserts or the steppes."

A man came to visit Abu Bakr al-Warraq, and when he was about to return, he said to him, "Counsel me." So he stated, "I have found the best of the world and the afterlife in retreat and paucity, and I have found the worst of the two [the world and the afterlife] in social intercourse and abundance."

Al-Jurayri, having been asked about seclusion, answered, "It is to enter into the crowd while guarding your inward being lest they beset you, secluding yourself from sins, and that your inward being be linked with God."

It was said, "Whoever chooses seclusion attains seclusion."

Sahl declared, "Retreat is only sound by eating licit foods, and eating licit foods is only sound by discharging what is due toward God." Dhu'n-Nun al-Misri said, "I have seen nothing that brings about sincerity better than retreat." Abu 'Abdallah ar-Ramli remarked, "Let your companion be solitude, your food be hunger, and your speech be intimate prayers. Then either you will die or you will reach God [may He be exalted]."

Dhu'n-Nun commented, "One who conceals himself from mankind through retreat is not like one who conceals himself from them by God."

Al-Junayd observed, "The hardship of seclusion is easier than the affability of company." Makhul said, "There is certainly goodness in associating with people. But there is safety in seclusion."

Yahya b. Mu'adh observed, "Solitude is the companion of the veracious."

Ash-Shibli would say, "Ruin . . . ruin, O people!" Someone asked him, "O Abu Bakr, what is the sign of ruin?" He replied, "One of the signs of ruin is being on familiar terms with people."

Yahya b. Abi Kathir stated, "Whoever mixes with people must be affable to them, and whoever is affable to them acts the hypocrite toward them."

Shu'ayb b. Harb related, "I went to see Malik b. Mas'ud in Kufa and he was alone in his house. So I asked, 'Are you not lonely and fearful by yourself?' He replied, 'I am not used to thinking that one is alone with God.'"

Al-Junayd said, "Whoever wants his religion to be sound and his body and heart to be soothed, let him withdraw from people. Truly, this is a time of fear, and the wise one is he who chooses solitude."

Abu Ya'qub as-Susi asserted, "Only the very strong ones should be alone. As for the likes of us, society is more abundant and beneficial so that awareness of each other may impel us to strive."

Ash-Shibli instructed Abu'l-'Abbas ad-Damaghani, "Make a practice of solitude, wipe out your name from the register of people, and turn your face to the wall until you die."

A man came to see Shu'ayb b. Harb, who inquired, "What brought you?" The man replied, "That I may be with you." Shu'ayb retorted, "O my brother! Surely worship endures not joining with anything else. One who has not become intimate with God will never be intimate with anything."

Someone was asked, "What is the most marvelous thing you have met on your journey?" He answered, "Al-Khidr* met me and he sought companionship with me. I was afraid lest he ruin my state of reliance on God."

One of them was asked, "Is there someone in this place with whom you feel intimate?" He said, "Yes," and stretched out his hand to his copy of the Qur'an. Putting

---

* The ubiquitous and immortal personification of the initiatic principle, generally identified with the anonymous figure mentioned in the Qur'an (18:65ff)

it in his lap, he declared, "This." As to its meaning they
recite this:

> *Your books around me do not leave my bed,*
> *for in them there is a cure for the*
> *sickness I conceal.*

A man asked Dhu'n-Nun al-Misri, "When will seclusion be right for me?" He responded, "When you are
able to seclude yourself from your own self." It was said
to Ibn al-Mubarak, "What is the remedy for the heart?"
He replied, "Having few encounters with people." And
it is said, "If God wishes to take the servant from the
shame of disobedience to the dignity of obedience, He
makes him intimate with solitude, rich with frugality,
and able to see the defects of his self. Whoever has been
given this has been given the best of the world and the
afterlife."

4

Fear of God

❧ Taqwa

God most High says, "Verily the noblest of you in the sight of God is the one who is the most God-fearing" (49:13).

It is reported on the authority of Abu Sa'id al-Khudri that a man came to the Prophet (may God's blessing and peace be upon him) and said, "O Prophet of God, counsel me." He replied, "May you have fear [taqwa] of God, for it is the aggregate of all good things. May you perform jihad, for it is the monkhood of the Muslim. And may you be occupied with remembrance of God, for it is a light for you."

Anas (may God be pleased with him) related, "Someone asked the Prophet of God, 'Who are the family of Muhammad?' He replied, 'Every God-fearing person.'" Taqwa is the gatherer of all goodnesses, and the inner truth of taqwa is protecting one's self from God's punishment by means of obedience to Him, just as it is said, "So-and-so protected himself with his shield." The origin of taqwa is wariness of shirk

25

(associating others with God), then after this, wariness of sin and evil things, then of dubious things. After that he leaves off all that is of no true concern. On this matter the master Abu 'Ali ad-Daqqaq (may God grant him mercy) declared, "Every one of these divisions could fill a chapter."

It has been said in commentary on His saying (may He be exalted and glorified) "O ye who believe! Fear God as He should be feared" (3:102), that it means, He should be obeyed and not disobeyed, remembered and not forgotten, and thanked and not be the object of ingratitude.

Sahl b. 'Abdallah asserted, "There is no helper other than God; there is no guide other than the Messenger of God; there are no provisions other than *taqwa;* and there is no work other than perseverance in *taqwa.*"

Al-Kattani stated, "The world is apportioned in accordance with affliction endured, and the afterlife is apportioned in accordance with *taqwa.*" Al-Jurayri said, "One who has not made *taqwa* and awareness his arbiter between himself and God will not reach illumination and contemplation." An-Nasrabadhi explained, "*Taqwa* is that the servant beware of whatever is other than God [may He be exalted and glorified]." Sahl said, "Whoever desires sound *taqwa,* let him abandon all sin." An-Nasrabadhi instructed, "Whoever perseveres in *taqwa* yearns for separation from the world because God [may He be exalted], says, 'Better is the abode of the afterlife for those who are pious; do you not understand?'" (6:32) A certain person asserted, "God makes turning away from the world easy for the heart of one who proves true in *taqwa.*" Abu 'Abdullah ar-

Rudhbari said, "*Taqwa* is shunning whatever makes you distant from God." Dhu'n-Nun al-Misri declared, "The God-fearing person is one who does not taint his outward being with resistance nor his inwardness with superfluous matters. He stands with God in a station of harmony."

Abu'l-Hasan al-Farisi observed, "*Taqwa* has an exterior and interior aspect. Its exterior aspect is preservation of the boundaries, and its interior aspect is intention and striving." Dhu'n-Nun recited:

> *There is no life except with men whose hearts*
> *long for taqwa and whose joy is in*
> *remembrance.*
> *Content are they with the spirit of certainty*
> *and its goodness*
> *like the nursing child in his mother's lap.*

It is said, "The *taqwa* of a man is indicated by three things: good trust with respect to what he has not been granted, good contentment with what he has been granted, and good patience in the face of what he has lost."

Talq b. Habib commented, "*Taqwa* is acting according to submissiveness to God upon a light from Him, dreading His penalty." Abu Hafs said, "*Taqwa* is restricting oneself to the indubitably permissible, and that is all." Abu al-Husayn az-Zanjani stated, "He whose greatest property is *taqwa* gains a profit tongues are unable to describe." Al-Wasiti asserted, "*Taqwa* is that one shun his *taqwa*, which is to say, avoid awareness of his *taqwa*."

The God-fearing one is like Ibn Sirin, who bought

forty vessels of butter. When his slave removed a mouse from one of the jars, Ibn Sirin asked him, "Which jar did you remove it from?" He replied, "I do not know!" Then Ibn Sirin proceeded to empty them all onto the ground. And the devout one is also like Abu Yazid al-Bistami, who purchased some saffron in Hamadan. There was a little left over, and when he returned to Bistam, he found two ants inside. So he returned to Hamadan and laid down the two ants.

Abu Hanifa would not sit in the shade of his debtor's tree. He would explain, "The *hadith* says, 'Every debt that brings about a benefit is usury.'"

Abu Yazid was washing his garment outside the city with a friend when his friend said, "Hang your garment on the orchard wall." Abu Yazid retorted, "No, you should not hammer nails in someone's wall." He suggested, "Let us hang it on the tree." Abu Yazid responded, "No, for it will break the branches." He said, "We will spread it on the plants." Abu Yazid answered, "No, they are fodder for the beasts of burden. We cannot cover them with it." Then he turned his back to the sun and threw the garment on his back until one side was dry; then he turned it around until the other side was dry.

Abu Yazid entered the mosque one day and thrust his staff in the ground. It fell upon the staff of an old man to his side who had also planted his in the ground, and caused it to fall. The old man bent down and took his staff. Abu Yazid went to the old man's house and asked him to forgive him, saying, "You were troubled on account of my negligence when you had to bend down."

'Utba al-Ghulam was seen breaking into a sweat in wintertime. When they asked him about it, he explained, "This is a place wherein I have rebelled against my Lord." They asked him to explain further, so he said, "I scraped off a chunk of clay from this wall so that a guest of mine could cleanse his hand with it, and I had not asked the owner of the wall for permission."

Ibrahim b. Adham related, "I was spending the night beneath the Rock in Jerusalem. When some of the night had passed, two angels descended. One of them asked the other, 'Who is this here?' He answered, 'Ibrahim b. Adham.' The other one said, 'This is the one whom God [may He be exalted] has lowered a degree.' So he inquired, 'Why?' He replied, 'Because when he bought some dates in Basra and one of the grocer's dates fell into his purchase, he did not return it to its owner.' Ibrahim reported, 'I left for Basra, bought some dates from the man, and dropped a date into his. I returned to Jerusalem and passed the night at the Rock. When part of the night had passed, behold, I saw two angels descend from the sky, and one of them asked his companion, 'Who is this here?' The other one answered, 'Ibrahim b. Adham.' He said, 'This is the one whom God has restored to his place and elevated his degree.'"

It is said that *taqwa* has different aspects: for the common people it is the shunning of *shirk;* for the elite it is the shunning of sins; for the saints it is the shunning of reliance on works; and for the prophets it is the shunning of attributing works [to other-than-God] for Him.

The Commander of the Believers, 'Ali (may God be

pleased with him), declared, "The most noble of mankind in the world are the generous, and the most noble in the afterlife are the God-fearing."

On the authority of Abu Umama, the Prophet (may God's blessing and peace be upon him) asserted, "Whoever gazes upon a woman's beauties and then lowers his eyes with the first look, God makes of this an act of worship the sweetness of which he experiences in his heart."

Al-Junayd was sitting with Ruwaym, al-Jurayri, and Ibn 'Ata'. Al-Junayd related, "One is saved only by sincerity in taking refuge with God. God Most High says, '[He turned in mercy also] to the three who were left behind, when the earth, vast as it is, was straightened for them. Their own souls were straightened for them, and they perceived that there is no refuge from God but toward Him. Then He turned unto them that they might turn [repentant unto Him], for God is Oft-Returning, the Merciful'" (9:118). Ruwaym (may God grant him mercy) commented, "One is saved only by sincere God-fearingness. God Most High says, 'And God will deliver the pious to their place of salvation. No evil shall touch them nor shall they grieve'" (39:61). Al-Jurayri observed, "One is saved only by observance of fidelity. God Most High says, 'Those who fulfill the pact of God and break not the covenant, for them is the final abode'" (13:20-22). Ibn 'Ata' declared, "One is saved only by the realization of shame. God Most High says, 'Does he not know that God sees?'" (96:14).

One is saved only by divine order and decree. God Most High says, "Those for whom kindness from Us has gone before will be removed far therefrom [Hell]"

(21:101). One is saved only by the election that has been decreed for him. God Most High says, "And We chose them, and We guided them to a straight way" (6:87).

5

Abstaining

❧ Wara'

On the authority of Abu Dharr, the Messenger of God (may God's blessing and peace be upon him), said, "Part of the goodness of a man's practice of Islam is that he abandon whatever does not concern him."

The master (may God be pleased with him), stated, "*Wara'* is the abandonment of whatever is dubious." Likewise, Ibrahim b. Adham explained, *"Wara'* is abandoning whatever is dubious, and the abandonment of whatever does not concern you means abandoning whatever is superfluous."

Abu Bakr as-Siddiq (may God be pleased with him) reported, "We used to foreswear seventy categories of the permitted, fearing to fall into a category of the forbidden." The prophet (may God's blessing and peace be upon him) told Abu Hurayra, "Be abstinent and you will be the most worshipful of mankind."

As-Sari said, "There were four people of *wara'* in their time: Hudhayfa al-Murta'sh, Yusuf b. Asbat, Ibrahim b. Adham, and Sulayman al-Khawwas. They took up *wara'* and when the acquisition of the permissible became difficult for them, they took recourse in the absolute minimum."

Ash-Shibli commented, *"Wara'* is that you abstain from everything other than God Most High." Ishaq b. Khalaf observed, "Abstaining from speech is more difficult than abstaining from gold and silver, and giving up power is more difficult than giving up gold and silver because you are ready to sacrifice them for the sake of power." Abu Sulayman ad-Darani remarked, "Abstaining is the beginning of renunciation *[zuhd]*, just as contentment is the chief part of satisfaction *[rida]*." Abu 'Uthman said, "The reward for abstaining is lightness of reckoning in the hereafter." Yahya b. Mu'adh stated, "Abstaining is restricting oneself to the immediate sense of religious decree without attempting to interpret it." 'Abdallah b. al-Jalla' related, "I know someone who lived in Mecca for thirty years without drinking the water of Zamzam except for what he drew with his own bucket and rope, and he did not eat food that was brought there from other cities." 'Ali b. Musa at-Tahirati reported, "A small coin belonging to 'Abdallah b. Marwan fell into a filthy well, and he hired a man to retrieve it for thirteen dinars. When someone asked him about it, he explained, 'The name of God Most High was upon it.'"

Yahya b. Mu'adh asserted, "There are two kinds of abstaining: abstaining in the external sense is that there be no outward movement except for God Most High, and abstaining in the internal sense is that nothing other than God Most High enter your heart." He also noted, "One who does not examine the subtleties of abstaining will not receive a generous gift." It is said, "The one whose gaze in religion is meticulous will find a great rank at the Resurrection." Ibn al-Jalla' declared, "One who does not associate God-fearing with his poverty eats the manifestly forbidden." Yusuf b. 'Ubayd said, "Abstaining is leaving behind every dubious thing and examination of the self with each moment." Sufyan ath-Thawri commented, "I have never seen anything easier than abstaining. Whatever your self devises, abandon it." Ma'ruf al-Karkhi instructs, "Guard your tongue from praise just as you guard it from censure." Bishr b. al-Harith observed, "The most difficult things to accomplish are generosity in times of hardship, abstaining in seclusion, and speaking the truth to one you fear and have hopes of."

The sister of Bishr al-Hafi came to Ahmad b. Hanbal and told him, "We were spinning on our roof, when the torch of the Tahirids passed by, and its light fell upon us. Is it permissible for us to spin by its light?" Ahmad inquired, "Who are you (may God Most High keep you in good health)?" She replied, "I am Bishr al-Hafi's sister." Ahmad wept and said, "Righteous abstinence arises from your family. Do not spin by that light."

'Ali al-'Attar related, "I was walking through Basra along a street, and I saw some sheikhs sitting while some boys played nearby. So I asked them, 'Are you not ashamed of playing in front of these sheikhs?' One of the boys answered, 'The abstinence of these sheikhs is so slight that we hold them in but slight awe.'"

Malik b. Dinar, who lived in Basra for forty years, did not regard it as correct to eat either the dried or the fresh dates of the city. Up to the time of his death, he did not even taste them. When the season for ripe dates was past, he would say, "O people of Basra, this stomach of mine has not missed anything and your stomachs have not gained anything."

Someone asked Ibrahim b. Adham, "Why don't you drink the water of Zamzam?" He responded, "If I had a bucket, then I would drink it." When al-Harith al-Muhasibi would reach out his hand for food of dubious permissibility, a vein in his fingertip would throb and he would know that it was not pure. Bishr al-Hafi was invited to a meal, and the food was placed in front of him. He strained to reach out his hand to it, but his hand would not move. He did this three times. A man who was familiar with this situation observed, "His hand never reaches out to touch dubious food. It was for nothing that the host invited this sheikh."

When Sahl b. 'Abdallah was asked about the pure *[halal],* he explained, "It is that which involves no sin against God Most High or forgetfulness of Him."

As Hasan al-Basri entered Mecca, he saw one of the children of 'Ali b. Abi Talib (may God be pleased with him) leaning his back against the Ka'aba and preaching to the people. Hasan rushed up to him, asking, "What is the foundation of religion?" He replied, "Abstention." So he inquired, "And what is the ruin of religion?" He answered, "Greed." So Hasan marveled at him, noting, "The weight of one dust speck of flawless abstention is better than one thousand weights of fasting and prayer."

God (may He be exalted) revealed to Moses (upon whom be blessings and peace), "The ones nearest to Me have drawn nigh to Me only through abstention and renunciation."

Abu Hurayra said, "The friends of God Most High on the morrow will be the people of abstention and renunciation." Sahl b. 'Abdallah declared, "If abstention does not accompany a man, even if he were to eat an elephant's head, he would still not be full."

Some musk from the spoils of war was brought to 'Umar b. 'Abd al-'Aziz, who held it to his nose and remarked, "The only benefit to this is its scent, and I hate to think that I alone should smell it without all the Muslims sharing in it."

When asked about abstention, Abu 'Uthman al-Hiri related, "Abu Salih Hamdun was with one of his friends who was in the agony of death. The man died, and Abu Salih blew out the lamp. Someone asked him about this, and he said, 'Until now it was his oil in the lamp, but from now on it falls to the lot of the heirs. Look for some oil that is not his.'"

Kahmas reported, "I have been lamenting for forty years over a sin I committed. One of my brothers visited me, and I bought a piece of broiled fish for him. When he finished eating it, I took a piece of clay from my neighbor's wall so he could wash his hands with it, without asking my neighbor for permission."

A man was writing a note while in a rented house, and he wanted to dry the writing using some dust from the wall. It occurred to him that the house was rented, but he thought that it was not important, so he dried the writing with dust. Then he heard a voice say, "He who makes light of the dust shall know what a lengthy reckoning is his!"

Ahmad b. Hanbal (may God have mercy upon him) pawned a bucket with a grocer in Mecca (may God

Most High watch over it). When he wanted to redeem it, the grocer brought out two buckets, saying "Take whichever of the two is yours." Ahmad replied, "I am not certain, so you may keep both the buckets and the dirhams." The grocer told him, "This is your bucket. I only wanted to test you." So he retorted, "I will not take it," and departed, leaving the bucket with the grocer.

Ibn al-Mubarak let a highly priced horse roam free while he prayed the noon prayer. The horse grazed in the cropland belonging to the village ruler. So Ibn al-Mubarak abandoned the horse without having ridden it. It is said that Ibn al-Mubarak came back from Marv to Syria because of a pen he had borrowed and not returned to its owner.

An-Nakh'i hired a horse. When his whip fell from his hand, he dismounted, tied the horse, and walked back to retrieve the whip. Someone commented, "It would have been easier for you if you had directed the horse to the place where the whip had fallen and then retrieved it." He retorted, "Not at all; I hired the horse to go in that direction, not this."

Abu Bakr ad-Daqqaq related, "I wandered about in the wilderness of the Children of Israel for fifteen days, and when I came to the road, a soldier met me and gave me a draught of water to drink. It induced hardness in my heart, and I suffered for thirty years."

Rabi'a al-'Adawiya sewed a tear in her dress by the light of the sultan's lamp, and then she lost her heart for a time until she remembered. So she ripped her dress and found her heart.

Sufyan ath-Thawri appeared in a dream with a pair of wings with which he flew in Paradise from tree to tree. Someone asked him, "By what means were you granted this?" He answered, "By abstention."

When Hassan b. Abi Sinan came upon the companions of al-Hasan, he inquired, "What is the most difficult thing for you?" They replied, "Abstaining." He said, "There is nothing easier for me than this." They asked, "How is that?" He responded, "I have not drunk from your stream for forty years."

Hassan b. Abi Sinan did not sleep lying down or eat fat or drink cold water for sixty years. He was seen in a dream, and someone asked him about what God had done with him. He explained, "He has done well, except that I am shut out of Paradise because of a needle I borrowed and never returned."

'Abd al-Wahid b. Zayd had a slave who served him for many years and devoted himself to worship for forty years. He had been a grain-measurer at first, and when he died, he was seen in a dream. When asked about what God had done with him, he reported, "He has done well, except that I am barred from Paradise because of the dust of the grain measure with which I dispensed forty portions."

As Jesus son of Mary (upon them both be peace) passed by a cemetery, a man called out from the tombs. God Most High restored him to life and Jesus asked him who he was. He replied, "I was a porter, and one day as I was transporting firewood for a man, I broke a small stick of the wood. I have been held accountable for that stick since I died."

Abu Sa'id al-Kharraz was speaking on abstention when 'Abbas b. al-Muhtadi passed by. He asked, "O Abu Sa'id, have you no shame? You sit beneath the roof of Abu ad-Dawaniq, drink from the pool of Zubayda, do business with spurious money, and talk about abstention!"

6

Renunciation

Zuhd

On the authority of Abu Khallad, the Prophet (may God's blessing and peace be upon him) said, "If you see a man who has been endowed with renunciation of the world and speech, then draw near to him, for he is infused with wisdom."

People differ concerning renunciation. Some people say, "Renunciation is of the forbidden because the licit is permissible in God's eyes. If God blesses His servant with licit property, and he devotes himself to God's service in gratitude for it, then deliberate renunciation of such property is not preferable to keeping it in accordance with His permission." Others say, "Renunciation of the forbidden is an obligation, whereas renunciation of the permitted is a virtue. If the servant has very little property, but is patient with this state of affairs, pleased with whatever God Most High has apportioned him, and content with what He gives him, it is better than striving for more and more in the world. God Most High has induced man to renounce worldly increase by His saying, 'Say: Little is the enjoyment of this world; the hereafter is best for those who fear God'" (4:77). Other verses can be found regarding the paltriness of the world and the call to renounce it.

Other people say, "If the servant spends his money in obedience, exhibits patience, and does not raise objections to what the law forbids him to do in the state of hardship, then it is preferable for him to renounce the permitted." Others comment, "It is fitting that the servant choose neither to abandon the permitted through deliberate effort nor to seek excess of his needs, being mindful of the portion [given him by God]. If God (may He be exalted and Most High) bestows upon him permitted property, he should thank Him. If God Most High fixes him at the limit of sufficiency, then he should not take it upon himself to seek surplus, for patience is most excellent for the possessor of poverty, and thankfulness is more proper for the possessor of permitted property." They say concerning the meaning of renunciation, "Each speaks from his own moment *[waqt]* and indicates his own limit. "

Sufyan ath-Thawri declared, "Renunciation of the world is reduction of hope for worldly gain, not eating coarse foods or wearing a rough cloak." Sari as-Saqati asserted, "God (may He be exalted) withdraws the world from His saints, denies it to His pure ones, and removes it from the hearts of those whom He loves, for He has not approved it for them."

It is said that renunciation is alluded to in His saying (may He be exalted and Most High), "In order that ye may not despair over matters that pass you by, nor exult over favors bestowed upon you" (57:23), because the renouncer does not delight in what he has of the world nor grieve over what he does not have. Abu 'Uthman remarked, "Renunciation is that you abandon the world and then not be concerned with those who take hold of it."

The master Abu 'Ali ad-Daqqaq said, "Renunciation is that you leave the world the way it is, not saying 'I will build in it a *ribat* [hospice] or construct a mosque.'" Yahya b. Mu'adh observed, "Renunciation causes generosity with possessions and love brings generosity with the spirit." Ibn al-Jalla' commented, "Renunciation is to regard the world with the eye of extinction so that it becomes low in your eyes. Then turning away from it will become easy for you." Ibn Khafif stated, "The mark of renunciation is the presence of repose in departing from property." He also remarked, "Renunciation is ridding the heart of secondary causes and shaking the hands loose from possessions."* It it said, "Renunciation is the soul's displeasure with the world without strenuous effort." An-Nasrabadhi declared, "The ascetic *[zahid]* is a stranger in the world, and the gnostic is a stranger in the hereafter." It is said, "To the one who is true in renunciation, the world will humbly present itself before him in wretchedness." For this reason it is said, "If a hat falls from the sky, it will only land on the head of someone who does not want it." Junayd instructed, "Renunciation is this: the heart is empty of that which the hand is empty of."

Abu Sulayman ad-Darani asserted, "Wool [garments] are one of the signs of renunciation, so it is not proper

---

* i.e., causes secondary to the divine will, which counts as the primary cause of all things.

for the ascetic to wear a woolen garment costing three dirhams when he has desire for five dirhams."

The ancestors have disagreed in the matter of renunciation. Sufyan ath-Thawri, Ahmad b. Hanbal, 'Isa b. Yunus, and others have stated, "Renunciation in this world is simply curtailment of hope for wordly gain." This has the meaning that the curtailment of hope is among the signs of renunciation, the causes that give rise to it, and the matters that necessitate it. 'Abdallah b. al-Mubarak commented, "Renunciation is trust in God Most High combined with the love of poverty." Shaqiq al-Balkhi and Yusuf b. Asbat have spoken similarly. So this is also among the signs of renunciation, for the servant is not able to give up the world except by trust in God Most High.

'Abd al-Wahid b. Zayd explained, "Renunciation is leaving behind the dinar and the dirham." Abu Sulayman ad-Darani observed, "Renunciation is abandoning whatever diverts you from God (may He be exalted and Most High)."

When Ruwaym asked al-Junayd about renunciation, he answered, "It is thinking little of the world and erasing its traces from the heart." Sari declared, "The life of the ascetic is not good if he is diverted from [concern with] his soul, and the life of the gnostic is not good if he is concerned with his soul." Al-Junayd said, "Renunciation is emptying the hand of possessions and the heart of attachments." When asked about renunciation, Shibli replied, "It is that you renounce whatever is other than God Most High." Yahya b. Mu'adh remarked, "One will not attain true renunciation until he possess these qualities: action without attachment, speaking without ambition, and glory without having power over men."

Abu Hafs said, "There cannot be renunciation except of the permitted. There is nothing permitted in the world, so there is no renunciation." Abu 'Uthman related, "God Most High gives the ascetic more than he desires, and He gives the desirous one less. He gives the moderate one exactly what he desires." Yahya b. Ma'adh stated, "The ascetic affronts your nose with the smell of vinegar and mustard, but the gnostic gives off the scent of musk and ambergris." Al-Hasan al-Basri explained, "Renunciation of the world is that you loathe its devotees and all it contains." One of them was asked, "What is renunciation of the world?" He replied, "It is leaving behind whatever is in it to whoever is in it. " A man asked Dhu'n-Nun al-Misri, "When may I renounce the world?" He answered, "When you renounce your self."

Muhammad b. al-Fadl said, "The unstinted giving of the ascetics is at the time of sufficiency, and that of the chivalrous is at the time of need." God Most High says, "[But those who before them had homes and had adopted the faith show their affection to such as came to them for refuge and entertain no desire in their hearts for things given] but they give them preference over themselves, even though poverty was their lot" (59:9).

Al-Kattani said, "Something to which the Kufans are not opposed, nor the Medinans, nor the Iraqis, nor the Syrians, is renunciation of the world, the generosity of the self, and wishing well to mankind." That is, no one says that these things are not praiseworthy.

A man asked Yahya b. Mu'adh, "When will I enter the tavern of trust, wear the cloak of renunciation, and be seated with the ascetics?" He replied, "When you come to a point, in the ascetic training of your soul in secret, that if God were to cut off your subsistence for three days, you would not weaken in your self. But when this goal is not attained, then sitting on the carpet of the ascetics is foolishness, and I do not guarantee you will not be disgraced among them."

Bishr al-Hafi asserted, "Renunciation is a king who does not dwell anywhere but in an emptied heart." Muhammad b. al-Ash'ath al-Bikandi declared, "Whoever speaks of renunciation and admonishes people while desiring what they own, God Most High removes the love of the hereafter from his heart." It is said, "When the servant renounces the world, God Most High entrusts him to an angel who implants wisdom in his heart." One of them was asked, "Why have you renounced the world?" He responded, "Because it has renounced me."

Ahmad b. Hanbal explained, "There are three kinds of renunciation: forswearing the forbidden is the renunciation of the common people; forswearing excess in the permitted is the renunciation of the elite; and foreswearing whatever diverts the servant from God Most High is the renunciation of the gnostics."

The master Abu 'Ali ad-Daqqaq related, "It was asked of one of them, 'Why have you renounced the world?' He said, 'Because I withdrew from most of it, I reject longing for the least of it.'"

Yahya b. Mu'adh observed, "The world is like the unveiled bride. The one who seeks the world becomes her lady's maid, and the one who renounces it blackens her face with soot, tears out her hair, and sets her dress on fire. The gnostic, preoccupied with God Most High, does not even turn his face in her direction."

As-Sari stated, "I carried out all the rules of renunciation and was granted whatever I wished of it except renunciation of people. I have not reached this, and I have not been able to endure it." It is said, "The ascetics have withdrawn only toward their own selves, because they abandon transitory bounties for abiding bounties." An-Nasrabadhi commented, "Renunciation spares the blood of the ascetics and sheds the blood of the gnostics."

Hatim al-Asamm remarked, "The ascetic consumes his purse before his self, and the one who strives to be abstemious uses up his self before his purse." Al-Fudayl b. 'Iyad related, "God placed all evil in one house and made its key love of the world. He placed all goodness in another house and made its key renunciation."

7

Silence

≈ Samt

On the authority of Abu Hurayra, the Prophet (may God's blessing and peace be upon him) is reported to have said, "Whoever believes in God and the Last Day, let him not harm his neighbor; whoever believes in God and the Last Day, let him honor his guest; and whoever believes in God and the Last Day, let him speak well or be silent." On the authority of Abu Umama, 'Uqba b. 'Amir is related to have asked, "O Messenger of God, what is salvation?" He replied, "Guard your tongue, be content with your house, and weep for your sins."

Silence represents security and it is the norm to be observed; remorse follows if one is compelled to abandon it. It is binding that the law, commands, and prohibitions be respected in it. Silence at the right time is the proper attribute for men, just as speaking on the right occasion is among the noblest qualities. The master Abu 'Ali ad-Daqqaq observed, "Whoever refrains from speaking the truth is a mute devil."

Silence is one of the manners proper in attending the

hadra [Sufi gathering], for God Most High says, "When the Qur'an is recited, listen to it with attention and hold your peace that ye may receive mercy" (7:204). God Most High said, recounting a meeting of the jinn with the Messenger (may God's blessing and peace be upon him), "When they stood in the presence of the Qur'an, they said: 'Listen in silence'" (46:29). God Most High says, "And voices are hushed for the Beneficent; nothing shall you hear but a faint murmur" (20:108).

How great a difference there is between a servant who is silent, protecting himself from lies and backbiting, and the servant who is silent because of his dominance by the monarch of awe. They have recited these verses as to its meanings:

> *I contemplate what I will say while we are*
> *apart*
> *And I continually perfect pleas of speech*
> *But then I forget them when we come together*
> *Speaking, when I do speak, absurdities.*

And they composed this:

> *O Layla, what a desperate need I have.*
> *But when I come to you, O Layla, I am not*
> *aware of what.*

And this:

> *How many words there were for you until*
> *when*
> *I was able to meet you, I was made to forget*
> *them.*

And this:

> *I perceived that speech adorns the young*
> *While silence is best for one who has*
> *become quiet.*
> *So then, how many letters bring death*
> *And how many speakers wished they had*
> *kept silent?*

There are two types of silence: outer silence and silence of the heart and mind. The heart of one who trusts completely in God is silent, not demanding any means for living. The gnostic's heart is silent in the face of divine decree through the attribute of harmony. The former is trusting by means of his goodly character, and the latter is content with all that He decrees.

They say as to the meaning of this:

> *His adversities afflict you*
> *But your worrying heart is content.*

The reason for silence might be the astonishment caused by a sudden insight, for when some matter is suddenly laid bare, words are muted and there is no eloquence, no speech at all. Witnesses are obliterated in that place, and there is neither cognition nor sensation. God Most High says, "One day God will gather the messengers together and ask, 'What was the response you received [from men]?' They will say, 'We have no knowledge'" (5:112).

Those engaged in striving *[mujahada]* prefer silence because they know the dangers inherent in words. They also know of the self's pleasure in speaking, displaying the qualities of praise and longing to be

known among his peers for the beauty of his eloquence. They realize that these are among the many
imperfections of mankind. This is the description of the
ones engaged in ascetic self-discipline, [silence being]
one of the basic principles for the wisdom of striving
and the refinement of character.

When Da'ud at-Ta'i wished to stay in his house, he
resolved to attend the gathering of Abu Hanifa (may
God have mercy on him) because he was one of his
students, sit among his peers of the *'ulama,* and say
nothing about the questions [under discussion]. When
his self was made strong in this trait and its practice for
a complete year, he then sat in his house and chose
seclusion.

When 'Umar b. 'Abd al-'Aziz (may God grant him
mercy) wrote something and found pleasure from its
wording, he would tear it to pieces and change it.

Bishr b. Harith instructed, "If speaking pleases you,
be silent! If silence pleases you, speak!" Sahl b. 'Abd allah asserted, "Nobody's silence is complete until he
imposes retreat on himself, and repentance is not
complete until he imposes silence on himself." Abu
Bakr al-Farisi declared, "If one's homeland is not
silence, he is talking to excess, even though he is silent
[with the tongue]. Silence is not confined to the tongue
but concerns the heart and all the limbs." One of them
commented, "One who makes no use of silence, when
he speaks, it is frivolity." Mamshad ad-Dinawari observed, "The wise have inherited wisdom by means of
silence and contemplation." When Abu Bakr al-Farisi
was asked about silence of the innermost being, he
replied, "It is to abandon concern with past and future."

He also said, "If the servant speaks only about what concerns him or is unavoidable, then he is within the bounds of silence." Mu'adh b. Jabal (may God be pleased with him) stated, "Speak little with men and much with God; perhaps your heart will behold Him." It was asked of Dhu'n-Nun al-Misri, "Among mankind, who is it that is the best protector of his heart?" He answered, "The one who is most in possession of his tongue." Ibn Mas'ud remarked, "There is nothing that deserves prolonged bondage more than the tongue."

'Ali b. Bukkar noted, "God made everything to have two doors, but He made four for the tongue: the two lips and the teeth."

It is said that Abu Bakr as-Siddiq (may God be pleased with him) would hold a stone in his mouth for some years so he would speak less. Abu Hamza al-Baghdadi (may God grant him mercy) was an excellent speaker. Once a voice called out to him, "You spoke, and you excelled in it. It remains to you now to be silent and excel at that." So he did not speak after this until he died, which happened about one week later. Sometimes silence is a chastisement for one who speaks because he had infringed the norms of the Path in some way.

When ash-Shibli sat in his circle of students and they were not questioning him, he would say, "And the word will be fulfilled against them because they have done wrong, and they will not speak" (27:85). Sometimes one accustomed to speaking is silent because there is someone present who is better with words.

Ibn as-Sammak relates that Shah al-Kirmani and Yahya b. Mu'adh were friends, and they lived in the same city, but Shah was not attending his gathering. When asked the reason, he replied, "This is only proper." They persisted until one day he attended his gathering and sat in a section where Yahya b. Mu'adh could not see him. Yahya began to speak; then suddenly he became silent. Then he announced, "There is someone here who speaks better than I do," and was at a loss to continue. So Shah asserted, "I told you it is better that I not come to his gathering."

Sometimes silence imposes itself on the speaker because of some state among those present. Perhaps someone present is not fit to hear that speech, so God Most High guards the speaker's tongue out of solicitude and protection of the speech.

It might be that the speaker's silence is due to the fact that God knows one of those attending to be capable of learning that speech but likely to be tempted by it, whether because he imagines it to come from his own state and it does not, or because it burdens his soul with what it cannot bear. Then God (may He be exalted and glorified) has mercy on him and preserves him from hearing that speech, either protecting him or preventing him from committing an error.

The sheikhs of this path have explained, "Sometimes the reason for someone's silence is because a jinn is present who is not to hear it. The gatherings of the Sufis are not free of the attendance of groups of jinn."

The master Abu 'Ali ad-Daqqaq (may God grant him mercy) related, "I fell ill in Marw one time, and I longed to return to Nishapur. I dreamed that a voice called out to me, saying, 'You cannot leave this city. There is a group of jinn attending your sessions and they are benefiting from the talks you give. For their sakes, stay where you are.'" One of the sages observed, "Man was created with only one tongue but two eyes and two ears. This is so he would listen and watch more than he speaks."

Ibrahim b. Adham was invited to a feast. When he sat down, the other guests began to gossip and slander others. He remarked, "It is our custom to eat the meat after the bread. You begin with the meat first." In this he referred to the words of God Most High, "[Do not slander one another.] Would any of you like to eat the flesh of his dead brother? You would abhor that" (59:12).

One of the Sufis said, "Silence is the language of forbearance." One of them instructed, "Learn silence just as you learned speech. If speech used to guide you, silence will protect you." It is said, "The modesty of the tongue is its silence." And "The tongue is like a wild beast. If you do not tie it up, it will attack you."

Abu Hafs was asked, "Which state is better for the saint, silence or speech?" He answered, "If the speaker knows of the harmful effects of speech, then let him remain silent, if he is able, as long as Noah's life span. And if the silent one knows of the harmful effects of silence, then let him ask God Most High for a life span double that of Noah's so that he may speak."

It is said, "Silence for the common people is with their tongues, silence for the gnostics is with their hearts, and silence for lovers is with restraining the stray thoughts that come to their innermost beings." It was said to one of them, "Speak!" He responded, "I do not have a tongue." So they commanded, "Listen!" He replied, "There is not a place in me wherein I can listen." One of them related, "I stayed for thirty years with my tongue hearing nothing but my heart, and then I stayed for thirty years with my heart hearing nothing but my tongue."

One of them stated, "If your tongue is silenced, then you have not been delivered from the words of your heart. If you become nothing but rotted bones, you still will not have rid yourself from the words of your self. And even if you strive greatly, your spirit still will not speak to you because it is the concealment for the secret."

It is said, "The fool's tongue is his key to death." It is also said, "If the lover is silent, he perishes, and if the gnostic is silent, he rules." Al-Fudayl b. 'Iyad declared, "Whoever reckons his words to be among his works [for which he will be requited], his words are few except in what concerns him."

8

Fear

❧ Khawf

God most High says, "They call on their Lord in fear and hope" (32:16).

On the authority of Abu Hurayra, the Messenger of God (may God's blessing and peace be upon him) is reported to have declared, "One who weeps out of fear of God Most High will not enter the Fire as long as milk continues to flow from breasts. [Moreover], dust from the path of God will never combine in the nostrils of a servant with the smoke of Hell." Anas reported that the Messenger of God asserted, "If you knew what I know, you would laugh little and cry much."

I say that fear is a matter pertaining to future events, for one fears only lest something undesirable befall him or something desirable pass him by. This occurs only in relation to the future. As for what already exists, fear does not pertain to it. Fear of God Most High is dreading His punishment in this life or in the hereafter. God has made fear a duty for His servants, demanding, "Fear Me if you are believers" (3:175). And He says, "[Take not two gods, there is only One God], so fear Me alone" (16:51). He praised the believers because of fear when He said, "They fear their Lord above them" (16:50).

The master Abu 'Ali ad-Daqqaq (may God grant him mercy) explained, "Fear has differing stages: *khawf, khashya,* and *hayba* [fear, dread, and awe]. *Khawf* is one of the conditions of faith and its criterion, for God Most High says, 'Fear Me if you are believers' (3:175). *Khashya* is one of the conditions of outer knowledge, for God Most High says, 'Truly they fear God, among His servants, who are learned' (35:28). And *haiba* is one of the conditions of inner knowledge, for God Most High says, 'God bids you beware [only] of Himself'" (3:28).

Abu Hafs stated, "Fear is God's whip with which He chastises those who rebelliously abandon His threshold." Abu'l-Qasim al-Hakim noted, "Fear is of two sorts: terror *[rahba]* and fear *[khashya]*. The possessor of *rahba* takes refuge in flight when he is afraid, but the possessor of *khashya* takes refuge in the Lord." It is correct that it is said that the words *"rahaba"* [to stand in terror] and *"haraba"* [to flee] have one meaning, just as is the case with *jadhaba* [to attract] and *jabadha* [the same]. When one flees *[haraba]*, he is attracted to his own desire, like the monks *[ruhban]* who follow their desires. But if their restraint is the rein of knowledge and founded on the truth of the law, then it is fear *[khashya]*.

Abu Hafs observed, "Fear is the lamp of the heart; by it one sees the good and evil of the heart." The master Abu 'Ali ad-Daqqaq (may God grant him mercy) commented, "Fear is that you leave off making excuses with *'asa* and *saufa* ['it might possibly be...' and 'it will be...'].'' Abu 'Umar ad-Dimashqi asserted, "The fearful one is he who is afraid of his own self more than he fears the devil." Ibn al-Jalla' remarked, "The one who fears [God] is he who feels safe from frightening things." It is said, "The fearful one is not he who weeps and wipes his eyes; on the contrary he is the one who abandons whatever he fears will bring punishment." It was asked of al-Fudayl, "How is it that we do not see the fearful ones?" He answered, "If you were fearing, then you would see them. Only the fearful one sees the fearful. It is the mother bereft of her child who likes to see other mourning mothers."

Yahya b. Mu'adh noted, "Poor son of Adam, if he feared the Fire as much as he fears poverty, he would enter Paradise." Shah al-Kirmani stated, "The mark of fear is constant sorrow." Abu'l-Qasim al-Hakim declared, "One fearful of something flees from it, and one fearful of God [may He be exalted and glorified] flees to Him." Dhu'n-Nun al-Misri (may God have mercy on him) was asked, "When does the way of fear become easy for the servant?" He replied, "When he considers his self to be in a state of illness, avoiding everything out of fear that his illness will be prolonged," Mu'adh b. Jabal (may God be pleased with him) related, "The believer's heart cannot be at peace, and his fear cannot be calmed until he leaves the bridge of Hell behind him." Bishr al-Hafi commented, "Fear of God is a king that resides only in the heart of a pious one." Abu 'Uthman al-Hiri observed, "The defect to which the fearful one is exposed is finding contentment in his fear because it is a hidden form of safety."

Al-Wasiti said, "Fear is a veil between God and the servant." This expression is problematic, but its meaning is that the fearful one expects the coming moment while the "sons of the present moment" have no expectation of the future. "The merits of the righteous are the sins of the near ones *[muqarrabun]*," An-Nuri asserted, "The fearing one flees from his Lord to his Lord." One of them remarked, "The token of fear is bewilderment and waiting at the gate of the unseen." When al-Junayd was asked about fear, he responded, "It is anticipation of punishment with each passing breath." Abu Sulayman ad-Darani noted, "Whenever fear leaves a heart, it is ruined." Abu 'Uthman said, "Sincerity of fear is abstaining from sins, inwardly and outwardly." Dhu'n-Nun stated, "People remain on the path as long as fear does not withdraw from them, for if fear abandons them, they lose their way." Hatim al-Asamm explained, "There is for everything an adornment, and the adornment of worship is fear. The mark of fear is the cutting short of hope for worldy success."

A man told Bishr al-Hafi, "I see that you fear death!" He replied, "Coming into the presence of God (may He be exalted and glorified) is hard." I heard the master Abu 'Ali ad-Daqqaq relate, "I went to visit Abu Bakr b. Furak when he was ill. When he saw me, his tears flowed, so I said to him, 'May God restore your health and cure you.' He retorted, 'You think that I fear death? On the contrary, I fear what is beyond death.'"

It is reported on the authority of 'Abd ar-Rahman b. Sa'id b. Mawhib that 'A'isha (may God be pleased with her) asked, "O Messenger of God, who are 'Those who give that which they give with hearts full of fear [because they will return to their Lord]' (23:60)? Are they people such as the man who steals and commits adultery and drinks wine?" He answered, "No, it is the man who fasts and prays and gives charity while fearing that it might not be accepted from him."

Ibn al-Mubarak (may God grant him mercy) declared, "That which arouses fear so that it comes to abide in the heart is continual observation *[muraqaba]*, secretly and openly." This report is confirmed by 'Ali ar-Razi. Ibrahim b. Shayban commented, "When fear dwells in the heart, the objects of desire are burned away from it and the desire for the world is exiled from it." It is said, "Fear is the force that propels knowledge down the paths of implementation." And "Fear is the movement and agitation of the heart due to the Lord's majesty." Abu Sulayman ad-Darani stated, "It is necessary that nothing gain supremacy over the heart except fear, for if hope gains supremacy over the heart, it becomes corrupted." Then he observed, "O Ahmad [his *murid*], they ascend through fear, and if they neglect it, they fall." Al-Wasiti asserted, "Fear and hope are reins on the self so that they are not left to their own frivolity." He also said, "If God triumphs over men's innermost beings, not a remnant remains for hope and fear." Let me remark that there is a subtlety in this. It means that when the signs of God Most High overcome the innermost beings of men, they master them so that no capacity remains for recalling created things and beings. Whereas fear and hope result from the continuance of the perception of human limitation.

Al-Husayn b. Mansur noted, "Whoever is afraid of something other than God [may He be exalted and glorified] or hopes for anything other than Him, all doors close upon him and fear predominates over him, veiling his heart with seventy veils, the least of which is doubt." That which has made them fear intensely is their thought of the final outcome and dread of the transformation of their states, for God Most High has said, "Say: 'Shall we tell you of those who lose most by their deeds?'—those whose efforts go astray in this life while they thought that they were performing good works" (18:103-104). So then, how many are they who will be pleased with their states when the state is turned against them and they are sorely tried by the association with despicable doings? Then intimacy is exchanged for frightening loneliness and absence for presence.

I often heard the master Abu 'Ali ad-Daqqaq (may God grant him mercy) recite:

> *You thought well of time when it was beautiful*
> *And you never thought in fear about the*
> *evil destiny brings.*
> *The nights kept peace with you so you were*
> *deceived by them.*
> *With the clear night comes sorrow.*

I heard Mansur b. Khalaf relate, "There were two men who kept each other's company while engaged in devotion. Then one of them departed and left his friend. After a long time passed, there had been no news of him. While the man who had stayed behind was in the army fighting the Byzantine troops, a man covered in armor attacked the Muslims looking for a duel. One of the Muslim champions came to him, and the Byzantine killed him. Then another came, and he was killed. Then a third Muslim came, and he also was killed. This Sufi came to him and they fought. The Byzantine's face was uncovered. It was his companion who had accompanied him in devotion and worship for some years! So he exclaimed, 'What is this?' The other replied, 'I have apostasized and married into these people and have many sons and a great fortune amassed.' He cried, 'And you are a person who used to recite the Qur'an in its different modes!' He replied, 'I do not remember one letter of it.' So the Sufi said to him, 'Desist! And return.' He retorted, 'I will not, for I have fame and money. So you leave me, or I will do to you what I have done to your friends.' The Sufi declared, 'Know that you have already killed three Muslims; there is no shame for you if you depart, so leave and I will grant you a respite.' So the man withdrew, turning his back, and the Sufi followed and stabbed him, killing him. After all that struggle and continuous spiritual discipline, the man died a Christian!"

It is said, "When what happened to Iblis [Satan] happened, Gabriel and Michael [peace be upon them] suddenly began to weep for a long time, so God Most High revealed to them, 'O you two, what is the matter with you that you are shedding all those tears?' They answered, 'O our Lord, we do not feel safe from Your cunning.' So God Most High said, 'Be like this, and do not feel safe from My cunning.'" Sari as-Saqati explained, "I look at my nose several times a day in this manner, fearful that it has become black out of what I fear in punishment." Abu Hafs related, "For forty years I firmly believed of myself that God Most High was looking upon me with wrath and my works proved that." Hatim al-Asamm asserted, "Do not be deceived by righteous places, for there is no place more righteous than Paradise, and consider what Adam [peace be upon him] met with in a righteous place! And do not be deceived by abundant acts of worship, for consider what Iblis came to after so much worship. And do not be deceived by large quantities of knowledge, for Balaam knew the Greatest Name of God, and consider what he met with!* And do not be deceived by meeting the pious, for there is no person with a greater destiny than Mustafa [may God's blessing and peace be upon him], and meeting him did not benefit [some of] his relatives and enemies."

Coming upon his companions one day, Ibn al-Mubarak reported, "I was bold with God [may He be exalted and glorified] yesterday—I asked Him for Paradise."

It is said that Jesus (peace be upon him) went on a journey, and with him was a pious man from the Children of Israel. A sinner, notorious among them for his degeneracy, followed them. Seating himself at a distance from them, he called out to God [may He be exalted] in utter humility, saying, "O my God, forgive me!" The pious man prayed, "O my God, spare me the company of that sinner on the morrow!" So God Most High revealed to Jesus, "I have answered both of their prayers; I have driven out the pious one from paradise and I have forgiven the sinner."

---

* An allusion to Qur'an 7:175, which speaks of an unnamed person who was led astray by Satan despite God's gift to him of His signs. Tradition has seen here a reference to Balaam.

Dhu'n-Nun al-Misri related, "I asked a learned one, 'Why do they say you are mad?' He said, 'When He shut me off from Him for a long time, I went mad for fear of becoming separated from Him in the hereafter.'" And they recite this as to its meaning:

Even if I were made of rock I would wither away.
So how can a being created from clay bear it?

One of them commented, "I never saw a man more hopeful for the Muslims or more fearful for himself than Ibn Sirin."

Sufyan ath-Thawri became ill. When the reason for his illness was suggested to the doctor, he replied, "This is a man whose liver has been torn apart by fear." The doctor came and felt his pulse. Then he said, "I did not know that there was such a person in Islam."

Shibli was asked, "Why does the sun pale at the time of sunset?" He answered, "Because it has been cut off from the place of perfection. It becomes yellow for fear of standing before God." This is like the believer: when his departure from the world draws near, his color becomes yellow because he fears standing before God. And when the sun rises, it rises luminous. Likewise the believer, when he is raised from his grave, emerges with his face shining.

Ahmad b. Hanbal (may God have mercy on him) said, "I asked my Lord [may He be exalted and glorified] to open for me the gate of fear. He opened it, and then I feared for my sanity. So I prayed, 'O Lord, give me fear only to the extent I am able to endure.' So that excess passed from me."

9

Hope

❧ Raja'

God Most High says, "For those who hope for the meeting with God [let them know] the time is surely coming" (29:5).

Al-'Ala' b. Zayd related, "I went to Malik b. Dinar and found Shahr b. Hawshab with him. When Shahr and I were coming away from our meeting with Malik b. Dinar, I said to Shahr, 'May God Most High grant you mercy, give me some counsel and enrich me. God Most High will enrich you.' He replied, 'Certainly. My aunt Umm ad-Darda' told me on the authority of Abu'd-Darda' that the Prophet of God [may God's blessing and peace be upon him] reported that Gabriel [peace be upon him] stated, "Your Lord [may He be exalted and glorified] declared, 'My servant, as long as you worship Me, hope for [meeting] Me, and do not associate partners with Me, I will forgive you for whatever you have done. Even if you come to Me with evil deeds and sins as great as the earth's expanse, I will receive you with that much forgiveness. I will forgive you, and not be concerned [with how much you have sinned].'"'"

64

Anas b. Malik reports that the Messenger of God (may God's blessing and peace be upon him) asserted, "God Most High will say on the Day of Resurrection, 'Come forth from the fire all you who have in your hearts as much as a barleycorn's weight of faith.' Then He will command, 'Come forth from the fire all you who have as much as a mustard seed's weight of faith in your hearts.' Then He will declare, 'I swear by My glory and majesty, My treatment of one who believed in Me for even one hour of the night or day will never be the same as My treatment of one who never believed in Me.'"

Hope is the heart's attachment to something it loves that will transpire in the future, just as fear relates to what will take place in the future. Therefore hope applies to something one expects to come about. The heart is enlivened by hope; it carries the heart's burdens. The distinction between hope and wishing for something is that wishing makes one lazy. One who only wishes for something will never put forth effort or serious intent [to achieve it]. The opposite is true for one who has hope. Hope is a commendable trait, but wishing for something is a deficiency in men.

The Sufis have spoken much about hope. Shah al-Kirmani observed, "The sign of hope is goodly obedience [to God]." Ibn Khubayq explained, "There are three kinds of hope: there is a man who does good works; his hope is that these works will be accepted by God. There is a man who does evil things and then repents; his hope is for forgiveness. Finally, there is a deceitful man who persists in his sinful deeds, all the while saying, 'I hope for forgiveness.' In the one who knows he is doing evil, fear should predominate over hope."

It is said, "Hope is relying on the bountifulness of the Generous, Loving One." It is said, "Hope is seeing the divine splendor with the eye of beauty." It is said, "Hope is the heart's nearness to the Lord's benevolence." It is said, "Hope is the heart's delight in the excellence of one's return [to God]." It is also said, "Hope means holding in view the all-embracing mercy of God Most High."

Abu 'Ali ar-Rudhbari commented, "Fear and hope are like the two wings of a bird. When they are equal, the bird is balanced and his flight is perfect. When one of them is lacking, this makes the bird lose its ability to fly. When both fear and hope are missing, the bird plummets to its death."

Ahmad b. 'Asim al-Antaki was asked, "What is the sign of hope in the servant?" He replied, "It is that when beneficence surrounds him, he is inspired to be thankful, full of hope for the completion of the blessings of God Most High in this world and for complete forgiveness in the hereafter."

Abu 'Abdallah b. Khafif stated, "Hope means taking the existence of His favors as a sure sign [of His mercy to come]." He also said, "Hope is the heart's delight in seeing the generosity of the Beloved in Whom hope is placed." Abu 'Uthman al-Maghribi declared, "Whoever impels himself to hope [alone] will fall into idleness. Whoever impels himself to fear [alone] will fall into despondency. But there is a time for hope and a time for fear; both have their place."

Bakr b. Salim as-Sawwaf related, "We went to visit Malik b. Anas on the evening he died. We asked, 'O Abu

'Abdallah, how do you find yourself?' He answered, 'I do not know what to say to you other than this: you will see with your own eyes forgiveness from God Most High in a measure beyond your imagination.' We stayed with him after this until we closed his eyes following his death."

Yahya b. Mu'adh asserted, "The hope that I place in You when I sin is almost greater than the hope that I place in You when I perform good works. This is because, when I perform good works, I find myself relying upon my sincerity in performing them. But how can I guard my works from faults, I who am marked with faults? When I engage in sin, I find myself relying on Your forgiveness. How can You not forgive my sins, You Who have the attribute of generosity?"

Some men were speaking to Dhu'n-Nun al-Misri while he was on the verge of death. He instructed them, "Do not concern yourselves with me, for I have marveled at the abundance of God Most High's benevolence toward me." Yahya b. Ma'adh remarked, "My God, the sweetest gift in my heart is hope for You. The most pleasant words my tongue makes are in praise of You. The hour I hold dearest is the hour in which I will meet You."

It is found in one of the commentaries that the Messenger of God (may God's blessing and peace be upon him) came to his companions through the gate of the Banu Shayba. He found them laughing and said, "Do you laugh? If you knew what I know, you would laugh little and cry much." He left them, and then he returned, saying, "Gabriel [peace be upon him] appeared to me after I left you. He brought these words of God, 'Tell My servants that I am Oft-Forgiving, Most Merciful'" (15:49).

On the authority of 'A'isha, the Messenger of God (may God's blessing and peace be upon him) is reported to have said, "God Most High laughs when His servants are seized with desperation and hopelessness when all the while His mercy is near to them." 'A'isha asked, "By my father and mother, O Messenger of God, does our Lord (may He be exalted and glorified) truly laugh?" He replied, "By the One in Whose hand is my soul, He certainly laughs." She noted, "He will not deprive us of the good if He laughs!" Know that laughter is an attribute pertaining to His actions. It is a manifestation of His bounty. This is like the saying, "The earth 'laughs' plants" [meaning it sprouts them forth]. His laughter at the hopelessness of men is a sign of the certainty of His bounty, which is many times greater than what they can ever imagine to expect from Him.

It is said that a Magian asked Abraham (peace be upon him) for hospitality. Abraham told him, "If you embrace Islam, I will be your host." The Magian responded, "If I embrace Islam, how will you favor me?" Then the Magian went away. God Most High said to Abraham, "O Abraham, you agree to feed him only if he changes his religion? We have fed him for seventy years despite his belief. If you were to receive him for one night, how would that trouble you?" Hearing this, Abraham went after the Magian and invited him to be his guest. When the Magian asked him why he had changed his mind, Abraham told him the story of what God had said. The Magian inquired, "Is this the way He treats me? Present Islam to me." Then he accepted Islam.

Abu Sahl as-Sa'luki (may God grant him mercy) dreamed of Abu Sahl az-Zajjaj. Abu Sahl az-Zajjaj used to speak much about eternal damnation. Abu Sahl as-Su'luki asked him in his dream, "What state do you find yourself in after death?" He answered, "The matter is easier than I had thought." Abu Bakr b. Ishkib related, "I dreamed of the master Abu Sahl as-Su'luki. His state was excellent beyond words. I inquired, 'O master, how did you attain this?' He told me, 'By my good opinion of My Lord.'" When Malik b. Dinar was seen in a dream, he was asked, "What has God done with you?" He replied, "I came before my Lord [may He be exalted and glorified] with many sins, but my good opinion of Him has erased all my sins from me."

On the authority of Abu Hurayra (may God be pleased with him) the Prophet (may God's blessing and peace be upon him) is reported to have said, "God [may He be exalted] says, 'I am as My servant thinks of Me, and I am with him when he makes remembrance of Me. If he makes remembrance of Me inwardly, I make remembrance of him to Myself. If he makes remembrance of Me in an assembly of men, I make remembrance of him in an assembly better than his. If he draws nearer to Me by a few inches, I draw nearer to him by one yard. If he draws nearer to Me by one yard, I draw nearer to him by two yards. If he comes to Me walking, I come to him running.'"

It is told that Ibn Mubarak was fighting one of the idolators one time. When the hour for the idolator's prayer came, he asked Ibn Mubarak for a respite. Ibn Mubarak let him go. When the man was prostrating to the sun, Ibn Mubarak had an urge to strike him with his sword. Suddenly he heard a voice in the wind commanding, "And keep the vow. Every vow will be inquired into" (17:34). So Ibn Mubarak held back his sword. When the idolator finished his ritual, he asked Ibn Mubarak, "Why did you stop before carrying out what you intended?" Ibn Mubarak told him about the voice. The idolator declared, "How perfect is the Lord who scolds his friend on behalf of his enemy!" Then he became a Muslim, and an excellent one.

It is said, "God caused men to sin when He gave Himself the name 'Forgiver.'" It is said, "If God had said, 'I will forgive no sin,' then no Muslim would ever commit a sin." For when He says, "God will not forgive [men who] associate partners with Him" (4:48), the Muslims never associate partners with Him. But when He declares, "But He will forgive anything else to whom He wishes" (4:48), then men expect His forgiveness [and commit sins].

Ibrahim b. Adham (may God be pleased with him) said, "One time I waited a long spell for the area around the Ka'ba to be free of crowds. It was a dark night and rain was falling heavily. At last the area was empty, so I began to walk around the Ka'ba crying, 'O my God, protect me from sin, protect me!' Then I heard a voice say, 'O Ibn Adham, you ask Me for protection from sin, as do all men. But if I were to render you all sinless, to whom could I be merciful?'"

When Abu'l-'Abbas b. Shurayh was ill with the sickness that caused his death, he dreamed that the Resurrection had taken place. The All-Powerful One (may He be exalted) asked, "Where are the scholars?" Abu'l-'Abbas continued, "All the scholars, including myself, came forward. God inquired, 'What have you done with what you have learned?' We replied, 'O Lord, we have been negligent and we have done evil.' Then God repeated the question as if He were displeased with the answer we had given and wanted another one. So I reported, 'As for myself, my record of deeds contains no acts of associating partners with You, and You have promised that You will forgive everything other than this.' God declared, 'Go now, all of you; I forgive you.'" Abu'l-'Abbas died three nights after having this dream.

There once was a drunkard, who gathered together a group of his drinking companions. He gave one of his slaves four dirhams and told him to buy some fruits for the gathering. The slave went out and passed by the gathering of Mansur b. 'Ammar, just as Mansur was asking the people to give charity for some pauper, saying, "Whoever gives four dirhams, I will make four prayers on his behalf." The slave gave the four dirhams he had with him to Mansur, who asked him, "What do you want me to pray for?" He answered, "I wish to be free from my master." Mansur prayed for that, then asked, "What else?" The slave said, "I want God Most High to recompense me for the four dirhams." Mansur prayed for that, then inquired, "What else?" The slave said, "I want God to induce repentance in my master." Mansur prayed for that. Then he said, "What else?" The slave responded, "I want God to forgive me, my master, you and all the people there." Mansur prayed for that. Then the slave returned to his master. When his master asked him why he was so late, the slave told him the story. The master asked, "And what did you pray for?" The slave answered, "I asked to be set free." The master declared, "You may go; you are free. And what was the second?" He said, "That God recompense me for the four dirhams." The master replied, "Here are four thousand dirhams for you. And what was the third." The slave said, "That God induce repentance in you." The master stated, "I repent unto God Most High. And what was the fourth?" The slave told him, "That God Most High forgive you, me, the people, and Mansur." The master said, "This is the only one that I have no power to carry out." When he went to sleep that night, the master perceived someone in his dream saying, "You have done what was in your power to do. Do you suppose that I will not do what is within My power? I forgive you, the slave, Mansur b. 'Ammar, and those people attending [the gathering]."

It is said that Rabah al-Qaysi used to perform the pilgrimage many times. One day he stood [next to the Ka'ba] under the drainspout and stated, "O my God, I give such-and-such a number of my pilgrimages to the Messenger [may Your blessings and peace be upon him], ten of them to his ten Companions, two of them to my parents, and the remainder to all the Muslims." He gave them all away without leaving any of his pilgrimages to his own credit. He heard an invisible caller declare, "Here is one who shows Us generosity! I forgive you, your parents, and all those who profess Islam."

'Abd al-Wahhab b. 'Abd al-Majid ath-Thaqafi related, "One time I saw a bier pass by carried by three men and a woman. I went up and took the woman's place. We proceeded to the graveyard; we prayed over the body and buried it. I asked the woman afterwards, 'What relation did he have to you?' She replied, 'He was my son.' I inquired, 'Do you not have any neighbors [who could have carried the bier]?' She said, 'Yes, but they all looked down on him.' I asked, 'How was that?' She answered, 'He was a catamite.' I felt sorry for her, so I brought her to my house and gave her some money, wheat, and clothing. In my sleep that night, I saw an apparition coming toward me looking like the full moon. He had on a white garment, and he made motions to thank me. When I asked him who he was, he explained, 'I am the catamite you buried today. My Lord has granted me mercy because of people's contempt for me.'"

Abu 'Amr al-Bikandi was passing down a street one day when he came upon a crowd of people who were calling for the banishment of a youth from the neighborhood for his immoral acts. A woman was there, crying. It was said that she was the boy's mother. Abu 'Amr felt compassion for her and pleaded with the crowd on behalf of the youth, "Release the youth this time, for my sake. If he repeats his immoral acts after this, then do with him as you wish." They let the boy go, and Abu 'Amr departed. After some days, he passed down that street again and he heard the woman crying from behind a door. He said to himself, "Perhaps the youth went back to his immoral ways, and they have banished him from the neighborhood." He knocked at the door and asked the woman what had happened to the youth. She came out and exclaimed, "He has died!" When Abu 'Amr asked her how he was when he died, she answered, "When he came near his time of death, he told me, 'Do not tell the neighbors about my death, for having suffered because of me, they will rejoice at my misfortune and not attend my funeral. When you bury me, take this ring engraved with "In the name of God" and bury it with me. When you are finished burying me, then plead on my behalf to my Lord [may He be exalted and glorified].' I did as he requested. As I was coming away from his graveside, I heard a voice calling out, 'Go now, O mother. I have come before a Lord Most Generous.'"

It is said that God revealed to David (peace be upon him), "Say to men that I have not created them so I could profit from them. I created them so they profit from Me."

Ibrahim al-Utrush related, "We were sitting one time on the banks of the Tigris with Ma'ruf al-Karkhi when a gang of young men passed by us in a boat. They were shaking tambourines, drinking wine, and playing boisterously. We asked Ma'ruf, 'Do you not see how they are openly rebelling against God Most High? Pray to God to punish them!' Ma'ruf raised up his hands in prayer, 'O my God, just as You have made them merry in this life, make them merry in the next life.' We exclaimed, 'But we asked you to pray for them to be punished!' He replied, 'If He makes them merry in the next life, then He will already have forgiven them.'"

Abu 'Abdallah al-Husayn b. 'Abdallah b. Sa'id reported, "Yahya b. Aktham al-Qadi was a friend of mine.

He loved me and I loved him. After he died, I longed to see him in my dreams so that I might ask him what God Most High had done with him. One night I did see him in my dreams, and I asked him. He answered, 'God has forgiven me. But He reprimanded me, saying, "O Yahya, you worked mischief against Me in the world." I responded, "This is true my Lord. I rely on a tradition related to me on the authority of Abu Hurayra that the Messenger [may Your blessings and peace be upon him] stated that You said, 'I am ashamed to punish one with white hair in the fire.'" God declared, "I pardon you, O Yahya, and the Prophet spoke the truth. But you acted unjustly toward Me when you were on earth."'"

10

Sorrow

?? Huzn

God Most High says, "And they will say [when in Paradise], 'Praise be to God Who has removed sorrow from us'" (35:34).

It is reported on the authority of Abu Sa'id al-Khudri that the Messenger of God (may God's blessing and peace be upon him) stated, "Whenever an evil befalls the believing servant, whether suffering, disease, sorrow, or a pain that troubles him, God Most High pardons him thereby for his sins."

Sorrow is a condition that rescues the heart from being scattered in the valleys of forgetfulness. And sorrow is one of the qualities of the people of the Path. The master Abu 'Ali ad-Daqqaq (may God have mercy on him) said, "The one full of sorrow travels along the path of God in one month [a distance] one deprived of sorrow cannot travel in years."

In the tradition it is said, "Verily God loves every sorrowful heart." The Torah states, "When God loves a servant, He places a mourner in his heart, and when He hates a servant, He places a flute in his heart." And it is told that the Messenger of God (may God's blessing and peace be upon him) was in a state of unceasing sorrow, endless reflection.

Bishr b. Harith observed, "Sorrow is a king who, when he dwells in a place, does not consent to have anyone dwell there with him." It is said, "If there is no sorrow in the heart, it becomes destroyed, just as the house falls to ruin if there is no one dwelling in it." Abu Sa'id al-Qarshi commented, "Tears of sorrow make one blind, but tears of longing dim the sight, not blind it. God Most High states, 'And his eyes became white with the sorrow that he was suppressing.'" (12:84).

Ibn Khafif explained, "Sorrow is restraining the self from arising to seek pleasure." Rabi'a al-'Adawiya heard a man crying, "O, alas for sorrow!" She asserted, "Say, 'Alas for the paltriness of our sorrow.' If you were [truly] filled with sorrow, you could not breathe." Sufyan b. 'Uyayna declared, "If there is one [who is] grief-stricken crying in a community, then God Most High has mercy on them all because of his tears." Da'ud at-Ta'i used to be overcome with sorrow, and he would say at night, "O God! Concern for You ruins for me the other concerns and comes between me and sleep." And He would answer, "How can one for whom afflictions are renewed with every moment seek consolation for sorrow?" It is said, "Sorrow holds one back from food, and fear prevents sins." One of them was asked, "By what is the sorrow of man judged?" He answered, "By the abundance of his groans."

Sari as-Saqati stated, "I wish that the sorrow of all mankind would be thrown upon me." Many have spoken about sorrow, and they all say that only sorrow inspired by concern for the Hereafter is praiseworthy, not the sorrow of this world. But Abu 'Uthman al-Hiri explains, "Sorrow in all its aspects is a virtue and an increase for the believer so long as it is not because of a sin. Even if it does not bring about a special rank, then it brings about forgiveness."

Whenever one of the companions of a certain sheikh would leave on a journey, he would instruct, "If you see one filled with sorrow, give him my greetings." The master Abu 'Ali al-Daqqaq said, "One of them would ask the sun as it was setting, 'Have you shone today on anyone full of sorrow?'"

One never saw al-Hasan al-Basri without supposing that he had recently experienced disaster. When al-Fudayl died, Waki' noted, "Sorrow has today vanished from the earth." One of the early generation of Muslims declared, "The majority of what the believer will find on his page of good deeds will be affliction and sorrow." Fudayl b. 'Iyad commented, "The ancestors used to say, 'There is *zakat* [almsgiving] due on everything, and the *zakat* of the heart is prolonged sorrow.'" When Abu 'Uthman al-Hiri was asked about sorrow, he replied, "The sorrowful one does not have time to be occupied with questions of sorrow. So strive in search of sorrow and then ask."

11

Hunger and the Abandonment of Passion

❧ Ju' wa Tark ash-Shahwa

God Most High says, "Be sure We shall test you with something of fear and hunger" (2:155). Then, at the close of the verse, He says, "But give glad tidings to those who patiently persevere." So He gave glad tidings to them of beautiful reward for patience in enduring hunger. And God Most High says, "They gave them preference over themselves even though poverty was their own lot" (59:9).

Anas b. Malik relates that when Fatima (may God be pleased with her) brought a small piece of bread to the Messenger of God (may God's blessing and peace be upon him), he asked, "What is this, O Fatima?" She answered, "A loaf of bread that I baked. My heart would not be still until I brought you this piece." He responded, "This is the first bit of food to enter your father's mouth for three days." (In one report, it was a loaf of barley bread that Fatima brought.)

For this reason hunger is among the qualities of this group of people [the Sufis] and one of the pillars of striving. Those on the Path proceed step by step to the habit of hunger and refraining from eating, and they find wellsprings of wisdom in hunger. The tales about them in this matter are many.

Ibn Salim observed, "The proper manner of hungering [as a practice] is that one continuously reduce his customary intake of food by a small amount. It is said that Sahl b. 'Abdallah ate only every fifteen days. When the month of Ramadan arrived, he did not eat until he saw the new crescent moon, and every night he would break his fast with nothing but water.

Yahya b. Mu'adh explained, "If one could purchase hunger in the marketplace, then the seekers of the Hereafter would not need to buy anything else there." Sahl b. 'Abdallah commented, "When God Most High created the world, He placed sin and ignorance within satisfaction of the appetite and knowledge and wisdom within hunger." Yahya b. Mu'adh stated, "Hunger is an ascetic exercise for the *murids,* a trial for the repentant, an ordeal for the renouncers, and a sign of nobility for the gnostics." The master Abu 'Ali ad-Daqqaq (may God have mercy on him) related, "Someone came to one of the sheikhs and, seeing him weeping, asked, 'Why are you weeping?' He replied, 'I am hungry.' The other one exclaimed, 'Someone like you weeps from hunger?' He retorted, 'Be silent. You do not know that His intended purpose in my hunger is that I should weep.'"

Mukhallid reported that Al-Hajjaj b. Furafisa was with them in Syria, and he stayed fifty nights without drinking water or taking his fill from anything he ate. Abu 'Abdallah Ahmad b. Yahya al-Jalla' said, "Abu Turab an-Nakhshabi came through the desert of Basra to Mecca [may God protect it], and we asked him about his food. He answered, 'I left Basra and I ate in Nibaj and then in Dhat 'Araq. From there I came to you.' So he crossed the desert eating only two times." 'Abd al-'Aziz b. 'Umayr related, "A flock of birds was starving for forty mornings. Then they flew into the air, and when they returned after some days, they gave off a scent of musk." When Sahl b. 'Abdallah hungered, he was powerful, and whenever he ate, he became weak. Abu 'Uthman al-Maghribi noted, "The one devoted to the Lord eats only every forty days, and the one devoted to the Eternal eats only every eighty days."

Abu Sulayman ad-Darani observed, "The key to this world is filling one's stomach, and the key to the Hereafter is hunger." It was asked of Sahl b. 'Abdallah, "What do you say of the man who eats once a day?" He said, "It is the eating of the believers." "And three times a day?" He retorted, "Tell your people to build you a trough."

Yahya b. Mu'adh commented, "Hunger is a light, and filling one's stomach is a fire. Passion is like firewood from which fire arises, never to subside until it consumes its owner." Abu Nasr as-Sarraj at-Tusi related, "A man from among the Sufis came upon a sheikh one day and presented him some food. Then he asked, 'How long has it been since you ate last?' He answered, 'Five days ago.' He observed, 'Your hunger is the hunger of greed. You wear [fine] garments while you hunger. This is not the hunger of poverty!'" Abu Sulayman ad-Darani asserted, "To leave even one morsel of dinner uneaten is more loved by me than standing in prayer through the night to its end."

Abu'l-Khayr al-'Asqalani craved fish for several years. Then some came to him from a licit source. But when he reached out his hand to eat it, a spike from its bones pricked his finger, so he drew back. Thereupon he declared, "O Lord, if this befalls one who reaches out his hand desiring a pure thing, how will it be for one who reaches for something forbidden?" I heard the master Abu Bakr b. Furak state, "To be kept busy by one's family is the result of pursuing desire in ways that are licit. How then will it be if you pursue it in ways that are illicit?"

I heard Rustam ash-Shirazi as-Sufi relate, "Abu 'Abdallah b. Khafif was attending a dinner, and one of those present, owing to his poverty, reached for food before the sheikh. One of the sheikh's companions, wishing to reproach him for the poor manners he showed in this, placed some [food] in front of this dervish. Knowing by this that he was being rebuked for his poor manners, he resolved not to eat for fifteen days as a punishment and discipline for his soul and as an outward sign of his repentance for his poor manners, despite the poverty that had been his lot before that."

Malik b. Dinar said, "Satan is terrified of the shadow of one who conquers the passions of the world." Abu 'Ali ar-Rudhbari instructed, "If the Sufi says after five days, 'I am hungry,' then send him to the marketplace to earn somthing."

I heard the master Abu 'Ali Ad-Daqqaq relate the saying of a certain sheikh that the passions of the people of the Fire overcame their aspiration, so they were disgraced. And I heard him relate, "Someone asked one of the sheikhs, 'Do you not desire?' He answered, 'I desire but I restrain myself.' Another one of them was asked, 'Do you not desire?' He replied, 'I desire not to desire.' And this is better."

Abu Nasr at-Tammar reported, "Bishr came to me one night, and I said, 'Praise be to God Who has brought you. Some cotton from Khurasan came to us; the girl has spun it, sold it, and bought some meat for us. So you can break the fast with us.' He replied, 'If I were to eat with anyone, I would eat with you.' Then he explained, 'I have craved eggplant for years, but it has not been destined for me to eat it.' So I assured him, 'But there is eggplant that is lawful in this dish.' He replied, '[I cannot eat it] until I am free from the longing for eggplant.'"

I heard 'Abdallah b. Bakawiya as-Sufi (may God grant him mercy) tell that he heard Abu Ahmad as-Saghir say, "Abu 'Abdallah b. Khafif ordered me to serve him ten raisins for breaking his fast each night. One night I felt pity for him, so I brought him fifteen raisins. He looked at me and asked, 'Who told you to do this?' He ate ten of them and left the rest."

Abu Turab An-Nakhshabi commented, "My soul never inclined to passions except once: it longed for bread and eggs while I was on a journey. So I turned to a village. Someone rose up and grabbed me, exclaiming, 'This one was with the robbers.' Then they clubbed me seventy times. A man among them recognized me and protested, 'This is Abu Turab an-Nakhshabi!' Then they apologized to me, and the man brought me to his house out of respect and compassion for me and he served me bread and eggs. So I told my soul, 'Eat! After seventy clubbings!'"

12

Humility and Submissiveness

Khushu' wa't-Tawadu'

God Most High says, "Successful indeed are the believers, those who humble themselves in their prayers" (23:1-2).

On the authority of 'Abdallah b. Mas'ud, the Prophet (may God's blessing and peace be upon him) declared, "The one who has even the smallest amount of arrogance in his heart will never enter Paradise, and the one who has even the smallest amount of faith in his heart will never enter Hell." Then a man observed, "O Messenger of God, man dearly wishes that his garments should be beautiful." So he said, "God Most High is beautiful and loves beauty; arrogance is turning away from God, and scorning man."

Anas b. Malik reported, "The Messenger of God [may God's blessing and peace be upon him] used to visit the sick, accompany funeral processions, ride a donkey, and accept invitations from slaves. On the days of battle against the Qurayza and Nadir, the Prophet was riding a donkey that was bridled with a rope of palm fiber, and upon it was a saddle of palm fiber."

Humility is submission to God, and submissiveness is surrender to God and forswearing objection to divine wisdom.

Hudhayfa stated, "Humility is the first thing you lose of your religion." When one of the Sufis was asked about humility, he answered, "Humility is the heart's standing before God [may he be Most High and exalted] with concentrated resolution." Sahl b. 'Abdallah asserted, "The devil will not come near to one whose heart is humble." It is said, "Among the signs of humility in the servant is that, when he is provoked, offended, or rejected, his duty is to meet [all] that with acceptance." One of the Sufis commented, "Humility of the heart is restraining eyes from glancing." Muhammad b. 'Ali at-Tirmidhi explained, "Humility is this: if the fires of a man's passion abate and the smoke of his breast subsides and the light of glorification shines in his heart, then his passion dies and his heart lives and all his limbs are humbled." Al-Hasan al-Basri noted, "Humility is constant fear accompanying the heart." When al-Junayd was asked about humility he replied, "[It is] that the hearts abase themselves before the One who knows the hidden matters."

God Most High speaks of "The servants of the Compassionate One, those who walk on the earth in humility" (25:63). The master Abu 'Ali ad-Daqqaq (may God have mercy on him) said that the meaning of this verse is that they [walk] in submissiveness and humility.

I also heard him say that they are the ones who do not make pretty the sound of the thong of their sandals when they walk.

They agree that the locus of humility is the heart. When one of the Sufis saw a man who was downcast in his outward manner, with lowered eyes and slumped shoulders, he told him, "O so-and-so, humility is here," and he pointed to his breast, "not here," and he pointed to his shoulders. It is related that the Messenger of God (may God's blessing and peace be upon him) saw a man playing with his beard during his prayers, and he declared, "If his heart were humble, his limbs would be humble too." It is said, "The condition of humility in prayers means that one does not know who is [standing] to his right or left."

One might say, "Humility is the silencing of one's innermost being while reverentially witnessing God [may He be exalted and Most High]." It is said, "Humility is a dejected state that comes upon the heart when the Lord is disclosed." And it is said, "Humility is the melting and hiding of the heart in the presence of the Sovereign of Truth." It is also said, "Humility is the prelude to being overpowered by awe." Or, "Humility is a tremor that comes upon the heart suddenly at the unexpected disclosure of the Truth."

Fudayl b. 'Iyad asserted, "It is offensive that there should be seen in the outward appearance of man more humility than what is in his heart." Abu Sulayman ad-Darani stated, "If all people were to join together in order to humiliate me, they could never equal the depth to which I abase my own self." It is said, "He who is not humble within his own soul cannot be humble with others."

'Umar b. 'Abd al-'Aziz would prostrate only upon the soil of the earth. On the authority of Ibn 'Abbas (may God be pleased with both of them), the Messenger of God (may God's blessing and peace be upon him) declared, "One who has as much as a mustard seed of arrogance in his heart will not enter Paradise."

Mujahid (may God have mercy upon him) remarked, "When God [may He be exalted] drowned the people of Noah, the mountains loomed proudly. But [the mountain] Judi behaved humbly, so God [may He be exalted] made it the resting place for Noah's ark [peace be upon him]." 'Umar b. al-Khattab (may God be pleased with him) used to walk at a quick pace, and he would explain that such walking would bring him swiftly to attend to [legitimate] needs and keep him far from vanity. 'Umar b. 'Abd al-'Aziz (may God be pleased with him) was writing something one night when there was a guest with him. Seeing that the lamp was about to go out, the guest offered, "I will go to the lamp and adjust it." But 'Umar replied, "No. It is not generous to use the guest as a servant." He suggested, "Then I will call the servant." 'Umar declined, "No, he has just gone to sleep." So he went to the container of oil and filled the lamp. The guest exclaimed, "You did it yourself, O Commander of the Believers!" So 'Umar told him, "I left and I was 'Umar, and I returned and still I am 'Umar."

Abu Sa'id al-Khudri (may God's blessing and peace be upon him) used to feed the camels, sweep the house, mend sandals, sew clothes, milk the sheep, eat with the servant, and help him to grind when he was weary. And shame never prevented him from carrying his goods from the market to his family. He would shake hands with the rich and the poor and be the first to extend greetings. He never scorned whatever it was he was invited to eat, even if it were dry, unripe dates. He was simple with regard to food, tender in character, noble in disposition, goodly of company, with a shining face [that] smiled without laughing, was sorrowful without frowning; he was humble without being meek, generous without being extravagant. He was gentle of heart and compassionate with each Muslim. He never gave signs of having eaten his fill or reached out his hand in greed."

Fudayl b. 'Iyad noted, "The scholars of the Merciful [may He be exalted and glorified], possess humility and submissiveness, and the scholars of the rulers possess pride and arrogance." He commented also, "Whoever considers his soul to be of any worth has no share of submissiveness." When Fudayl was asked about submissiveness, he instructed, "Submit to the Truth; obey it and accept it from whoever says it." He also said, "God [may He be exalted and Most High] revealed to the mountains, 'I will speak to a prophet upon one of you.' So the mountains raised themselves high in pride while Mount Sinai lowered itself humbly. Then God spoke to Moses (peace be upon him) on this mountain because of its humility."

When Al-Junayd was asked about submissiveness, he answered, "It is extending one's protective care to all beings and being forbearing toward them." Wahb said, "It has been written in one of the revealed books, 'Verily I extracted particles [all of mankind] from the loins of Adam, and I did not find a more submissive heart than that of Moses [upon whom be peace]. So I chose him and spoke to him directly.'" Ibn al-Mubarak declared, "Pride toward the rich and submissiveness toward the poor are part of submissiveness." Abu Yazid was asked. "When has a man reached submissiveness?" He replied, "When he does not attribute a station or state to his self and considers none among mankind worse than himself." It is said, "Submissiveness is a divine favor that is not envied. And insolence is an affliction that evokes no pity. Dignity lies in submissiveness, and one who seeks it in pride will never find it." Ibrahim b. Shayban stated, "Honor lies in submissiveness; dignity lies in piety; and freedom lies in contentment."

Ibn al-'A'rabi said that he heard the report that Sufyan ath-Thawri remarked, "Five souls are the most dignified in creation: an abstemious scholar, a Sufi jurisprudent, a humble rich person, a thankful poor one, and a noble who follows the Sunna." Yahya b. Mu'adh asserted, "Humility is an excellent quality for everyone, but it is most excellent for the rich. Arrogance is disgusting for everyone, but it is most disgusting for the poor." Ibn 'Ata' commented, "Humility is acceptance of the Truth from whomever it may be." It is said that Zayd b. Thabit was riding, and Ibn 'Abbas drew near to him so that he could take hold of his bridle. So he told him, "Stop, O son of the uncle of the Messenger of God!" Then Ibn 'Abbas reported, "This is what we have been ordered to do with our learned ones." So Zayd b. Thabit took Ibn 'Abbas's hand and kissed it, saying, "This is how we have been commanded to treat the family of the

Messenger of God [may God's blessing and peace be upon him]."

'Urwa b. az-Zubayr related, "When I saw 'Umar b. al-Khattab [may God be pleased with him] with a full waterskin on his shoulder, I told him, 'O Commander of the Believers, this is not fitting for you.' He responded, 'When deputations came to me, listening and obedient, a certain arrogance entered my soul, and I wished to break it.' So he proceeded with the waterskin to the chamber of a woman from the Ansar and emptied it into her water jug."

Abu Nasr as-Sarraj at-Tusi reported, "Abu Hurayra was seen while he was governor of Medina with a bundle of firewood on his back, saying, 'Make way for the governor!'"

'Abdallah ar-Razi explained, "Humility is the abandonment of distinctions in serving." Abu Sulayman ad-Darani said, "One who ascribes any value to his soul will never taste the sweetness of service." Yahya b. Mu'adh declared, "Arrogance toward one who is arrogant to you on account of his property is humility." Ash-Shibli (may God have mercy on him) commented, "My lowliness exceeds the lowliness of the Jews." A man came to Ash-Shibli, who asked him, "What are you?" He answered, "O my master, I am the dot under the letter *ba'*." Shibli replied, "You are my witness because you have made little of your station."

Ibn 'Abbas (may God be pleased with him and his father) observed, "One part of humility is that a man drink the portion left behind by his brother." Bishr instructed, "Greet the worldly by not greeting them."

Shu'ayb b. Harb related, "While I was circling the Ka'ba, a man jabbed me with his elbow, so I turned to him. It was Fudayl b. 'Iyad, who stated, 'O Abu Salih, if you were thinking that there was someone attending this Hajj worse than me or you, then how wretched is what you thought.'" One of them remarked, "I saw a man, during the circumambulation of the Ka'ba, surrounded by people praising him. Because of this, they blocked others from making the circumambulation. Then I saw him some time after that on a bridge in Baghdad begging passersby for charity, and I was surprised. He told me, 'I was proud in a place where people were humble, so God [may He be exalted] afflicted me with self-abasement in a place where people are proud.'"

'Umar b. 'Abd al-'Aziz heard that one of his sons had purchased a valuable jewel for one thousand dirhams. So 'Umar wrote to him, "I have heard that you have bought a gem for one thousand dirhams. When this letter reaches you, sell the ring and fill one thousand stomachs. Then make a ring out of two dirhams, make its stone out of Chinese iron, and write upon it, 'God has mercy upon the one who knows his true value.'"

It is said that a slave was presented to one of the rulers for one thousand dirhams. But when the money was brought out, he thought it too much. He changed his mind about buying him, and returned the money to the treasury. Then the slave pleaded, "O my lord, buy me, for within me, for every dirham of these dirhams, is a quality worth more than one thousand dirhams." He inquired, "And what might they be?" The slave replied, "The very least of them is that if you were to buy me and then favor me over all your slaves, I would not mistake

my true state; I would still know that I am your slave."
So the sale was made.

It is said that Raja' b. Haya commented, "I appraised
the garments of 'Umar b. 'Abd al-'Aziz, while he was
delivering a sermon, at twelve dirhams. These consisted of an outer garment, a turban, a tunic and
trousers, a pair of slippers, and a hood."

It is said that when 'Abdallah b. Muhammad b. Wasi'
walked with a strutting gait, his father told him, "Do you
know how much I paid for your mother? Three
hundred dirhams; and as for your father, may God not
increase the likes of him among the Muslims. And with
such parents, you walk this way!" Hamdun al-Qassar
declared, "Submissiveness is that you not see anyone
needful of you either in the world or in the hereafter."

Ibrahim b. Adham observed, "I delighted in Islam
only three times. One time I was on board a ship and
there was a man who laughed often. He would remark,
'We used to grab an infidel in the land of the Turks thus,'
and he would tug at my hair and shake me back and
forth. This would please me because there was no one
baser in his eyes on board ship. Another time I became
ill in a mosque. The man who made the call to prayer
came in and told me to get out, but I could not. So he
grabbed me by my foot and dragged me out of the
mosque. The third time, I was in Syria, and I was
wearing a fur. I looked at it, and I could not distinguish
between its hair and the lice, such was their abundance.
That delighted me." And in another tale about him, he
reported, "My joy was never greater than the day I was
sitting down and a man came and urinated on me."

It is said that Abu Dharr and Bilal (may God be

pleased with them) were quarreling and Abu Dharr chided Bilal for his black skin. Then Bilal complained about Abu Dharr to the Messenger of God (may God's blessing and peace be upon him), who said, "O Abu Dharr, surely something of Jahili insolence remains in your heart!" At that, Abu Dharr threw himself down and swore that he would not lift his head until Bilal had stepped on his cheek with his foot. And he did not get up until Bilal did so.

Al-Hasan b. 'Ali (may God be pleased with him) passed by a group of youths who had some pieces of bread. They invited him to be their guest, and he dismounted and ate with them. Then he brought them to his house, fed them, clothed them, and said, "I am indebted to them because they did not gain any more than what they offered to me while I gained more than that."

It is said, "'Umar b. al-Khattab [may God be pleased with him] divided up the clothing from the spoils of war among his companions. Then he sent a Yemeni garment to Mu'adh, who sold it and bought six slaves and freed them. This reached 'Umar, and when he divided up the clothing the next time, he sent him a less valuable garment. When Mu'adh reproached him for that, 'Umar asked him. 'Why reproach me? You sold the first one.' Mu'adh demanded, 'What is the matter with you? Hand over my share, for I have sworn I will wind it around your head.' 'Umar declared, 'Here, my head stands before you; the old deal kindly with the old.'"

13

Opposition to the Self and Remembering Its Failings

❧ Mukhalafat an-nafs wa dhikr 'uyubiha

God Most High says, "And for one who fears the standing before his Lord and restrains his soul from passion, the Garden will be his abode" (79:40).

It is reported on the authority of Jabir (may God be pleased with him) that the Prophet (may God's blessing and peace be upon him) stated, "The things I most fear for my community are following passion and limitless expectation [of worldly gain]. Following desire turns one away from God, and limitless expectation makes one forget the afterlife." Know therefore, that opposing the self is the beginning of worship.

When the sheikhs have been asked about Islam, they have explained, "It is slaughtering the self with the swords of opposition [to it]. And know that for one whose calamities of self rise, the sun of intimacy sets."

Dhu'n-Nun al-Misri declared, "The key to worship is reflection. The sign of attaining the goal is opposing the self and passion, and this is abandoning their desires." Ibn 'Ata' observed, "The self is naturally disposed to evil manners. At the same time the servant is commanded to perseverance in [proper] manners. So the self behaves in accordance with its nature through opposing [proper manners], and the servant repels the soul by his fight against its evil demands. For one who lets free the self's reins is partner to it in its corruption." Junayd commented, "The self that is constantly urging to evil is the summoner to perdition, the helper to enemies, the follower of desire, and charged with all varieties of evil." Abu Hafs instructed, "One who does not suspect his self in all conditions, oppose it in all states, and impose upon it what it dislikes in all his days is deluded. And one who looks upon it, approving a part of it, has ruined it."

How can it be right for one possessed of intellect to be pleased with his self! The noble Joseph, son of the noble offspring of a noble lineage, said, "I have never cleared my self from guilt; truly the self is constantly urging to evil" (12:53).

Al-Junayd related, "I could not sleep one night, so I got up to recite my *wird* [litany]. But I found none of the sweetness or delight I usually experience in my intimate conversation with my Lord. So I was at a loss and wished that I could sleep but I could not. Then I sat, but I could not bear the sitting, so I opened the door and went out. There was a man wrapped in a cloak who was lying on the road. When he sensed my presence, he lifted his head, saying, 'O Abu'l-Qasim, look to the hour! [You are late!]' So I replied, 'But sir, [there was] no appointed time.' He responded, 'Nay, I had asked the Awakener of hearts to move your heart to me.' I said, 'He has done so! What is your wish?' He answered, 'When does the self's disease become its remedy?' I said, 'When the self opposes its passion, its disease is its remedy.' Then he turned to his own self and said to it, 'Listen, I answered you thus seven times, but you refused to accept it until you heard it from al-Junayd, and now you have heard.' Then he left me. I knew not who he was and I never met him again thereafter."

Abu Bakr at-Tamastani declared, "The greatest blessing is emerging from the self, because it is the greatest veil between you and God [may He be exalted and glorified]." Sahl b. 'Abdallah asserted, "There is no worship of God like that of opposing the soul and passion." When asked about the most loathsome thing in the sight of God Most High, Ibn 'Ata' said, "Paying heed to the self and its states. And worse than that is anticipating recompense for its actions."

Ibrahim al-Khawwas related, "I was on the mountain al-Lakam, where I saw some pomegranates, and I craved one. So I went up and picked one of them and split it open, but I found that it was sour. So I went away and left the pomegranates. Then I saw a man lying on the ground with wasps buzzing around him, and I said, 'Peace be upon you.' He replied, 'And upon you be peace, O Ibrahim.' I asked, 'How do you know me?' He answered, 'Nothing is hidden from one who knows God Most High.' I remarked, 'I see that you have a state with God Most High. Why have you not asked Him to protect you and shelter you from the annoyance of these wasps?' He said, 'And I too, see that you have a state with God Most High. Why have you not asked Him to shelter you from the craving for pomegranates? Man will experience pain from the sting of [desiring] pomegranates in the Hereafter, while he feels the pain of the wasp's sting in the world!' I left him and passed on."

It is related that Ibrahim b. Shayban reported, "For forty years I did not sleep one night under my roof or in a locked place, but I would wish at times that I could eat my fill of lentils. However, it never happened.... Then one time when I was in Syria, a large bowl of lentils was brought to me. I ate from it and departed. Then I saw hanging glass containers in which there was some sort of liquid, and I supposed it to be vinegar. One of the people exclaimed, 'What are you thinking! These are drops of wine, and this is a wine jug!' Then I told myself, 'It is my duty . . .' so I entered the tavern and kept emptying those jugs. He thought I was emptying them on orders of the sultan. When he learned the truth, he brought me to Ibn Tulun, who commanded that I be given two hundred lashes and be thrown into prison. I stayed there a while until Abu 'Abdallah al-Maghribi, my teacher, came to that country and pleaded on my behalf. When he saw me, he asked, 'What did you do? What is this?' I answered, 'A stomach full of lentils and two hundred lashes!' He declared, 'You have been saved, free of charge.'"

On the authority of al-Junayd, Sari as-Saqati is said to have related, "For thirty or forty years my self has begged me to dip a carrot in date honey, but I have not eaten it!" Abu 'Abd an-Rahman as-Sulami related that his grandfather once said, "The servant's calamity is his contentment with the state of his self." 'Isam b. Yusuf al-Balkhi sent something to Hatim al-Asamm, who accepted it. Someone asked, "Why did you accept it?" He replied, "In taking it I felt my shame and his pride. And in refusing it I felt my pride and his shame. So I chose his pride over my pride and my shame over his." A man said to one of the Sufis, "I want to make the pilgrimage in a state of deprivation." He replied, "First deprive your heart of negligence, your self of levity, and your tongue of vain talk; then travel wherever you please."

Abu Sulayman ad-Darani observed, "One who passes his nights in a goodly fashion is recompensed in his days, and one who spends his days in a goodly fashion is recompensed in his nights. One who is sincere in renouncing passion is spared the burden of feeding it. God is more generous than to punish a heart that renounces passion for His sake."

God (may He be exalted) revealed to David (upon whom be peace), "O David, caution and warn your companions against freely indulging the passions, for the understanding of hearts that are fastened to the passions of the world is veiled from Me."

It is said that a man was sitting suspended in the air, and someone asked, "How did you achieve this?" He explained, "I abandoned passion *[hawa]*, so He made the air *[hawa']* subservient to me."

It is said, "If [the fulfillment of] one thousand desires were offered to the believer, he would drive them away with fear [of God]. But if [the fulfillment] of one single desire were to come to the sinner, it would expel from him fear [of God]." It is also said, "Do not place your reins in the hand of passion, for it will certainly lead you into darkness."

Yusuf b. Asbat remarked, "Only an alarming fear or a restless yearning can extinguish passions in the heart." Al-Khawwas declared, "One who abandons a passion but does not experience its recompense in his heart is a liar in claiming to have abandoned it." Ja'far b. Nasir reported, "Al-Junayd gave me a dirham and commanded me to buy him a certain kind of fig. I bought some, and when he broke his fast, he took one of them and put it in his mouth. Then he threw it down, wept, and said, 'Take them away.' When I asked him what had happened, he answered, 'A voice cried out in my heart, "Have you no shame! You renounced a desire for My sake and then you took it up again!"'"

They recite: "The *nun* of *hawan* [abasement] has been stolen from *hawa* [passion]. Succumbing to every passion is falling victim to abasement." Know that the self possesses blameworthy characteristics, and among them is envy.

14

Envy

❧ Hasad

God Most High says, "Say, 'I seek refuge in the Lord of the dawn from the evil of that which He has created,'" and then He says, "'And from the evil of the envier when he envies'" (113:1 and 5). So He concludes the chapter He made as a plea for protection with the mention of envy.

It is reported on the authority of Ibn Masʿud that the Prophet (may God's blessing and peace be upon him) commented, "There are three things at the root of all sin. Guard yourselves against them and beware of them. Beware of pride, for pride caused Iblis to refuse to prostrate before Adam. Beware of greed, for greed caused Adam to eat of the tree. And beware of envy, for it was from envy that one of the two sons of Adam killed his brother."

One of the Sufis stated, "The envier is an unbeliever [denier] because he is not content with the divine decree of God." It is said, "The envier never prevails."

It is said in the words of God Most High, "Say, 'My

Lord has forbidden only abominations, those that are apparent and those that are within'" (7:33). It is said that "Those that are within are envy." It is written some-where that "The envier is an enemy of My blessing." And it is said, "The marks of envy appear in you before they appear in your enemy."

Al-Asma'i related, "I saw a Bedouin who was one hundred twenty years old, and I exclaimed, 'How long your life is!' He replied, 'I have abandoned envy, so I live on.'" Ibn al-Mubarak declared, "Praise be to God, Who has not placed in the heart of my commander what He has placed in the heart of my envier." In one of the traditions it is said, "There is an angel in the fifth heaven by whom the deed of a servant passed, and it had a glow like that of the sun. The angel commanded it, 'Stop, for I am the angel of envy. Strike the doer of this deed in the face with it, for he is an envier.'" Mu'awiya observed, "I am able to please every man except the envier. He is never content with anything less than the cessation of favors to all except himself." It is said, "The envier is a most unjust wrong-doer; he lets nothing remain in its place." 'Umar b. 'Abd al-'Aziz asserted, "The envier resembles more the oppressed than any oppressor I have seen, [for he is all] constant sorrow and heaving breaths." It is said, "Among the signs of the envier are that he flatters others when he is with them, slanders them when he is apart from them, and savors their misfortune when it befalls them." Mu'awiya noted, "Among the attributes of evil, none is more just than envy. The envier is vanquished before the one who is envied." It is said that God (may He be exalted) revealed to Solomon, son of David (peace be upon them), "I direct you to do seven things: do not slander on of My righteous servants, do not envy one of My servants...." So Solomon replied, "O my Lord, this suffices me." It is said that Moses (peace be upon him) saw a man close to the throne. Because he wished to be in his place, he asked, "How has he attained this?" It was said, "He was not envying people for what God has bestowed of His Bounty."

It is said: "The envier is confounded when he sees in another a blessing and rejoices when he sees a fault." "If you wish to be safe from the envier, then conceal your affairs from him." "The envier is enraged over one who has no sin and stingy with what he does not posess." "Beware lest you toil in loving one who envies you, for he will surely not accept your kindness." "When God Most High wishes to empower a pitiless enemy over one of His servants, He gives his envier power over him."

They have composed:

> *Warning example enough it is for you to see*
> *A man pitied by his enviers.*

They recite:

> *The killing of all enmity may be hoped for*
> *Except for the enmity of one who is hostile*
> *from envy.*

Ibn al-Mu'tazz said:

> *Say reproachfully to the envier in the midst of*
> *his sighs,*
> *"O oppressor," and it's as if he's oppressed.*

They recite:

> *When God wishes to unfold a virtue [for*
> *someone]*
> *He decrees [for that person] that the envious*
> *tongue be rolled up.*

Among the blameworthy characteristics for the self is the habit of backbiting.

15

Backbiting

❧ Ghiba

God Most High says, "And do not slander one another. Would any of you like to eat the flesh of his dead brother? You would abhor that. But fear God, for God is most forgiving, merciful" (49:12).

Abu Hurayra reported that a man had been sitting with the Messenger of God (God's blessings and peace be upon him) and then rose and left. One of the assembly observed, "What a feeble man he is." The Messenger asserted, "You eat your brother's flesh when you backbite him."

God (may He be exalted) revealed to Moses (upon whom be peace), "Whoever dies penitent over backbiting will be the last one to enter the Garden, and whoever dies persisting in it will be the first one to enter the Fire."

'Awf related, "I came to Ibn Sirin, and I slandered al-Hajjaj. Ibn Sirin declared, 'Verily God Most High is a just arbiter, for as much as He takes away from al-Hajjaj, He gives to him. When you meet God [may He be exalted] on the morrow, the smallest sin that you have committed will be more grievous for you than the greatest sin al-Hajjaj has committed.'"

It is told that Ibrahim b. Adham was invited to a feast, which he attended. When they mentioned a man who had not come, it was said, "He is so tedious." Ibrahim remarked, "This is what this soul of mine has done to me: I find myself in a gathering where backbiting takes place." He left, even though he had not eaten for three days.

It is said, "He who slanders people is like unto the one who prepares a catapult. He shoots his good deeds with it to the east and the west. He slanders one from Khurasan, another from the Hijaz, one from Syria, another from Turkistan. He scatters his good deeds, and he rises on the Day of Judgment with nothing."

It is said, "A certain servant will be given his tablet on the Day of Resurrection, but he will not see one good deed on it. He will ask, 'Where are my prayers, my feasts, and my acts of worship?' He will be told, 'All your works have vanished because you engaged in backbiting.'"

It is said, "God forgives half the sins of one who falls victim to backbiting." Sufyan b. al-Husayn reported, "I was sitting with Iyas b. Mu'awiya, and I slandered a man. He asked me, 'Have you attacked the Byzantines or the Turks this year?' I replied, 'No.' He exclaimed, 'The Turks and the Byzantines are safe from you while your Muslim brother is not!'" It is said, "A certain man will be given his tablet on the Day of Judgment, and he will find on it good deeds he never performed. It will be said to him, 'These are for the people's slander of you of which you were unaware.'"

106

Sufyan ath-Thawri was asked about the saying of the Prophet (God's blessings and peace be upon him), "Verily God loathes the family of the flesheaters." He commented, "They are the ones who backbite; they eat people's flesh." Backbiting was mentioned in the presence of 'Abdallah b. al-Mubarak, who remarked, "If I were to slander anyone, I would slander my parents, because they are the most deserving of my good deeds." Yahya b. Mu'adh stated, "Let the Muslim's benefit from you be these three qualities: If you cannot be helpful to him, then do not harm him. If you cannot bring him delight, then do not cause him sorrow. If you cannot praise him, then do not find fault with him." It was told to al-Hasan al-Basri, "So-and-so has slandered you." He sent a tray of halva [sweets] to the man, noting, "I hear that you have bestowed upon me your good deeds. I would like to repay you."

On the authority of Anas b. Malik, the Messenger of God (God's blessing and peace be upon him) is related to have said, "If one casts off the covering of shame from his face, the question of backbiting does not arise." Al-Junayd related, "I was sitting in the ash-Shuniziya mosque waiting for a funeral procession so I might pray the funeral prayer. The people of Baghdad in their different classes were seated waiting for the procession. Then I saw a poor man bearing the marks of asceticism who was begging from the people. I told myself, 'If this one would work in order to sustain himself, it would be better for him.' When I returned to my home, as customary, I began to recite my litany at night, to engage in weeping and prayer and other things. But all my litanies weighed heavily upon me, so

I was sleepless and was sitting up. When sleep overcame me, I saw that poor man. They were laying him out on a large cloth, and they commanded me, 'Eat his flesh, for you have slandered him.' His state was revealed for me, and I protested, 'But I did not slander him! I only said something to myself.' Then it was said to me, 'This sort of thing is not acceptable from you. Go and ask his forgiveness.' In the morning I continued to search until I found him gathering leaves left in the water used for washing vegetables. When I greeted him he asked, 'O Abu'l-Qasim, have you returned to slander?' I answered, 'No.' He declared, 'May God forgive both of us.'"

Abu Ja'far al-Balkhi reported, "A youth from the people of Balkh was with us, and he was striving and devoting himself to the service of God, except that he was constantly engaged in backbiting. He would say, 'So-and-so is like this; So-and-so is like that.' One day I saw him visiting some washers of the dead known to be catamites. When he came away from them, I asked, 'O So-and-so, what has happened?' He replied, 'This is what happened because of my backbiting. It brought me down to this. I have become infatuated with one of those catamites and I serve them on his account. All my previous states of devotion have gone, so ask God to forgive me.'"

16

Contentment

❧ Qanaʻa

God Most High says, "Whoever works righteousness, whether male or female, and is a believer, We shall quicken with a life that is good" (16:97). Many of the commentators say that "a life that is good" in this world is one of contentment.

On the authority of Jabir b. ʻAbdallah, the Messenger of God (may God's blessing and peace be upon him) observed, "Contentment is an inexhaustible treasure." On the authority of Abu Hurayra (may God be pleased with him), the Messenger of God declared, "Be one who abstains, and you will be the most thankful of people. Wish for others what you wish for yourself, and you will be a believer. Be an excellent neighbor to the one who lives near you, and you will be a Muslim. And be moderate in your laughter, for much laughter kills the heart."

It is said, "The poor are dead, except the ones God Most High revives with the glory of contentment." Bishr al-Hafi stated, "Contentment is a king who dwells only in the believing heart." Abu Sulayman ad-Darani commented, "Contentment is to satisfaction as the station of abstinence is to renunciation; contentment is the beginning of satisfaction, and abstinence is the beginning of renunciation." It is said, "Contentment is calm in the absence of that to which one is accustomed." Abu Bakr al-Maraghi explained, "The intelligent one is he who arranges the concerns of the world with contentment and at a slow pace, the concerns of the afterlife with greed and haste, and the concerns of religion with knowledge and striving." Abu 'Abdallah b. Khafif remarked, "Contentment is to abandon desire for what is lost and for what one does not have, and to avoid dependence on what one does have."

It is said as to the meaning of the saying of God Most High, "God will bestow on them a goodly sustenance" (22:88), that this refers to contentment. Muhammad b. 'Ali at-Tirmidhi asserted, "Contentment is the satisfaction of the soul with the sustenance that has been apportioned to it." It is said, "Contentment is finding sufficiency in what is at hand and ceasing to covet what is not at hand." Wahb related, "Dignity and wealth went wandering about searching for a companion. They met with contentment, and they alighted with him." It is said, "One whose contentment is plump finds every broth to be delicious." It is also said, "The one who returns to God in every state is provided by God with contentment."

It is told, "Abu Hazim passed by a butcher who had some fatty meat. He said to him, 'Take some, O Abu Hazim, for it is fatty.' He replied, 'I have no dirhams with me.' The butcher responded, 'I will give you time to pay.' He observed, 'My soul is still more patient with me than you are.'"

It was asked of one of the Sufis, "Who is the most content of mankind?" He answered, "He who is the most helpful to mankind and the least demanding upon them for sustenance." It is said in the Psalms, "The contented one is rich even if he be hungry." It is said, "God Most High place these five things in five places: glory in worship, vileness in sin, awe in rising at night, wisdom in the empty stomach, and wealth in contentment." Ibrahim al-Maristani declared, "Take revenge on your greed with contentment just as you take revenge on your enemy with retribution." Dhu'n-Nun al-Misri stated, "One who is content is saved from his contemporaries and prevails over all." It is said, "One who is content will find rest from anxiety and prevail over all." Al-Kattani remarked, "Whoever sells greed for contentment gains glory and valor." It is said, "Sorrow and distress are prolonged for one whose eyes pursue what is in the possession of others."

They recite:

> *Better for the youth than a day of disgrace*
> *bringing him wealth*
> *Is hunger nobly endured.*

And it is related, "A man saw a wise man eating the pieces of vegetables discarded after washing and observed, 'If you were to serve the sultan, you would not need to eat this.' The wise man replied, 'And you, if you were content with this, would not need to serve the sultan.'" It is said that when flying, the eagle is mighty and beyond the sight and bait of the hunter, but when he craves a carcass suspended in a snare, he descends from his flight and becomes caught in the net."

It is said that Moses (upon whom be peace) spoke of greed, saying, "If you had wished, you could have taken payment for it" (18:77). Al-Khidr then told him, "This is the parting between you and me" (18:78). It is said that when Moses spoke those words, a gazelle stopped in front of Moses and al-Khidr (peace be upon them). They were hungry; the side facing Moses was not roasted, and the side facing al-Khidr was roasted.

It is said about the words of God Most High, "Truly the righteous are in bliss" (82:13), that they refer to contentment in the world. "And truly the wicked are in fire" (82:14) means greed in the world. It is said about the words of God Most High, "And what will explain to you the steep path? It is the unshackling of the neck" (90:12-13), that this means unshackling from the lowliness of covetousness. It is said that the words of God Most High, "God wishes only to remove uncleanness far from you, people of the house" (33:33), mean "[to remove] miserliness and covetousness," and "And [He wishes] to purify you thoroughly" (33:33) means "by means of generosity and unstinted giving." With regard to the words of God Most High, "He [Solomon] cried, 'O my Lord! Forgive me, and bestow on me a sovereignty such as will not be fitting for any after me'" (38:35), it is said that this means "Bestow on me a rank in contentment in which I will stand alone, none others in likeness to me, and by means of which I will be satisfied with Your decree." It is said about the words of God Most High, "I [Solomon] will certainly punish him [the hoopoe] with a severe penalty" (27:21), that this means "I will strip him of contentment and try him with greed," that is, "I will ask God Most High to do that to him."

Abu Yazid was asked, "How have you arrived where you are?" He replied, "I gathered the things of this world and tied them to the rope of contentment. Then I placed them in the catapult of sincerity and hurled them into the sea of despair. Thus I found rest." 'Abd al-Wahhab, the uncle of Muhammad b. Farhan, related, "I was sitting with al-Junayd during the days of Hajj, and around him was a great crowd of non-Arabs, including some who had grown up among the Arabs. A man came to him with five hundred dinars and put them before al-Junayd, instructing him, 'Divide them among the poor people here.' He asked, 'Do you have more dinars?' He affirmed, 'Yes, I have many.' So he asked, 'Do you wish for more than you possess?' He answered, 'Yes,' and al-Junayd told him, 'Take them, for you are more in need of them than us.' And he did not accept them."

17

Trust in God

❧ Tawakkul

God Most High says, "Whosoever puts his trust in God, He will suffice him" (65:3). And He says, "Let those who believe trust in God" (5:26). He also says, "Put your trust in God if you are believers" (5:26).

On the authority of 'Abdallah b. Mas'ud (may God be pleased with him), the Messenger of God (God's blessing and peace be upon him) is reported to have said, "I was shown all the communities at the gathering place of the Hajj. I saw that my community had filled the plain and the mountain. Their number and appearance pleased me. I was asked, 'Are you content?' I said, 'yes.' Together with them will be seventy thousand who will enter Paradise without reckoning. They never had themselves tattooed nor sought omens in birds nor uttered spells; rather, they trusted in God." Then 'Ukkasha b. Muhsin al-Asadi stood up and requested, "O Messenger of God, pray to God to make me one of them." The Messenger of God, prayed, "O God, make him one of them." Then another stood up and said, "Pray to God to make me one of them." Then he replied, "'Ukkasha came ahead of you."

Abu 'Ali ar-Rudhbari related, "I said to 'Amr b. Sinan, 'Tell me something about Sahl b. 'Abdallah.' He told me, 'He said that there are three signs of the one who trusts in God. He does not ask. He does not turn anything away. He does not withhold anything.'"

Abu Musa ad-Dabili reported, "Abu Yazid was asked, 'What is trust in God?' So he asked me, 'What do you say?' I replied, 'Our companions say, "Even if beasts of prey and serpents were on your right and left, your innermost being would not waver on their account."' Abu Yazid observed, 'Yes, this is close. But if the people of the Garden were living the life of ease in the Garden and the people of the Fire were tormented in the Fire, and then it occurred to you to prefer one to the other, you would leave the sphere of trust in God.'"

Sahl b. 'Abdallah explained, "The first station in trust in God is that the servant be between the hands of God [may He be exalted and glorified] exactly as the dead body is between the hands of the one who washes the dead. He turns him however he wishes; the body has no movement or control." Hamdun declared, "Trust is clinging to God Most High."

Ahmad b. Khidruya related, "A man asked Hatim al-Asamm, 'Who is it that feeds you?' He answered, 'The treasures of the heavens and earth belong to God, but the hypocrites do not comprehend'" (63:7).

Know that the locus of trust in God is the heart. Outward action does not preclude trust in God in the heart after the servant has become certain that destiny is from God Most High, so that if something is withheld,

115

he sees God's determination therein, and if something is granted, he sees God's facilitation therein.

On the authority of Anas b. Malik, it is told that a man came riding his camel, and he asked, "O Messenger of God, shall I leave my camel untied and trust in God?" He replied, "Both tie your camel and trust in God."

Ibrahim al-Khawwas commented, "Whoever genuinely trusts in God when dealing with himself will also trust in God when dealing with others." Bishr al-Hafi reported, "One of the Sufis said, 'I have placed my trust in God Most High,' but he was lying to God Most High. If he were to trust in God, he would be satisfied with whatever God does with him."

Yahya b. Mu'adh was asked, "When is a man trusting in God?" He answered, "When he is satisfied with God Most High as a guardian." Ibrahim al-Khawwas related, "While I was traveling in the desert, a voice called out and there was a Bedouin walking along. He said to me, 'O Ibrahim, among us there is trust in God. Stay with us until your own trust is sound. Do you not know that your hope to reach a city for the sake of different varieties of food is impelling you there? Cease hoping for cities and trust in God.'"

When Ibn 'Ata' was asked about the true nature of trust in God, he explained, "It is that anxious desire for things of the world should not appear in you, despite the severity of your need for them, and that you should always remain truly content with God, despite your dependence on those things." Abu Nasr as-Sarraj observed, "The condition of trust in God is what Abu Turab an-Nakhshabi has noted, 'Casting down the body in worship, attaching the heart to lordship, and being serene as to [the matter of] sufficiency. If something is given, he is thankful, and if it is withheld, he is patient.'"

As Dhu'n-Nun al-Misri has said, "Trust in God is abandoning the stratagems of the soul and stripping off power and strength, for the servant is only capable of trust in God when he knows that God [may He be exalted] knows and sees all of his states." Abu Ja'far b. Abu al-Faraj related, "I saw a ruffian known as ''A'isha's Camel' who was receiving a lashing. I asked him, 'When does the pain of your beatings become easier?' He replied, 'When the one on whose account we are beaten sees us.'"

Al-Husayn b. Mansur asked Ibrahim al-Khawwas, "What have you accomplished during your journeys and crossings of the deserts?" He answered, "I remained in a state of trust in God, curing my self thereby." So al-Husayn asked, "You have annihilated your lifetime in the cultivation of your inner being, but what about annihilation [of the self] in the Oneness of God?"

Abu Nasr as-Sarraj stated, "Trust in God is, as Abu Bakr ad-Daqqaq has said, 'Restricting concern for livelihood to one day and refraining from aspirations for the morrow.'" He affirmed, "It is as Sahl b. 'Abdallah has said, 'Trust in God is abandoning oneself to God Most High in whatever He wishes.'" Abu Ya'qub an-Nahrajuri remarked, "Trust in God, in its perfect essence, is the state manifested by Abraham [peace be upon him] when he answered Gabriel's offer of help [peace be upon him], 'From you, I need help.' For his self had withdrawn to God Most High and with God, he did not see anything other than God [may He be exalted]."

A man asked Dhu'n-Nun al-Misri, "What is trust in God?" he replied, "Deposing all masters and abandoning causality." The man requested, "Say more." He continued, "It is casting the self into servitude to God, ousting it from lordship."

When Hamdun al-Qassar was asked about trust in God, he explained, "If you had ten thousand dirhams, and you owed one-sixth of a dirham, you would not rest easy lest you might die and that debt remain on your head. And if you had a debt of ten thousand dirhams, and were unable to leave enough to cover your debt, you would not give up hope that God Most High might settle it for you."

When asked about trust in God, Abu 'Abdallah al-Qarshi commented, "It is being attached to God Most High in every state." The questioner requested, "Say more." He instructed, "Abandon dependence on every cause that leads to another so that God Himself takes possession of those causes."

Sahl b. 'Abdallah observed, "Trust in God is the state of the Prophet [God's blessing and peace be upon him], and earning is his Sunna. So whoever maintains his state will never abandon his Sunna." Abu Sa'id al-Kharraz stated, "Trust in God is agitation without contentment and contentment without agitation." It is said, "Trust in God is that abundance and paucity are one and the same for you."

Ibn Masruq declared, "Trust in God is surrendering oneself to the flow of destiny and decrees." Abu 'Uthman al-Hiri asserted, "Trust in God is contentedness with God Most High together with reliance upon Him." Al-Husayn b. Mansur noted, "The one who truly trusts in God does not eat anything while there is someone in the land who is more deserving of it than he."

'Umar b. Sinan related, "Ibrahim al-Khawwas passed by us, and we said to him. 'Tell us about the strangest thing you saw in your travels.' He replied, 'Al-Khidr [upon whom be peace] met me and asked to keep me company, and I was afraid lest my trust in God might be corrupted by my staying with him. So I parted from him.'"

When Sahl b. 'Abdallah was asked about trust in God, he explained, "It is a heart that lives with God Most High without other attachment." The master Abu 'Ali ad-Daqqaq (may God have mercy upon him) said, "There are three degrees for the one trusting in God: trust, then surrender, and then assignation [to God of one's affairs]." The one who trusts in God is at peace with His promise, the one who surrenders is content with His knowledge, and the one who assigns his affairs to God is satisfied with His wisdom. I heard him say, "Trust in God is the beginning, surrender is the middle, and assigning one's affairs to God is the end." Ad-Daqqaq was asked about trust, and he commented, "It is eating without greed."

Yahya b. Mu'adh declared, "Donning wool garments is a shop, speaking about renunciation is a profession, and accompanying a caravan is desire. These, all of them, are attachments."

A man came to ash-Shibli complaining about his many dependents, and ash-Shibli commanded, "Go back to your house and drive away from you the ones whose sustenance is not by virtue of God Most High." Sahl b. 'Abdallah stated, "Whoever criticizes activity [in earning a livelihood] criticizes the Sunna. And one who criticizes trust in God criticizes faith."

Ibrahim al-Khawwas reported, "I was on the road to Mecca, and I saw a terrifying person. I asked, 'Are you a jinn or a man?' He replied, 'I am a jinn.' I inquired, 'Where are you going?' He answered, 'To Mecca.' And I asked, 'Without any provisions?' He affirmed, 'Yes. Among us, too, are ones who journey in a state of trust in God.' I asked him, 'And what is trust in God?' He replied, 'Receiving from God Most High.'"

Al-Farghani related, "Ibrahim al-Khawwas was without peer in trust in God. He took great care in observing it. He would never be without a needle and thread, a small bucket for ablutions, and scissors. Someone asked him, 'O Abu Ishaq, why do you carry these things while you abstain from all else?' He responded, 'These kinds of things do not destroy trust in God because God [may He be exalted] has made religious duties binding on us. The dervish has but one robe, and his robe may be torn. If he has no needle and thread with him, his private parts show, and his prayer is rendered invalid. And if he has no bucket for ablutions, then his purity is sullied. So if you see a dervish without a bucket for ablutions or a needle and thread, then you should worry about the completeness of his prayer.'"

The master Abu 'Ali ad-Daqqaq (may God have mercy upon him) said, "Trusting in God is the quality of the believers, surrender is the quality of the saints, and assigning one's affairs to God is the quality of those who assert His unity." So trust in God is the quality of the common people, surrender is the quality of the elite, and assigning one's affairs to God is the quality of the elite of the elite. I also heard him say, "Trust in God is the attribute of the prophets [generally], surrender is the attribute of Abraham [upon whom be peace], and assigning one's affairs to God is the attribute of our Prophet Muhammad [God's blessings and peace be upon him]."

Abu Ja'far al-Haddad related, "I stayed for some ten years firmly believing in trust in God while I was working in the marketplace. Every day I would take my wages, and without using any part of them for a draught of water or for going to the baths, I would bring them to the dervishes in ash-Shuniziya, and I remained in my state."

Al-Husayn, the brother of Sinan, said, "I made the pilgrimage fourteen times while I was barefoot, trusting in God. When a thorn pierced my foot, I would remember that I had enjoined upon my soul trust in God, scrape my foot on the ground, and walk on." Abu Hamza stated, "I feel ashamed to enter the desert when I am full, having resolved to trust in God, lest my traveling while relying upon a full stomach be itself a provision with which I have supplied myself."

When Hamdun was asked about trust in God, he answered, "This is a degree I have not reached yet, and how can one who has not completed the state of faith speak about trust in God?" It is said, "The one who trusts in God is like an infant. He knows of nothing in which he can seek shelter except his mother's breast. Like that is the one who trusts in God. He is guided only to his Lord Most High." One of the Sufis related, "I was in the desert, and I was proceeding ahead of a caravan. I saw someone in front of me, so I hurried to catch up with him. It was a woman, holding a staff, who was walking along slowly. Because I thought she was feeble, I reached in my pocket, brought out twenty dirhams, and instructed, 'Take these. Then wait until the caravan reaches you and hire a camel with this money.' But she lifted her hand in the air thus, and suddenly there were dinars in her palm. She observed, 'You pull dirhams from a pocket, but I pull dinars from the Unseen.'"

Abu Sulayman ad-Darani saw a man in Mecca who was consuming nothing but the water of Zamzam. After several days, Sulayman asked him, "What do you think: if the water of Zamzam were to dry up, what would you drink?" The man stood up, kissed his forehead, and declared, "May God reward you with goodness, as much as you have guided me, for truly I had been worshiping Zamzam for days." Then he passed on.

Ibrahim al-Khawwas reported, "I saw a young man on the road to Syria who was excellent in outward manner. He asked me, 'Would you like companionship?' I replied, 'But I have no food.' He declared, 'If you hunger, I will hunger with you.' So we stayed for four days together. Then something was granted to us, and I invited him, 'Come now [partake of this].' He told me, 'I have resolved not to accept anything by an intermediary.' So I exclaimed, 'O lad, how exacting you are toward yourself!' He retorted, 'Ibrahim, do not flatter me, for surely the One Who calls to account is watching. What do you know of trust in God?' Then he observed, 'The beginning of trust in God is that even when need arises in you, you long for nothing except the One Who has all sufficiency.'"

It is said, "Trust in God is negating doubts and

surrendering one's affairs to the King of Kings." And it is said, "A group of people came to al-Junayd [may God grant him mercy] and inquired, 'Where should we seek sustenance?' He answered, 'If you know where it is, go seek it there.' They said, 'But we *do* ask God Most High.' He instructed, 'If you think that He is forgetting you, then remind Him.' They asked, 'Should we go home and then trust in God?' He stated, 'Testing is doubting.' They asked, 'Then what measure should we try?' And he replied, 'Abandonment of all measures.'"

Abu Sulayman ad-Darani said to Ahmad b. al-Hawari, "O Ahmad, verily the paths to the Hereafter are many, and your sheikh knows many of them except this blessed trust in God, for I have never caught a whiff of it."

It is said, "Trust in God is reliance on what is in God Most High's hand and despairing of whatever is in the hands of men." It is also said, "Trust in God is emptying the innermost being of [even] the thought of demanding fulfillment in one's search for sustenance."

Al-Harith al-Muhasibi (may God grant him mercy) was asked about the one who trusts in God, "Does desire affect him?" He replied, "Perils arising from natural characteristics affect him, but they do him no harm at all, and despairing of all that is in the hands of men gives him strength to overcome desire."

It is said that an-Nuri was in the desert in a state of hunger when an invisible voice called to him, "Which do you love more: the causes [of sufficiency] or sufficiency [itself]?" He responded, "There is nothing but sufficiency." So he remained seventeen days without eating.

Abu 'Ali ar-Rudhbari remarked, "If, after five days, the dervish says, 'I am hungry,' then send him to the marketplace and order him to take a job and earn something." It is said that Abu Turab an-Nakhshabi once observed a Sufi reaching for a melon rind to eat after three days of hunger. He told the Sufi, "Sufism is not suitable for you! Keep to the marketplace."

Abu Ya'qub al-Basri related, "One time I went hungry for ten days in the sacred mosque in Mecca, and I felt weak, and my self tempted me. So I went to the river valley that I might find something to abate my weakness. I saw a discarded turnip lying on the ground and picked it up. I felt a frightening agitation in my heart from that, as if someone were saying to me, 'You were hungry for ten days, and now your lot is a rotting turnip!' So I threw it down, entered the mosque area, and sat. Then a Persian appeared. He sat before me and put down a satchel, saying, 'This is for you.' I asked him, 'Why have you chosen me for this?' He told me, 'Know that we were at sea for ten days, and one time the ship was on the brink of capsizing. Each one of us made a vow that if God Most High saved us, he would give something as charity. I vowed that if God Most High saved me, I would give this to the first person my eyes fell upon among those living near the mosque, and you are the first one I have met.' Then I instructed him, 'Open it.' He opened it, and inside were Egyptian sesame cakes, shelled almonds, and cubed sweetmeats. I took some of each and said, 'Take the remainder to your young men. It is my gift to you for I have accepted yours." Then I told my self, 'Your sustenance was on the way to you for ten days, and you were looking for it in the river valley!'"

Abu Bakr ar-Razi reported, "I was with Mamshad ad-Dinawari when talk of debts came up. He remarked, 'I had a debt once, and my heart was preoccupied with it. Then I perceived someone saying to me in a dream, "O miser! You deprive us of this amount. Take more… the taking is on your head, and the giving is upon us." From then on I never dealt with a grocer, butcher, or anyone else.'"

It is told about Bunan al-Hammal that he related, "I was on the road to Mecca, coming from Egypt, and had provisions with me. A woman came to me, observing, 'O Bunan, you are a porter; you carry provisions on your back, imagining that He will not provide for you!' So I threw down my things. But then it came to my mind three times that I had not eaten. I found an anklet on the road and said to myself, 'I will hold onto this until its owner comes. Maybe he will give me something when I return it to him.' Then the same woman appeared and told me, 'Now you are a merchant! You say, "Maybe the owner will come back, and I will get something from him!"' So she threw some dirhams at me, saying, 'Spend them.' They lasted me all the way to to Mecca."

It is related about Bunan that he was in need of a slave girl to serve him, so he revealed his need to his brothers. They gathered her price together for him and announced, "Here it is. A group of slaves is coming, so purchase whichever suits you." When the group arrived, all eyes were drawn to one of them, and they said, "She is the right one for him." They asked her owner, "How much is this one?" He replied, "She is not for sale." They implored him, but he declared, "She is for Bunan al-Hammal. A woman from Samarqand is making him a present of her." So she was brought to Bunan, and she related the story to him.

Al-Hasan al-Khayyat reported, "I was with Bishr al-Hafi when a party of travelers came and gave him greetings. He inquired, 'Where are you from?' They answered, 'We are from Syria. We have come to give you greetings and we wish to make the pilgrimage.' He exclaimed, 'Thanks be to God Most High for you.' They asked, 'Will you go with us?' He replied, 'On three conditions: we will carry nothing with us; we will not ask anyone for anything; and if someone gives us something, we will not accept it.' They stated, 'As for not carrying anything with us, so be it. As for not asking, so be it. But as for not accepting anything if it is given to us, that we cannot do.' So he said, 'You have come with your trust in the provisions of the pilgrims.' Then he explained, 'O Hasan, there are three types of dervishes. There is the dervish who does not ask and if he is given something, does not take it. Such a one subsists by means of his spirit. Then there is the dervish who does not ask, and if he is given something, accepts it. For such a one are feasts laid out in the shrine of sanctity. Then there is the dervish who asks, and if he is given something, accepts the amount of sufficiency. His penance is to give alms.'"

Habib al-'Ajami was asked, "Why have you given up trading?" He answered, "I found the [divine] surety to be reliable."

It is said that long ago there was a man on a journey who had with him a loaf of bread. He declared, "If I consume this, I will die." So God entrusted him to an angel, commanding, "If he eats the bread, provide for him. If he does not eat it, then do not give him a thing." That loaf of bread remained with him until he died [of starvation], never having eaten it. The loaf of bread was still with him.

It is said, "To the one who goes about fully assigning all his affairs to God, the goal is brought, just as the bride is brought in procession to her bridegroom's family." The distinction between *tadyi'* (deliberately forfeiting what God has given one) and *tafwid* (assigning one's affairs to God) is that *tadyi'* relates to the rights of God Most High and is a blameworthy practice; *tafwid* relates to your own rights, and it is a praiseworthy practice.

'Abdallah b. al-Mubarak observed, "Whoever receives a single penny from an illicit source is not trusting in God."

Abu Sa'id al-Kharraz related, "I went into the desert one time with no provisions and I was overcome by extreme need. Off in the distance, I saw a way station, so I was happy that I had arrived. Then I thought to myself, 'I have become complacent, and I have trusted in something other than Him.' I swore that I would enter the town only if I were carried to it. I dug a hole for myself and covered my body with sand up to my chest. In the middle of the night a loud clamor arose, and it was said, 'O people of the town, one of the friends of God Most High has buried himself in the sand. Find him!' Then a crowd came to me, and dug me out, and brought me to the town."

Abu Hamza al-Khurasani reported, "I went on the

pilgrimage one year. As I was walking along the road, I fell into a well. My soul urged me to call for help, but I said, 'No, by God, I will not call for help.' I was scarcely finished with this thought when two men passed by. One of them suggested to the other, 'Come, let us block up the opening to this well so that no one may fall into it.' They came with reeds and matting and filled up the mouth of the well with dirt. I wanted to cry out, but I told myself, 'I will cry to the One Who is nearer than these two.' So I remained silent. After one hour, suddenly something came, uncovered the top of the well, and lowered its leg into it. Then it was as if I were instructed, 'Hold onto me,' in a growl. I knew what was meant. So I held on and it pulled me out of the well. Lo and behold, it was a lion! Then it passed on. An invisible caller cried out to me, 'O Abu Hamza, is this not better? One peril saved you from another.' I walked on, saying:

> *I cry aloud to You that I may utter to You*
> *whatever I conceal.*
> *My inner being utters what my glance says*
> *to it.*

> *My shame before You forbade me to conceal*
> *the passion,*
> *And You made me dispense with unveiling*
> *through my perceiving You.*

> *You were kind toward me. Then you showed*
> *my outer state*
> *To my concealed one, and kindness was*
> *followed by kindness.*

You presented Yourself to me unseen, so that it
was as if
You gave me glad tidings in the unseen that
You were in my grasp.

Now I see you and a sense of abandonment
overcomes me from my awe for You.
Then You grant me intimacy by your kind-
ness and affection.

And You revive a lover whose love for You is
his death.
That is wondrous: the existence of life
together with death."

Hudhayfa al-Mar'ashi, who had been serving and accompanying Ibrahim b. Adham, was asked, "What is the strangest thing you witnessed with him?" He answered, "We had been on the road to Mecca for some days and had not found any food. We came into Kufa and sought shelter in a ruined mosque. Ibrahim b. Adham looked at me and observed, 'O Hudhayfa, I see in you the marks of hunger.' I replied, 'It is as the sheikh sees.' He instructed, 'Bring me an inkwell and paper.' So I brought them, and he wrote, 'In the name of God, the Compassionate, the Merciful. You are the One desired in every state and the One indicated in every sign.

I am praising, I am thankful, I am invoking
[Your name].
I am hungry, I am thirsty, I am naked.

> *That makes six qualities, and I will be a surety*
> *for half of them,*
> *So You be the surety for the other half, O*
> *Creator.*

> *Asking, too, for me is like the fire, so please—*
> *Do not compel me to enter the fire.'*

Then he handed me the sheet of paper, commanding, 'Go out and do not attach your heart to anything other than God Most High. Give this paper to the first one you meet.' I went, and the first one I met was a man on a mule. So I gave him the paper. He took it and wept. He asked where was the one who had written it. I told him, 'He is in Such-and-such mosque.' He gave me a bag filled with six hundred dinars. Then I met another man and asked him who the man on the mule was. He told me that he was a Christian. I came to Ibrahim b. Adham and told him the story. He declared, 'Do not touch it, for he is on his way here.' After an hour the Christian appeared, bent over Ibrahim b. Adham's head [to kiss him], and became a Muslim."

18

Thankfulness

❧ Shukr

God Most High says, "If you are thankful, I will give you more" (14:7).

On the authority of Abu Khabab, 'Ata' related, "I came with 'Ubayd b. 'Umayr to 'A'isha [may God be pleased with her] and said, 'Tell us of the most wondrous thing you saw of the Messenger of God [God's blessing be upon him].' She wept and asked, 'What did he do that was not wondrous? He came to me one night, and we went to my bed [or she said, 'under my covers'], so that his body touched mine. After a time he said, "O daughter of Abu Bakr, let me be now, so that I may worship my Lord." I replied, "I so love being near to you," but I gave him permission. Then he got up, went to the waterskin and made his ablutions, pouring out much water, and stood to pray. He began weeping, until the tears fell onto his chest, then he bent in prayer and wept, then he prostrated and wept, then he lifted his head and wept. He continued in that manner until Bilal came and called him to the morning prayer. I asked him, "What makes you weep when God has forgiven your sins early and late?" He said, "Should I not be a thankful servant? Why should I not weep when God has sent this verse to me, 'Verily in the creation of the heavens and earth . . . are signs for people who reflect' [2:164 and cf. 3:190]?'"

The real nature of thankfulness, in the view of the people who have attained truth, is recognition of the bounty of the Bounty-Giver, in an attitude of submissiveness and in accordance with this saying, "God [may He be exalted] is described as thankful *[shakur]* in the sense of widely extending His favors, not in a literal sense." This means that He rewards the servant for thankfulness. So He has designated the recompense for thankfulness as thankfulness [on His part], just as He has stated, "The recompense for an offense is one equal thereto" (42:40).

It is said that God's thankfulness is His bestowing of abundant reward for slight deeds, as in the saying, "A beast is thankful when it looks plump beyond the [measure] of fodder it is given." We might say that the true nature of thankfulness is praise for the Beneficent by remembering the beneficence He has shown to one. So then thankfulness of the servant toward God Most High is appreciation for Him by remembering His beneficence to him. And the thankfulness of God (may He be exalted) to the servant is praise of him by remembering his beneficence to Him. As for the beneficence of the servant, it is obedience to God Most High, and the beneficence of God is His bestowing blessing on the servant by enabling him to render thanks to Him.

Thankfulness of the servant, in the true sense, includes both mention by the tongue and affirmation by the heart of the Lord's bestowal of blessings. Thankfulness is divided thus: thankfulness by the tongue, which is recognition of blessings with a degree of submission, thankfulness of the body and limbs, which means taking on the characteristics of fidelity and service, and thankfulness of the heart, which is withdrawal to the plane of witnessing by constantly observing respect. It is said that the learned are thankful with their words, the worshippers are thankful in their deeds, and the gnostics are thankful in their steadfastness toward Him in all of their states.

Abu Bakr al-Warraq declared, "Thankfulness for blessings is to bear witness to favor and to observe respect." Hamdun al-Qassar asserted, "Thankfulness for blessings is that you see yourself as a parasite in thankfulness." Al-Junayd commented, "There is a defect in thankfulness because the thankful one seeks an increase for himself; thus he is aware of his allotted share even as he is aware of God." Abu 'Uthman remarked, "Thankfulness is recognizing one's inability to be thankful." It is said, "Thankfulness for the ability to be thankful is more complete than thankfulness." This is because you see that your thankfulness comes by means of His enabling, and that enabling is among the most sublime blessings for you. Thus you give thanks for thankfulness, and then you give thanks for the thankfulness of thankfulness, and so on, ad infinitum.

It is said, "Thankfulness is attributing the blessings to their proper owner with a quality of submission." Al-Junayd observed, "Thankfulness is that you do not regard yourself as worthy of blessings." Ruwaym explained, "Thankfulness is that you exhaust all your capacities [in the effort to give thanks]." It is said, "The thankful one *[shakir]* is he who is thankful for what is, and the very thankful one *[shakur]* is he who is thankful for what is not." It is said, "The *shakir* is thankful for a gift, and the *shakur* is thankful for rejection." It is also said, "The *shakir* is thankful for benefits, and the *shakur* is thankful for deprivation." And it is said, "The *shakir* is thankful for gifts, and the *shakur* is thankful for adversity." "The *shakir* is thankful when blessings are granted, and the *shakur* is thankful when blessings are delayed."

Al-Junayd (may God have mercy on him) related, "One time when I was seven years old, I was playing in front of as-Sari, and a group was gathered before him speaking about thankfulness. He asked me, 'O lad, what is thankfulness?' I replied, 'That one not disobey God using the blessings [He has given].' He declared, 'Soon your destiny from God will be your tongue.'"Al-Junayd remarked, "I still weep over these words." Ash-Shibli explained, "Thankfulness is awareness of the Giver of blessings, not of the blessings." It is said, "Thankfulness is a shackle for what one possesses, and a snare for what one does not yet possess." Abu 'Uthman observed, "The common people give thanks for being fed and clothed while the elite give thanks for meanings that enter their hearts."

It is said that David (upon whom be peace) asked, "O my God, how can I thank You when my very act of thanksgiving is a blessing from You?" God revealed to him, "You have just given the thanks." It is said that

Moses (upon whom be peace) stated in his intimate prayer, "O my God, You created Adam by Your hand, and You did this and You did that [for him]. How did he thank You?" He replied, "He knew that that was from Me, and so his knowledge of that was his thankfulness to Me."

It is said that one of the Sufis had a friend who was arrested by the sultan. The Sufi was sent for, and his friend told him, "Give thanks to God Most High." Then the man was beaten, and he wrote to his friend [the Sufi], "Give thanks to God Most High." Then a Magian who had a stomach disorder was brought and shackled, and one cuff of the chain was put on the foot of this man and the other cuff on the foot of the Magian. The Magian would get up many times at night, which meant that he had to stand over him until the Magian was finished. He wrote to his friend, "Give thanks to God." His friend inquired, "How long will you say this? What trial could be more severe than this?" The man replied, "If the girdle the infidel wears around his waist were placed around your waist, just as the shackle on his foot were placed on your foot, then what would you do?"

A man came to Sahl b. 'Abdallah and told him, "A robber broke into my house and stole my belongings!" Sahl declared, "Give thanks to God Most High. If a robber [that is, Satan] entered your heart and corrupted your belief in God's Oneness, then what would you do?"

It is said, "Thankfulness of the eyes is that you conceal a fault you see in your companion, and thankfulness of the ears is that you conceal a fault you hear about him." It is also said, "Thankfulness is delighting in praising Him for giving what you do not deserve." Al Junayd related, "When as-Sari wished to instruct me, he would ask me a question. One day he asked me, 'Al-Junayd, what is thankfulness?' I replied, 'It is that not one part of the blessings of God Most High be used in disobeying Him.' He inquired, 'How did you come to this [knowledge]?' I answered, 'From sitting with you.'"

It is said that al-Hasan b. 'Ali clung to a column and stated, "O my God, You have blessed me, and You do not find me thankful. You have tested me, and You do not find me patient. But You have not withheld blessings because I have ceased being thankful, and You have not prolonged hardship because I have ceased being patient. O my God, there is only generosity from the Generous One."

It is said, "If your hand cannot reach out to gain a reward, your tongue should give thanks more profusely." It is said, "There are four useless acts: confiding a secret to a deaf man, giving to one who is thankless, sowing seeds in a salt marsh, and lighting a lamp in the sunlight." It is also said that when Idris (upon whom be peace) was given tidings of forgiveness, he asked for [long] life. When he was asked about this, he replied, "So that I may thank Him, because before this I had been striving for forgiveness." Then an angel spread its wings and carried him to the sky.

It is told that one of the prophets (peace be upon them) passed by a small stone from which much water was coming forth. This amazed him. Then God made it speak to him, and it said, "When I heard God Most High say, 'A Fire whose fuel is men and stones' [66:6],

I wept out of fear." The prophet then prayed that God would protect the stone, and God Most High revealed to him, "I have already saved it from the Fire." So the prophet passed on, and when he returned, he saw water gushing forth from the stone in the same way, which amazed him. Again God made the stone speak, and he asked it, "Why are you crying when God has forgiven you?" It replied, "Those were tears of sorrow and fear, and these are tears of thankfulness and joy."

It is said, "The thankful one has increase because he is in the presence of blessing." God Most High says, "If you give thanks, I will increase you" (14:7). And the patient one is with God Most High because he is in the presence of the One Who imposes trials. God (may He be exalted) says, "Verily God is with those who are patient" (2:153, 8:46, and 8:66).

It is said that a delegation came to 'Umar b. 'Abd al-'Aziz (may God be pleased with him). Among them was a youth, who began to speak. 'Umar instructed, "Let the elders speak," whereupon the youth told him, "O Commander of the Believers, if command were to be given according to years, then there are many among the Muslims older than you." So he ordered, "Speak." He explained, "We are not a delegation of desire nor a delegation of fear. As for desire, your generosity has brought it to us, and as for fear, your just manner has safeguarded us against it." So he asked him, "Then who are you?" He answered, "The delegation of thankfulness. We have come to thank you, and now we will depart." And they recited:

> *"A misfortune it is that my thankfulness is
>   silent*
> *For what you have done while your kind-*
>   *ness speaks.*
> *I see the favor from you and then I conceal it;*
> *I am, therefore, robbing the hand of the*
>   *generous one."*

It is said, God Most High revealed to Moses (upon whom be peace), "I have mercy upon My servants: the ones tested with adversity and those spared from it." Moses asked, "Why those who are spared from it?" He replied, "Due to the paltriness of their thankfulness for My sparing them from it."

It is said, "Praise of God *[hamd]* is for the breaths, and thankfulness is for the blessings of the senses." It is also said, "Praise begins with Him, and thankfulness is your following this lead." In an authentic tradition it is said that "The first to be called to Paradise will be those who give praise to God in every state." It is said, "Praise is for what is withheld and thankfulness is for what is done."

It is related that one of the Sufis reported, "On a journey I saw a great sheikh advanced in years, so I asked him about his state. He replied, 'In my early years I was struck with love for my cousin, and she also loved me. It so happened that they married her to me. The night they brought her to me in the wedding procession we said, "Come let us spend this night giving thanks to God Most High for having joined us." We spent that night in prayer and neither of us had time for the other. The second night we said the same, and for seventy or eighty years we have done the same every night. Is it not like that, O lady?' The old woman affirmed, 'It is as the sheikh says.'"

19

Certainty

Yaqin

God Most High says, "[This is the book . . . for] those who believe in that which is revealed to you and that which was revealed before you and [who] are certain of the Hereafter" (2:2-4).

On the authority of 'Abdallah b. Mas'ud, the Prophet (may God's blessing and peace be upon him) is reported to have said, "Do not seek to please anyone at the price of God's wrath, do not offer thanks to anyone for the bounty of God [may He be exalted and glorified], and do not find fault with anyone for something God Most High has withheld from you, for the sustenance of God is not brought to you by the greed of the greedy nor is it driven away from you by the hatred of one who hates. By means of His justice and fairness, God Most High has placed repose and delight in contentment and certainty, and distress and sorrow in suspicion and anger."

Abu 'Abdallah al-Antaki stated, "The smallest [benefit] of certainty is that, when it enters the heart, it fills the heart with light and banishes every doubt from it, and by it the heart becomes filled with thankfulness and fear of God." Ja'far al-Haddad related, "Abu Turab an-Nakhshabi saw me while I was in the desert sitting next to a pool of water. It had been sixteen days since I had eaten or drunk. He asked me, 'Why are you sitting here?' I answered, 'I have been [alternating] between knowledge and certainty, waiting to see which will triumph so that I may act accordingly. If knowledge wins out over me, I will drink. If certainty wins out, I will pass on.' He told me, 'Great rank awaits you.'"

Abu 'Uthman al-Hiri explained, "Certainty is lack of concern for the morrow." Sahl b. 'Abdallah declared, "Certainty comes from an abundance of faith and its inward realization." Sahl also said, "Certainty is a branch of faith and short of confirming the truth of faith *[tasdiq]*." One of the Sufis commented, "Certainty is the knowledge entrusted to the hearts for safekeeping." This person indicates that it is not acquired [but given].

Sahl observed, "The beginning of certainty is unveiling." Therefore one of the ancestors remarked, "If the curtain were drawn away, I would not increase in certainty." It is, then, viewing and witnessing. Abu 'Abdallah b. Khafif asserted, "Certainty is ascertainment by the innermost heart of the affairs of the Unseen." Abu Bakr b. Tahir noted, "Knowledge comes by way of opposing doubts, but in certainty there is no doubt at all." Thereby he contrasted acquired knowledge with whatever comes by way of intuition. Thus the Sufis' knowledge in the beginning is acquired, and in the end is intuited.

One of the Sufis stated, "The first of the stations is

knowledge, then certainty, then attesting the Reality of God, then sincerity of belief, then bearing witness, and then obedience. And 'faith' is the term that combines all these." This person points out that the first thing needed is knowledge of God Most High, which is not attainable except by fulfilling its conditions. Those conditions consist of correct vision. Then when proofs follow upon each other and evidence results, one becomes, through the continuous succession of lights and the obtaining of inward vision, free of all need for reflection on proofs; such is the state of certainty. As for the attestation of the Reality of God (may He be exalted), it is concerning what He informs one provided that one be attentive to the answer of the One Who invites concerning what He informed one of His actions in the future, for attestation presupposes being informed. Then as for sincerity of belief, it lies in what follows of the performance of commands. After that is the disclosure of the response [of God] to the goodly bearing of witness. And then comes the performance of acts of obedience, asserting God's unity in all one has been commanded to do and shunning all one has been forbidden from doing. Imam Abu Bakr b. Furak alluded to this meaning when I heard him say, "Remembrance of the tongue is an excellent thing by which the heart overflows."

Sahl b. 'Abdallah commented, "It is illicit for the heart to smell the scent of certainty while contentment with other-than-God dwells therein." Dhu'n-Nun al-Misri declared, "Certainty calls one to cut short expectation for worldly fulfillment, cutting short this expectation calls one to renunciation, renunciation bequeaths wisdom, and wisdom bequeaths discernment of the outcome." He also noted, "There are three signs of certainty: reducing one's intercourse with people, abandoning praise of them for gifts, and avoiding finding fault with them when they withhold [gifts]. And there are three signs of the certainty of certainty: looking to God Most High for everything, returning to Him in every matter, and turning to Him for aid in every state."

Al-Junayd (may God grant him mercy) declared, "Certainty is the constancy of knowledge in the heart: it does not vanish or change." Ibn 'Ata' stated, "To the degree that they attain fear of God, they will attain whatever they can of certainty. The foundation of fear of God is opposing prohibited things, and opposing prohibited things is opposing the self. Thus whatever is the degree of their separation from the self, [this] they reach in certainty."

One of the Sufis said, "Certainty is unveiling, and unveiling takes place in three ways: by means of informing, by means of disclosure of the power [of God], and by means of the truths of faith." Know that in their way of speaking, unveiling consists of the revelation of something to the heart when it is possessed by remembrance of Him with no doubt remaining. Sometimes by unveiling they mean something similar to what is seen between waking and sleep. Many times they designate this state as steadfastness.

Imam Abu Bakr b. Furak related, "I asked Abu 'Uthman al-Maghribi, 'What is this I hear that you have said?' He replied, 'I see certain people like this and that.' So I inquired, 'You see them with your vision or by an unveiling?' He answered, 'By an unveiling.'" 'Amir b. 'Abd Qays explained, "Were the curtain to be withdrawn, I would not increase in certainty." It is said, "Certainty is direct vision vouchsafed by the strength of faith" and "Certainty is the extinguishing of acts of resistance."

Al-Junayd (may God grant him mercy) observed, "Certainty is the cessation of doubt in the witnessing of the Unseen." The Prophet (may God's blessing and peace be upon him) said about Jesus, son of Mary (peace be upon him), "If he had increased in certainty, he would have walked through the air as I have done." The master Abu 'Ali ad-Daqqaq explained that the Prophet was referring to his own state on the night of the Mi'raj because it was concerning the mysteries of the Mi'raj that he (may God's blessing and peace be upon him) said, "I saw [that] Buraq* remained behind and I walked on."

Al-Junayd reported that when as-Sari was asked about certainty, he replied, "It is your motionless tranquillity when thoughts move through your breast because of your certainty that any motion on your part would neither benefit you nor repel from you whatever may be decreed."

'Ali b. Sahl declared, "Being in the presence [of God] is preferable to certainty because being in the presence [of God] is actual and certainty is conceptual." It is as if he placed certainty at the beginning of being in the presence [of God], and made being in the presence [of

---

* The miraculous steed the Prophet rode on the Night Journey and the Ascent from Jerusalem to the heavens. (See 17:1-2)

144

God] the continuation of certainty. It is as if he regarded as possible the attainment of certainty apart from being in the presence [of God], and the converse as impossible. Therefore an-Nuri stated, "Certainty is witnessing." He means that in witnessing there is a certainty beyond all doubt, because nobody witnesses Him Most High unless he trusts in what comes from Him.

Abu Bakr al-Warraq commented, "Certainty is the foundation of the heart, and by it is faith perfected. God Most High is known by certainty, and the intellect comprehends that which comes from God." Al-Junayd remarked, "By means of certainty, some men walk on water, but someone who dies of thirst may surpass them with respect to certainty." Ibrahim al-Khawwas related, "I met a youth in the desert as handsome as an ingot of silver and I asked, 'Where are you going, O lad?' He answered, 'To Mecca.' I asked, 'Without provisions or camel or money?' He exclaimed, 'O one weak in certainty, is the One Who can preserve the heavens and the earth not able to convey me to Mecca without material provision?'" Ibrahim reported, "When I came to Mecca, there he was circumambulating the Ka'ba saying:

> *'O my everlastingly tearful eye,*
> *O my soul dying in grief,*
> *Do not wish for anyone*
> *Other than the One Majestic and*
> *Everlasting.'*

And when he saw me, he inquired, 'O sheikh, after this are you still in that [state] of weak certainty?'"

An-Nahrajuri declared, "If the servant perfects the inner meanings of certainty, trials become a blessing for him and comfort a misfortune." Abu Bakr al-Warraq observed, "There are three aspects of certainty: certainty of informing, certainty of proofs, and certainty of witnessing." Abu Turab an-Nakhshabi related, "When I saw a youth walking in the desert without provisions, I remarked, 'If he has no certainty, then surely he will perish.' I asked him, 'O lad, you are in this sort of place without any provisions?' He replied, 'O sheikh, raise your head. Do you see [anything] other than God [may He be exalted and glorified]?' I told him, 'Go wherever you wish.'"

Abu Sa'id al-Kharraz explained, "Knowledge is what enables you to act, and certainty is what impels you [to act]."

Ibrahim al-Khawwas commented, "I sought a livelihood that would enable me to eat licit food. So I engaged in fishing. One day a fish swam into the net, and I took it out and flung the net back into the water. Then another swam into it, and again I tossed the net in the water, and then I waited. Then an invisible caller cried out, 'Could you find no livelihood other than capturing those who remember Us, and then killing them?' So I tore apart the nets and abandoned fishing."

20

Patience

≈ Sabr

God (may He be exalted and glorified) said, "And be patient, and your patience is only by God" (16:127).

On the authority of Abu Hurayra, 'A'isha (may God be pleased with her) related this tradition from the Prophet (God's blessing and peace be upon him), "Patience is at the time of the first obstacle." Patience is, then, of different kinds: patience with what the servant acquires [through his deeds] and patience with what is not by his acquisition. As for patience with acquired things, it is of two kinds: patient perseverance in what God commands and patient perseverance in shunning what He prohibits. With regard to patience with things not acquired by the servant, his patience is enduring a decree of God that results in hardship for him.

Al-Junayd asserted, "The journey from the world to the Hereafter is easy for the believer, but relinquishing creation for the sake of God Most High is difficult. And the journey from the self to God Most High is intensely difficult, but patience with God is still more difficult."

When asked about patience, al-Junayd replied, "It is drinking down bitterness without a frowning look." 'Ali b. Abi Talib (may God be pleased with him) declared, "The relation of patience to faith is like that of the head to the body."

Abu'l-Qasim al-Hakim explained, "The words of God Most High 'And be patient' are a command to worship, and His words 'And your patience is only by God' (16:127) are to servitude. Thus one who ascends from the degree of 'for You' to the degree of 'by You' has been advanced from the degree of worship to the degree of servitude." The Prophet (God's blessing and peace be upon him) stated, "By You I live and by You I die."

Ahmad related, "I asked Abu Sulayman about patience, and he said, 'By God, we are not patient with what we like, so how will it be with what we dislike?'" Dhu'n-Nun remarked, "Patience is keeping away from transgressions and remaining content while imbibing the agony of affliction, and it is showing detachment when poverty assails one's livelihood." Ibn 'Ata' observed, "Patience is remaining constant in a state of misfortune with a goodly manner." It is said, "Patience is the soul's passing away in trials without complaint."

Abu 'Uthman commented, "The one most steadfast is he who accustoms his soul to assaulting adversity." It is said, "Patience is to abide with trials as a good companion as one does with well-being." And Abu 'Uthman also said, "The best reward for acts of worship is the reward for patience. There is no reward above it. God Most High promises, 'We will bestow on those who are patient their reward according to the best of their actions'" (16:96). 'Amr b. 'Uthman noted, "Patience is perseverance with God [may He be glorified and Most High] and accepting His trials in a welcoming and calm manner." Al-Khawwas explained, "Patience is adherence to the ordinances of the Book and the Sunna."

Yahya b. Mu'adh asserted, "The patience of lovers is greater than that of the abstemious. [This is] astonishing. How can they be patient?" They have recited:

> *Patience is praiseworthy in every time and place.*
> *Except for You, surely that is not praiseworthy.*

Ruwaym said, "Patience is to abandon complaint." Dhu'n-Nun declared, "Patience is seeking help from God Most High." The master Abu 'Ali ad-Daqqaq (may God have mercy on him) stated, "Patience is like its name." Ibn 'Ata' recited:

> *I will be patient to please You while longing destroys me;*
> *It suffices me that You are pleased while my patience destroys me.*

Abu 'Abdallah b. Khafif remarked, "Patience is of three kinds: that of the one who strives to be patient, that of the patient one, and that of the very patient one." 'Ali b. Abi Talib (may God be pleased with him) observed, "Patience is a mount that never stumbles." 'Ali b. 'Abdallah al-Basri related, "A man came upon ash-Shibli and asked, 'Which kind of patience is most difficult for the patient?' He replied, 'Patience toward

God [may He be exalted and glorified].' But the man said, 'No.' Then ash-Shibli suggested, 'Patience for God.' But he said, 'No.' Ash-Shibli answered, 'Patience with God.' But again he said, 'No.' Ash-Shibli asked, 'Then what is it?' He responded, 'Patience away from God,' and ash-Shibli let out such a cry that his spirit was almost destroyed."

Al-Jurayri explained, "Patience is not distinguishing a state of blessing and a state of suffering, together with peace of mind in both of them. And patient forbearance is the experience of peace while being tried despite awareness of the burdens of suffering."

One of the Sufis has recited:

> I was patient when I knew not of Your desire
> for my patience.
> And I concealed out of patience the afflic-
> tion You visited on me,
> Fearing that my heart might complain of my
> longing
> In secret to my tears so they might flow
> when I knew not.

The master Abu 'Ali ad-Daqqaq (may God have mercy on him) commented, "The patient ones will achieve high rank in both worlds because they attain from God His company. God Most High says, 'Verily God is with the patient ones'" (2:153 and 8:46).

It is said as to the meaning of the words of God Most High, "[O you who believe,] be patient and persevere in patience and connect [yourselves to God] " (3:200), that patience *(sabr)* is less than persevering in patience *(musabara)*, and this is less than connecting [yourselves to God] *(murabata)*. It is also said, "Be patient" with your souls in obedience to God Most High, "persevere in patience" with your hearts in the trials concerning God, and "connect" your innermost beings to the yearning for God. And it is said, "Be patient" toward God, "persevere in patience" by God, and "connect" [yourselves] with God.

It is said that God Most High revealed to David (upon whom be peace), "Adopt My characteristics. Among them is that I am the Most Patient." It is said, "Imbibe patience. If it kills you, you will die like a martyr. If it quickens you, you will live like a noble." It is also said, "Patience for God is a hardship, patience by God is [an act of] abiding [with Him], patience toward God is a trial, and patience away from God is loathsome." They recite:

> *Blameworthy is the outcome of patience in*
> *being away from You*
> *But praiseworthy is patience in all else.*

They also recite:

> *How could I be patient in separation from one*
> *Who is as close to me as the right hand to*
> *the left?*
> *When men play tricks with all things*
> *I see that love plays tricks with them.*

It is said, "Patience in seeking fulfillment of a desire is a sign of victory, and patience in hardship is the token of deliverance." Mansur b. Khalaf al-Maghribi (may God have mercy on him) related, "A man was scourged with a whip. When he returned to the prison, he called out to one of his friends and spat into his hand. He spat out from his mouth small pieces of silver. When asked about this, he replied 'There were two dirhams in my mouth. Among the spectators was someone I knew, and I did not want to cry out when he was looking at me. So I was biting the dirhams, and they shattered in my mouth.'"

It is said, "Your present state is your stronghold, and all that is other than God is your enemy. So the best form of warfare takes place in the stronghold of your state." It is said, "Being constant in patience is being patient in being patient until patience is immersed in patience, and patience despairs of patience, as it is said:

He persevered in patience so patience ap-
pealed to him for help.
So the lover called out to patience: Patience!"

It is told that one time Shibli was confined to the lunatic asylum, and a group of people came to him. He asked, "Who are you?" They answered, "We are your dear friends who have come to visit you." Then Shibli started to pelt them with stones, so they ran away. He cried, "O liars, if you were my dear friends, you would have been patient when I tested you."

It is told in one of the reports, "What those who are burdened bear for My sake is within My sight." God Most High says, "And be patient for your Lord's decree, for surely you are in Our sight" (52:48).

One of the Sufis reported, "I was in Mecca, and I saw a dervish circumambulating the House. He drew a slip of paper from his pocket, looked at it, and passed on. The next day he did the same. I watched him for some days, and he continued to do the same. Then one day he walked around [the Ka'ba], looked at the paper, retreated a few paces, and then fell dead. I took the paper out from his pocket. Written on it was, 'And be patient for your Lord's decree, for surely you are in Our sight.'"

It is told that a youth was seen hitting an old man in the face with his shoe. They asked him, "Are you not ashamed? Why are you striking the old man in the middle of his face like this?" He replied, "He has committed a grave offense." They asked, "And what is that?" He answered, "This old man told me he cared for me, and he has not seen me for three days."

One of the Sufis related, "I went to India, and I saw a man with one eye known as 'So-and-so the Patient.' When I asked about him, I was told, 'When he was in the prime of his youth, a friend of his left on a journey. When he bade him farewell, one of his eyes started to weep, but the other did not. So he said to his tearless eye, 'Why are you not weeping at the departure of my companion? I forbid you to look at the world." He closed his eye, and for sixty years he has not opened it.'"

It is said as to the words of God Most High, "Therefore be patient with a comely patience" (70:5), that a "comely patience" is one that prevents the victim of affliction from being known. 'Umar b. al-Khattab remarked, "If patience and thankfulness were two camels, it would be one to me as to which of them I would ride." When afflicted by trials, Ibn Shubruma (may God have mercy on him) would exclaim, "These are clouds," and then they would disperse.

It is related that the Messenger of God (may God's blessing and peace be upon him) was asked about faith, and he explained, "[It is] patient perseverance and generosity." As-Sari was asked about patience, and he began to speak. Then a scorpion crawled on his foot and stung him many times; yet Sari did not move. Someone asked him, "Why do you not brush it away?" He answered, "I am ashamed before God Most High to speak on patience while I myself am not patient." In one of the traditions it is said, "The patient poor ones will be the companions of God Most High on the Day of Resurrection."

God Most High revealed to one of His prophets, "I sent down My trial to My servant, so he prayed to Me. But I deferred answering his prayer. Then he complained to Me. So I inquired, 'O My servant, how can I in My mercy withold from you something by which I am being merciful?'"

Ibn 'Uyayna commented as to the meaning of the words of God Most High, "And We appointed them leaders giving guidance under Our command because they persevered in patience" (32:24), [that is] "Because they grasped the essential concern, We appointed them leaders." I heard the master Abu 'Ali ad-Daqqaq declare, "The condition of patience is that you not object to what has been decreed, and as for letting trials become apparent, but without complaining, this does not negate patience. God Most High says in the story of Job, 'Truly We found him patient. How excellent in servitude! Ever did he turn [to Us]' (38:44), despite what God Most High has said about him, that he said, 'Distress afflicts me'" (21:83). And I heard him state,

"God elicited these words from Job so that they might be a way of escape for the weak ones of this community." One of the Sufis remarked, "[God said] Truly We found him patient *[sabir].*" He did not say "most patient *[sabur]*" because Job was not patient at all times. On the contrary, at times he took pleasure in the trials and found them pleasant. At the time of taking pleasure, he was not patient; therefore God did not say "most patient."

The master Abu 'Ali (may God grant him mercy) asserted, "The inner truth of patience is to emerge from trials in the same manner as entering them, just as Job [upon whom be peace] said at the end of his trial, 'Distress afflicts me, and You are the Most Merciful of those who show mercy' (21:83). He maintained the proper manner of speaking because he made an allusion by saying, 'and You are the Most Merciful of those who show mercy,' but he was not explicit, [as he might have said:] 'Be merciful to me.'"

Patience is of two kinds: the patience of the worshipers and the patience of the lovers. As for the patience of the worshipers, it is better that it be preserved. As for that of the lovers, it is better that it be abandoned. As to the meaning of this, they recite:

> *It became clear on the Day of Separation that*
> *his resolve*
> *To be patient was a lying fancy.*

As to this meaning, I heard the master Abu 'Ali (may God have mercy on him) relate, "Jacob [upon whom be peace] awakened, and he had promised himself to be patient. So he said, 'Then let it be a comely patience'

(12:83). That is, 'So my way will be that of comely patience.' Then it was not evening before he said, 'How great is my grief for Joseph!'" (12:84)

21

Vigilant Awareness

❧ Muraqaba

God Most High says, "God is watchful over all things" (33:52).

On the authority of Jarir b. 'Abdallah al-Bajalli, it is told that Gabriel came to the Prophet (God's blessing and peace be upon him) in the form of a man. He asked, "O Muhammad, what is *iman?*" He replied, "It is that you believe in God, His angels, His books, His messengers, and destiny—its good and evil, its sweetness and bitterness." He said, "You have spoken the truth." Jarir remarked, "We were astonished at his confirming the truth of what the Prophet said, when he had asked him a question and then confirmed the answer." He then commanded, "Tell me, what is *islam?*" He replied, "*Islam* is that you establish regular prayer, give the *zakat,* fast the month of Ramadan, and perform the pilgrimage to the House." He confirmed, "You have spoken the truth." He then asked, "Tell me, what is *ihsan?*" The Prophet replied, "*Ihsan* is that you worship God as if you see Him, for if you do not see Him, yet

He sees you." He averred, "You have spoken the truth." The saying of the Prophet, "For if you do not see Him, yet He sees you," is an indication of the state of vigilant awareness, because vigilant awareness is the servant's knowledge of the Lord's constant awareness of him. So his constancy in this knowledge is vigilant awareness of his Lord, and this is the source of all good for him. He will come to this vigilant awareness only after he has fully called himself to account, for when he has called himself to account for what has happened in the past, makes right his state in the present, keeps firmly to the path of Truth, makes good his relationship with God by compliance of his heart, and guards his breaths against forgetfulness of God Most High, observing God Most High in all his states, then he knows that God (may He be exalted) is watchful over him and that He is near to his heart. He knows his states, He sees his deeds, and He hears his words. The one who is heedless of all this is distant from the beginning of attainment and [how much more so] from the inner truths of nearness.

Al-Jurayri declared, "One who has not made firm his fear of God and vigilant awareness between himself and God will not attain unveiling and witnessing." The master Abu 'Ali ad-Daqqaq (may God have mercy on him) said, "A ruler once had a vizier who was in his presence one day. The vizier turned to one of the servants standing there, not due to some suspicion, but because he sensed a movement or sound from them. It happened that the ruler looked at this vizier at that moment. The vizier feared that the ruler would imagine that he looked at them due to suspicion, so he continued to look at them. After this day the vizier would always come to the ruler looking to one side so that the ruler supposed that it was in his nature always to look to one side. This is man's vigilant awareness of men, so how is it with the awareness of the servant of his Master?"

I heard one of the dervishes report, "There was a ruler who had a servant for whom he cared more than his other servants; none of them was more valuable or more handsome than this one. The ruler was asked about this, so he wanted to make clear to them the superiority of this servant over the others in service. One day he was riding with his entourage. In the distance was a snow-capped mountain. The ruler looked at that snow and bowed his head. The servant galloped off on his horse. The people did not know why he galloped off. In a short time he came back with some snow, and the ruler asked him, 'How did you know that I wanted snow?' The servant replied, 'Because you looked at it, and the look of the sultan comes only with a firm intention.' So the ruler said, 'I accord him special favor and honor, because for every person there is an occupation, and his occupation is observing my glances and watching my states of being attentively.'"

One of the Sufis commented, "One who is aware of God in his thoughts, God will restrain in his limbs." Abu'l-Husayn b. Hind was asked, "When does the shepherd chase away his sheep from the pastures of ruin with the staff of preservation?" He answered, "When he knows that someone is watching."

It is said that Ibn 'Umar (may God be pleased with him) was on a journey when he saw a boy tending some sheep. He asked him, "Will you sell one of these sheep?" The boy replied, "They are not mine." So Ibn 'Umar suggested, "[You could] tell the owner of the flock that a wolf made off with one of them." The boy said, "And where is God?" After that for some time Ibn 'Umar would repeat, "That slave said, 'And where is God?'"

Al-Junayd declared, "One who achieves vigilant awareness fears only the loss of reward from his Lord."

One of the sheikhs had some disciples, and he would favor one by giving him more attention than the others. When he was asked about that, he replied, "I will show you why this is so." He gave each of his disciples a bird and instructed him, "Slaughter it someplace where no one can see." They departed; then each returned, having slaughtered his bird. But the favored one brought back his bird alive. When the sheikh asked, "Why have you not slaughtered it?" he responded, "You ordered me to slaughter it where no one would see, and I did not find such a place." So the sheikh stated, "This is why I favor him with my attention."

Dhu'n-Nun al-Misri observed, "The sign of vigilant awareness is choosing what God Most High chooses, making great what God Most High makes great, and belittling what God Most High belittles." An-Nasrabadhi asserted, "Hope impels you to obedience, fear removes you from disobedience, and vigilant awareness leads you to the paths of inner truths." Abu'l-'Abbas al-Baghdadi related, "When I asked Ja'far b. Nasir about vigilant awareness, he told me, 'It is watchfulness over the innermost being because of awareness of the gaze of God [may He be exalted] with every thought.'"

Al-Jurayri explained, "Our way is founded on two parts: that you compel your soul to vigilant awareness of God Most High and that this knowledge be visible in your outward movements." Al-Murta'ish commented, "Vigilant awareness is watchfulness over the innermost being because of awareness of the Unseen with every glance and utterance." When Ibn 'Ata' was asked, "What is the best act of worship?" he answered, "Vigilant awareness of God at all times." Ibrahim al-Khawwas said, "Observance bequeaths vigilant awareness; this awareness bequeaths inner and outer devotion to God Most High." Abu 'Uthman al-Maghribi noted, "The best things man imposes on his soul in this path are calling the self to account, vigilant awareness, and regulating his actions by knowledge." Abu 'Uthman related, "Abu Hafs told me, 'When you sit instructing the people, be a preacher to your heart and soul and do not allow their gathering around you to beguile you, for they are attentive to your external being, while God is attentive to your inner being.'"

Abu Sa'id al-Kharraz reported, "One of the sheikhs said to me, 'You must watch over your innermost being and have vigilant awareness of God. One day I was traveling in the desert, and suddenly there was a crashing noise behind me, which frightened me. I wanted to turn around, but I did not. Then I saw something falling upon my shoulders, so I ran away. I was watching my innermost being . . . then I turned around, and there was a huge lion.'"

Al-Wasiti declared, "The best act of worship is watchfulness of the moments. That is, that the servant not look beyond his limit, not contemplate anything other than his Lord, and not associate with anything other than his present moment."

22

Satisfaction

ﻌ Rida

God Most High says, "God is well pleased with them, and they are well pleased with Him" (98:8).

Jabir reports that the Messenger of God (may God's blessing and peace be upon him) declared, "The inhabitants of Paradise will be in a gathering when a light from the gate of Paradise will shine on them. They will lift their heads, and the Lord Most High will look upon them and say, 'O people of Paradise, ask Me for what you wish.' They will reply, 'We ask that You be pleased with us.' He Most High will respond, 'My pleasure has brought you to My abode, and I have honored you. This is the proper time, so ask Me.' They will answer, 'We ask You for increase [beyond this].'" He stated, "They will be brought powerful steeds made of ruby, their reins of green emeralds and rubies. They will ride upon them, the steeds kicking their hooves faster than the eye can see. Then God [may He be exalted] will order the fruit-bearing trees and houris to be brought, and they will say, 'We are young and tender, and we will never grow withered. We are eternal, and we will not die—mates for a noble, believing people.' And God will call for piles of fragrant white musk, and they will whirl all about in a wind called 'al-Muthira' (the Arouser) until they are brought at length to the Garden of Eden, which is the center of Paradise. The angels will announce, 'O our Lord, the people have come.' God will exclaim, 'Welcome to the truthful ones, welcome to the obedient ones.'" He said, "And so the veil will be lifted for them. They will look upon God, and they will enjoy the Light of the Compassionate One so that they will no longer see one another. Then He will command, 'Return them to their palaces with the gifts.'" He continued, "They will be brought back home, and they will be able to see one another." Then the Messenger of God explained, "That is what is meant by His words, 'A gift from the Forgiving One, the Compassionate One'" (41:32).

The 'Iraqis and the Khurasanis differ concerning satisfaction. Is it a state or a station? The people of Khurasan assert, "Satisfaction is one of the stations. It is the culmination of trust in God. This means that it is attributable to what the servant attains by his own effort." The 'Iraqis state, "Satisfaction is one of the states, not something attained by the servant. Rather it is something that alights in the heart, as with the other states." A synthesis of the two views is possible. It would be stated thus, "The beginning of satisfaction is attained by the servant and is a station, although in the end it is a state and not something to be attained." When people speak about satisfaction, each one expresses his state and his own allotted shares. So their expression differs, just as people differ in their experience and allotted shares. As for what is known beyond any possible doubt, it is that the one who is satisfied with God Most High is the one who does not object to his destiny.

The master Abu 'Ali ad-Daqqaq declared, "Satisfaction is not that you experience no trials; satisfaction is only that you not object to the divine decree and judgment."

Know that it is binding on the servant that he be satisfied only with the destiny with which he has been commanded to be satisfied, because it is not possible nor necessary that he be satisfied with all parts of his destiny, such as acts of disobedience and the numerous trials of the Muslims.

The sheikhs comment, "Satisfaction is the greatest gate of God." They mean that whoever is honored with satisfaction is met with the most perfect welcome and is honored with the highest favor.

'Abd al-Wahid b. Zayd explained, "Satisfaction is the greatest gate of God and the paradise of this world." Know that the servant will not approach being satisfied with God (may He be exalted) until God is satisfied with him, because God Most High says, "God is well pleased with them, and they are well pleased with God" (98:8). The master Abu 'Ali ad-Daqqaq related, "A disciple asked his master, 'Does the servant know if God is pleased with him?' The answer was, 'No. How could he know that when His pleasure is hidden?' The disciple protested, 'But he does know that!' So he was asked, 'How is that?' He replied, 'If I find my heart pleased with God Most High, I know that He is pleased with me.' Then the master remarked, 'Well have you spoken, young man.'"

It is said that Moses (upon whom be peace) prayed, "O my God, direct me to a deed whose performance would please You." He was told, "You would not be able to do that." Moses fell down prostrate to Him, imploring. So God Most High revealed to him, "O Son of 'Imran, My pleasure is in your pleasure with My decree."

Abu Sulayman ad-Darani declared, "If the servant rids himself of the memory of passions, then he will be satisfied." An-Nasrabadhi stated, "Whoever wishes to reach the place of satisfaction, let him adhere to that in which God has placed His satisfaction."

Muhammad b. Khafif explained, "There are two kinds of satisfaction: satisfaction with Him and satisfaction with what proceeds from Him. Satisfaction with Him is that one be satisfied with Him as Arranger [of one's affairs], and satisfaction with what proceeds from Him concerns whatever He decrees."

I heard the master Abu 'Ali ad-Daqqaq observe, "The path of the wayfarer is longer, and it is the path of spiritual exercises. The path of the elite is shorter but more difficult, and it requires that you act in accord with satisfaction and that you be satisfied with destiny." Ruwaym remarked, "Satisfaction is that if God were to place Hell at one's right hand, one would not ask that He change it to one's left." Abu Bakr b. Tahir commented, "Satisfaction is eliminating reluctance from the heart so that nothing remain there but happiness and joy." Al-Wasiti instructed, "Make use of satisfaction to your utmost, and do not allow satisfaction to make use of you lest its sweetness and vision veil you from the inner truth of that in which you are engaged." Know that these words of al-Wasiti are momentous. In them may be found a subtle warning for the people because contentment with their states is itself a veil from the Giver of states. If a man finds pleasure in his satisfaction and experiences the comfort of satisfaction in his heart, he is veiled by his state from witnessing its inner truth.

Al-Wasiti also warned, "Beware of being delighted with acts of worship, for they are a deadly poison." Ibn Khafif stated, "Satisfaction is tranquillity of the heart with His ordinances and conformance of the heart with what pleases God and what He chooses for one."

Rabi'a al-'Adawiya was asked, "When is the servant satisfied?" She replied, "When afflictions delight him as much as blessings." It is said that ash-Shibli asserted in front of al-Junayd, "There is no power or might except by God," and Junayd told him, "This speech of yours comes from dejectedness, and dejectedness comes from abandoning satisfaction with destiny." Ash-Shibli fell silent.

Abu Sulayman ad-Darani said, "Satisfaction is that you not ask God Most High for Paradise or take refuge in Him from the Fire." Dhu'n-Nun al-Misri (may God grant him mercy) explained, "There are three signs of satisfaction: having no preference before a decree has been decided, feeling no bitterness after the decree has been decided, and feeling stirrings of love in the very midst of trials."

It was said to al-Husayn, (son of) 'Ali b. Abi Talib (may God be pleased with them), "Abu Dharr stated, 'Poverty is more beloved to me than wealth, and illness is more beloved to me than health.'" He responded, "May God have mercy on Abu Dharr. As for me, I say, 'One who trusts God's good choice for him will not wish for other than what God [may He be exalted and glorified] has chosen for him.'"

Al-Fudayl b. 'Iyad told Bishr al-Hafi, "Satisfaction is better than asceticism in this world because one who is satisfied never wishes for anything beyond his station." When Abu 'Uthman was asked about the saying of the Prophet (may God's blessing and peace be upon him), "I ask You to grant me satisfaction after the decree has been decided," he explained, "This is because satisfaction before the decree has been decided would mean there is a resolution to be satisfied, but satisfaction after the decree has been decided is [true] satisfaction."

Abu Sulayman remarked, "I wish that I knew some small part of satisfaction. Even if it caused me to enter the Fire, then I would be satisfied by that." Abu 'Umar ad-Dimashqi observed, "Satisfaction is the elimination of sorrow concerning whatever a command might be." Al-Junayd commented, "It is removal of choice." Ibn 'Ata' asserted, "Satisfaction is directing the heart's attention to God's preexistent choice for the servant, and it is abandoning displeasure." Ruwaym said, "Satisfaction is tranquillity of the heart beneath the flow of decrees." An-Nuri declared, "Satisfaction is the delight of the heart with the bitterness of fate." Al-Jurayri said, "Whoever is satisfied without measure, God will raise him beyond limit." Abu Turab an-Nakhshabi noted, "One who has esteem for the world in his heart will not be granted satisfaction."

On the authority of al-'Abbas b. 'Abd al-Mutallib, the Messenger of God (may God's blessing and peace be upon him) explained, "He who is satisfied with God as Lord experiences the taste of faith."

It is said that 'Umar b. al-Khattab wrote to Abu Musa al-Ash'ari (may God be pleased with them both), "All goodness is in satisfaction. If you are able, then be satisfied; if not, then be patient." It is said that 'Utba al-Ghulam would spend the night until morning exclaiming, "If You punish me, I love You, and if You have mercy on me, I love You." I heard the master Abu 'Ali ad-Daqqaq relate, "Mankind is made of clay, and clay has no worth by means of which the judgment of God Most High could be opposed."

Abu 'Uthman al-Hiri reported, "For forty years whatever state God [may He be exalted and glorified] placed me in, I did not dislike it, and whatever state He moved me to, I did not resent it." The master Abu 'Ali ad-Daqqaq said, "A man was angry with one of his slaves, so the slave asked another man to intercede for him. When he was forgiven, the slave began to weep, and the intercessor inquired, 'Why are you weeping, when your master has forgiven you?' The master told him, 'He is seeking satisfaction from me, [not mere forgiveness,] and there is no way for him to gain it. Thus he weeps."

23

Servitude

✤ 'Ubudiya

God Most High says, "Serve your Lord until [the Day of] Certainty comes to you" (15:99).

It is related on the authority of Abu Hurayra that the Messenger of God (may God's blessing and peace be upon him) said, "Seven are the ones God will shade in His shade on the day there will be nothing but His shade: a just *imam,* a youth who grew up in service to God Most High, a man whose heart is attached to the mosque from the moment he leaves it until he returns, two men who love one another for the sake of God and who meet and take leave of one another for this purpose, a man who makes remembrance of God without restraint so that his eyes overflow with tears, a man who answers a beautiful woman who would seduce him by saying, 'I fear God, Lord of the worlds,' and a man who gives charity in secret such that his left hand knows not what his right hand gives."

The master Abu 'Ali ad-Daqqaq (may God grant him mercy) observed, "Servitude *['ubudiya]* is more perfect than worship *['ibada]*, so first comes worship, then servitude, and finally, adoration *['ubuda]*." Worship is the practice of the common people, servitude is the practice of the elect, and adoration is the practice of the elect of the elect. He also said, "Worship is for one who possesses knowledge of certainty, servitude is for one who possesses the eye of certainty, and adoration is for one who possesses the truth of certainty." He also commented, "Worship is for those who strive, servitude is for those who excel in bearing hardships, and adoration is for the people of witnessing." So one who does not begrudge God his soul is in the state of worship, one who does not begrudge God his heart is in the state of servitude, and one who does not begrudge God his spirit is in the state of adoration.

It is said, "Servitude is establishing true acts of obedience, performing them without limit, ascribing little worth to whatever you offer, and being aware that your virtuous deeds come only by means of God's prior decree." It is said, "Servitude is abandoning personal choice in the face of divine fate." It is also said, "Servitude is emptying oneself of [belief in one's own] power and might and acknowledging the wealth and blessings He grants you." And it is said, "Servitude is embracing whatever you are commanded to do and separating yourself from whatever you are told not to do."

Muhammad b. Khafif was asked, "When is servitude sound?" He replied, "When a man surrenders himself completely to his Master and has patience with Him in the tribulations He imposes." Sahl b. 'Abdallah declared, "Devotion is not sound for anyone until he feels no concern for four things: hunger, nakedness, poverty, and disgrace." It is said, "Servitude is that you submit your entire being to Him and that you attribute to Him all your [praiseworthy] deeds." It is also said, "One of the signs of servitude is that you abandon your schemes and bear witness to the divine decree."

Dhu'n-Nun al-Misri explained, "Servitude is that you be His slave every instant, just as He is your Lord every instant." Al-Jurayri noted, "Many are the slaves of bounteous blessings, but rare are the slaves of the Bestower of blessings." The master Abu 'Ali ad-Daqqaq stated, "You will be the slave of whoever holds you in bondage. If you are in bondage to your self, you will be the slave of your self. If you are in bondage to your earthly life, you will be the slave of your earthly life." The Messenger of God (may God's blessing and peace be upon him) remarked, "Wretched are the slaves of money; wretched are the slaves of fine clothing."

Abu Zayn saw a man and asked him, "What is your occupation?" He answered, "I serve the donkeys." Abu Zayn retorted, "May God Most High make your donkeys die so you may serve Him, not donkeys." Abu 'Amr b. Nujayd asserted, "Not a single step can be pure on the path of servitude until a man sees that his good works are hypocrisy and his states pretensions." 'Abdallah b. Munazil declared, "Man is a slave of God so long as he does not seek for things to be subservient to him. If he seeks for things to be subservient to him, then he has left the fold of servitude [to God] and forsaken its practices." Sahl b. 'Abdallah commented, "Devotion is right for the servant only when no trace of wretchedness is seen in him when he is destitute and no sign of richness when he has plenty." It is said, "Servitude is bearing witness to divine lordship." An-Nasrabadhi observed, "The slave's worth is in proportion to his master's worth, just as the knower's nobility is in proportion to the nobility of the object of his knowledge."

Abu Hafs stated, "Servitude is the beautiful adornment of the servant. Whoever abandons servitude is shut off from beauty." An-Nibaji said, "Worship is based upon three things: that you not refuse any of His rulings, that you withhold nothing from Him, and that He not hear you asking others to answer your needs." Ibn 'Ata' explained, "Servitude is found in four traits: fidelity to one's vows, preserving the [divinely set] limits, contentment with whatever one has, and patience with whatever is withheld." 'Amr b. 'Uthman al-Makki related, "Among the many men I met in Mecca and elsewhere, or those who came to visit me at various times, none was greater in striving or more persevering in worship than al-Muzani [may God grant him mercy]. I never saw anyone better in glorifying the commands of God Most High than him, or anyone who restrained his soul as he did, or was as generous with people as he was." I heard the master Abu 'Ali ad-Daqqaq remark, "There is nothing more noble than servitude, nor is there a more perfect title for the believer than 'slave.' For this reason God [may He be exalted] said, in describing the Prophet [may God's blessing and peace be upon him] on the night of the Mi'raj—and it was his noblest moment in this world—'Glory be to the One who brought His slave by night from the sacred mosque' (17:1). Then God Most High said, 'And then

He revealed to His slave what He revealed' (53:10). So if there were a title more sublime than 'slave,' He would have used it for him."As to the meaning of this, they recite:

> *O 'Amr, to averge my blood is Zahra's right.*
> *Any who hear and see know this.*
> *Call me nothing but 'Zahra's slave,'*
> *For it is my noblest name.*

One of the Sufis commented, "If you cast off two things from yourself, you will be a true servant of God: tranquillity in pleasure and dependence on outward action." As al-Wasiti warned, "Beware the pleasure obtained from the gift, for it is a veiling for the people of purity." Abu 'Ali al-Juzjani said, "Being satisfied with God's decree is the abode of servitude, patience is satisfaction's door, and giving over all power to God is satisfaction's house. There is clamor at the door, apprehension in the abode, and repose in the house." The master Abu 'Ali ad-Daqqaq observed, "Just as 'lordship' is an eternal quality of God [may He be exalted], so is 'servitude' a quality of man that stays with him as long as he lives." One of the Sufis recited:

> *If you ask for me I will say, "Here I am, His*
> *slave."*
> *And if they ask Him He will say, "There is*
> *My bondsman."*

An-Nasrabadhi asserted, "Acts of worship are closer to seeking pardon and forgiveness for shortcomings than they are to being pleas for compensation and reward." He also said, "Servitude means losing awareness of serving in witnessing the One served."

Al-Junayd stated, "Servitude is abandoning all activity other than the work that is the root of repose."

24

Desire

❧ Irada

God Most High says, "Do not send away those who call upon their Lord morning and evening desiring His face" (6:52).

The Prophet (may God's blessing and peace be upon him) is related by Anas to have stated, "If God desires good for a servant, He uses him." Someone asked, "How does He use him, O Messenger of God?" He replied, "He grants him success in performing a righteous work before his death."

Desire is the beginning of the path of the wayfarers and the name of the first station of those who seek God Most High. This quality is called "desire" only because desire precedes every matter such that if a servant does not desire a thing, he will not do it. When this occurs at the beginning of the path, it is named "desire" by analogy with the intention that precedes all matters. The *murid* is so named because he has *irada* (desire), just as the *'alim* (scholar) is he who has *'ilm* (knowledge). They are both derived active participles. But in

the usage of the Sufis, the *murid* is one who has no
desire. One who has not stripped the self of desire is not
a *murid*. In the strict etymological sense, however, one
who has no desire is not a *murid*.

People have spoken concerning the meaning of
desire, each expressing what has come to his heart.
Most sheikhs explain, *"Irada* is to part from habitual
practices." The habit of most people is to stay in
forgetfulness, inclining to the calls of instinct, and to
remain in the realm of desire. But the *murid* is detached from all this. His detachment is itself a token and
proof of the soundness of his desire, so the state is
called *'irada,'* being the abandonment of habitual
practices.

The inner truth of desire is that it is a restive motion
in the heart in search of God. For this reason it is said,
"Irada is a painful rapture that makes every fear appear
paltry." Mamshad ad-Dinawari related, "From the time
I learned that all the states of the dervishes are very
serious, I have not jested with them. One time a dervish
came to me and said, 'O sheikh, I have a desire for you
to get me some sweet porridge.' Then I repeated the
words *'irada* [desire] and *'asida* [porridge]' in a jesting
way. The dervish withdrew, but I did not notice. I
ordered the porridge and looked around for the
dervish, but I could not find him. When I sought news
of him, they told me, 'He left immediately, saying to
himself, *"Irada* and *'asida, irada* and *'asida."* He
wandered aimlessly about until he went into the desert,
and he continued to say these words until he died.'"

One of the sheikhs reported, "I was alone in the
desert one time and I became depressed. I cried, 'O

men, speak to me! O jinn, speak to me!' Then an invisible caller called out to me, 'What do you desire?' I replied, 'I desire God Most High.' He asked, 'When is it that you desire God?'" That is, anyone who calls out to men and jinn, saying, "Speak to me!"—how can he be desiring God (Glorious and Majestic)?

The *murid* never slackens in his desire, day or night. He strives outwardly, while inwardly he suffers. He forsakes his bed, he is inwardly absorbed at all times, he bears hardship, he takes on burdens, he cultivates good moral qualities, he practices asceticism, he embraces terror, and he leaves behind all considerations of form. Just as it is recited:

> *I spent the night in the desert*
> > *But neither lions nor wolves alarmed me.*
> *I was overwhelmed by my longing, giving me*
> > *swiftness in the journey.*
> *This one filled with longing is still over-*
> > *whelmed.*

I heard the master Abu 'Ali ad-Daqqaq declare, "Desire is painful rapture in the inner heart, a sting in the heart, a violent passion in the intuitive senses, an anxious desire in the inward being, fires burning in the hearts." Yusuf b. al-Husayn related, "There was an agreement between Abu Sulayman and Ahmad b. Abi al-Hawari that Ahmad would follow Abu Sulayman's command in all things. He came to Abu Sulayman one day when Abu Sulayman was lecturing his students. Ahmad reported, 'The oven is fired. What do you command?' Abu Sulayman did not answer him. Ahmad repeated it two or three more times, until finally Abu

Sulayman exclaimed, 'Go sit in it!' as if he were angry with him. Then he forgot about Ahmad for a time. When he remembered, he ordered, 'Go fetch Ahmad. He is in the oven because he swore he would obey me.' So they went, and there he was in the oven, not one hair burned." I heard the master Abu 'Ali ad-Daqqaq assert, "When I was young, I burned with desire. I would say to myself, 'I wish I knew the meaning of desire!'"

It is said that among the signs of the *murids* are that they love to perform supererogatory prayers, they are sincere in wishing the community well, they are attached to solitude, they are steadfast in fulfilling the precepts of religion, they give generously according to His command, they have shame before His eyes, they are diligent in doing what He loves, they embark on all things that will bring them to Him, they are content with anonymity, and they experience restlessness in their hearts until they reach their Lord.

Abu Bakr al-Warraq remarked, "There are three things that torment the *murid*: marriage, writing *hadith*, and travel." Someone asked him, "Why have you stopped writing *hadith*?" He answered, "Desire [for God] prevents me from continuing." Hatim al-Asamm instructed, "If you come upon a *murid* who desires anything other than his *murad* [one desired], you may be certain that he has revealed his baseness." Al-Kattani noted, "The proper regime of the *murid* entails sleeping only when overcome by drowsiness, eating only in urgent necessity, and speaking only when compelled to do so." Al-Junayd observed, "If God desires good for the *murid*, He brings him into contact with the Sufis and keeps him from the company of professional scholars."

Ar-Raqqi related, "I heard ad-Daqqaq say, 'In the final stage of desire, you make a motion toward God Most High and you find Him with that motion.' So I asked, 'What embraces the whole subject of desire?' He replied, 'That you find God without a motion.'" Abu Bakr ad-Daqqaq explained, "The *murid* is not a *murid* until the angel on his left shoulder has not written anything for twenty years." Abu 'Uthman al-Hiri declared, "If one's desire is not pure in the beginning, the passage of time will only bring more misfortune." Abu 'Uthman asserted, "The *murid* is one who acts accordingly when he hears something of the Sufi sciences, and it becomes wisdom in his heart. If he speaks on it, those who hear gain benefit. One who hears something of their sciences and does not act accordingly [proves that] it was nothing but a story he remembered for a time and then forgot."

Al-Wasiti commented, "The first station of the *murid* is desire for God [may He be exalted], arrived at by throwing away his own desire." Yahya b. Mu'adh stated, "The most difficult thing for the *murids* is having to mix with those who oppose them." Yusuf b. al-Husayn said, "If you see a murid engaged in earning his living and acts permitted but not corresponding to the full rigor of the law, be assured that nothing will come of him."

Someone asked al-Junayd, "Is it good for the *murids* to listen to pious tales?" He replied, "Pious tales are one of God's legions, and the hearts are strengthened by them." He was asked, "Is there proof for what you say?" He affirmed, "Yes, the words of God Most High, 'All that We relate to you of the tales of the messengers is to strengthen your heart'" (11:120). Al-Junayd noted, "The sincere *murid* has no need of the learning of the ulama."

It may be said on the subject of the difference between *murid* and *murad* that every *murid* is, in truth, a *murad*. If he were not a *murad* [desired by] God (Glorious and Majestic), he would not be a *murid* because naught comes to be save by God's desire. Then again, every *murad* is a *murid* because if God desires him especially, He grants him success in having desire [for Him]. The Sufis do, however, distinguish between *murid* and *murad*. In their opinion, the *murid* is the beginner and the *murad* is at the highest degree. The *murid* is guided to take on works of exhausting proportions and is plunged in hardships; for the *murad*, a command [from God] is sufficient, without cause for hardship to himself. The *murid* is compelled to labor, and the *murad* is granted felicity and ease.

God's ways of dealing with those traveling His path are various: Most of them achieve success in striving and then, after lengthy hardships, attain sublime inner truths. But many of them are shown the splendor of inner truths at the start, attaining what the ones who perform many spiritual exercises have yet to reach. But most of these [former] return and strive following these [latter] so that they may obtain the benefits of spiritual exercises that they missed before.

The master Abu 'Ali ad-Daqqaq explained, "The *murid* is made to bear and the *murad* is borne." He also commented, "Moses [peace be upon him] was a *murid* because he said, 'O my Lord, expand for me my breast' (20:25). Our Prophet [may God's blessing and peace be upon him] was a *murad* because God Most High says of him, 'Have We not expanded for you your breast, lifted from you your burden that weighed down your back, and exalted your fame?' (94:1-4). Moses also requested, 'O my Lord, show Yourself to me that I may look upon You.' [God said,] 'You will never see Me [directly]' (7:143). God told our Prophet, 'Do you not see your Lord, how He extends the shadow?' (25:45). The words 'Do you not see your Lord' and 'how He extends the shadow' are intended as a veil for the real story [of what happened to the Prophet] and as a means of strengthening his state."

When Al-Junayd (may God grant him mercy) was asked about the *murid* and the *murad,* he replied, "The *murid* is controlled by the rules and regulations of scholarly learning, and the *murad* is controlled by the care and protection of God. The *murid* walks; the *murad* flies. When will the earthbound overtake the one who flies?"

It is said that Dhu'n-Nun sent a man to Abu Yazid, telling him, "Ask Abu Yazid, 'How long will this slumber and lazy repose go on? The caravan has passed by.'" Abu Yazid sent his reply, "Tell my brother Dhu'n-Nun, 'A man is he who sleeps the whole night through and then awakens in the last stopping-place before the caravan arrives.'" Dhu'n-Nun exclaimed, "Excellent! We in our present state cannot answer this."

25

Steadfastness

❧ Istiqama

God Most High says, "Those who say, 'Our Lord is God' and then are steadfast, [the angels descend upon them]" (41:30).

Thawban, who was a client of the Prophet (may God's blessing and peace be upon him), relates that he instructed, "Be steadfast even though you will never be able to be so completely. Know that the best part of your religion is the prayer, and only the believer will preserve his [bodily] purity."

Istiqama is a degree that makes one's affairs sound and complete and enables him to achieve benefits in a steady and orderly manner. The effort and striving of one who is not steadfast are wasted. God Most High says, "Be not like a woman who unravels her thread into fine strands after she has made it strong" (16:92). One who is not steadfast in his manner of being will never rise from one station to another, and his wayfaring on the path will never be firm.

One of the conditions necessary at the beginning of

the path is steadfastness in fulfilling the requirements of commencing the path, just as it is a duty for the gnostic to be steadfast in his behavior at the end of the path.

A mark of the steadfastness of those beginning the path is that their outer deeds not be marred by lassitude. For those at the middle stage, a mark of their steadfastness is that there be no pause in their wayfaring. A mark of the steadfastness of those in the final stage is that no veils come between them and their continuance on the path.

I heard the master Abu 'Ali ad-Daqqaq explain, "There are three degrees of steadfastness: setting things upright *[taqwim]*, making things sound and straight *[iqama]*, and being upright *[istiqama]*. *Taqwim* concerns discipline of the soul; *iqama*, refinement of the heart; and *istiqama*, bringing the inmost being near to God."

Abu Bakr (may God be pleased with him) commented, "The meaning of His words, 'and then are steadfast' (41:30) is that they do not associate partners with God." 'Umar taught, "It means that they did not swindle others like foxes." Abu Bakr's opinion refers to observing the principles of monotheism, and 'Umar's opinion refers to refraining from forced interpretations and to observing the conditions of contracts. Ibn 'Ata' said the verse means, "They were firm in confining their hearts to God." Abu 'Ali al-Juzjani declared, "Be content with the state of steadfastness, not seeking miraculous deeds, for your lower self is moved to seek miracles while your Lord [may He be exalted] demands of you steadfastness."

Abu 'Ali ash-Shabbuwi related, "I saw the Prophet in a dream, and I told him 'It is reported that you said, "The *sura* Hud has made my hair turn white." What is it that made your hair turn white: the stories of the prophets and the obliteration of nations?' He replied, 'No. It was God's words, "So be steadfast as you have been commanded."'" (11:112).

It is said, "Only the great men can maintain steadfastness because it entails leaving behind what is familiar and abandoning convention and habits. It means that one stands before God firm in the inner reality of truthfulness. For this reason the Prophet commanded, 'Be steadfast, although you will never be able to be so completely.'"

Al-Wasiti observed, "Steadfastness is the quality that perfects characteristics, the absence of which renders them ugly." Ash-Shibli remarked, "Steadfastness means that you face every moment as if it were the Resurrection." It is said, "Steadfastness in speech means to forsake slander, in actions it means refraining from innovation, in good works it means abandoning laxity, and in inward states it means being rid of the veil."

I heard the master Abu Bakr Muhammad b. al-Hasan b. Furak explain, "The verbal form of *istiqama* means asking for something." That is to say, they seek steadfastness from God in their monotheism, then in being faithful to their oaths, and in preserving the limits [of behavior set by God].

Know that steadfastness engenders continual miraculous signs. God Most High says, "And if they are steadfast on the path, We will give them water to drink in abundance" (52:16). He did not state, "We will let them drink water." He said, "We will give them water to drink in abundance," indicating thereby continuity.

Al-Junayd reported, "I met one of the young seekers in the desert under an acacia tree and asked him what made him sit there. He replied, 'I am looking for something.' Then I passed on and left him where he was. When I was returning from the pilgrimage, I found he had moved to a spot closer to the tree. I asked, 'Why are you sitting here?' He answered, 'I found what I had been looking for in this place, so I stuck to it.' I do not know which was more noble, his persistence in seeking his state or his perseverance in staying at the place where he attained his desire."

26

Sincerity

❧ Ikhlas

God Most High says, "Is it not to God that sincere devotion is due?" (39:3).

Anas b. Malik (may God be pleased with him) relates that the Messenger of God (may God's blessing and peace be upon him) declared, "Rancor will not invade the heart of the Muslim if he conform to three things: sincerity toward God in actions, giving honest counsel to those in command, and keeping to the community of Muslims."

Sincerity is having God as one's sole intention in worship. It means that one desires nearness to God by one's worship, to the exclusion of all else, whether it be making a show before men, trying to earn their praise, or loving to receive glory from them—anything other than desire for nearness to God Most High. It is said, correctly, "Sincerity means purifying actions of any awareness of fellow creatures." It is also said, "Sincerity means protecting oneself from [concern for] the regard of men."

An authentic tradition states that the Prophet (may God's blessing and peace be upon him) related, on the authority of Gabriel (peace be upon him), who related about God (may He be exalted) that He said, "Sincerity is a secret taken from My secret. I have placed it as a trust in the hearts of servants I love."

The master Abu 'Ali ad-Daqqaq stated, "Sincerity is guarding oneself from [concern for] the opinions of men and truthfulness is cleansing oneself of awareness of self. The sincere one is not hypocritical, and the truthful one is not conceited."

Dhu'n-Nun al-Misri commented, "Sincerity is complete only by being truthful in it and having patience for it. Truthfulness is complete only by sincerity in it and constancy throughout." Abu Ya'qub as-Susi observed, "When they perceive sincerity in their sincerity, their sincerity is in need of sincerity." Dhu'n-Nun explained, "There are three signs of sincerity: one sees praise and blame from men as being equal, one loses the awareness of doing good works while doing them, and one forgets the claim to reward in the afterlife for good works."

Abu 'Uthman al-Maghribi remarked, "Sincerity is a state in which the self takes no pleasure. This is the sincerity of the common people. As for the sincerity of the elect, it comes to them not by their own doings. Good deeds come forth from them, but they are detached from them. They neither experience awareness of the deeds nor have any regard for them. That is the sincerity of the elect." Abu Bakr ad-Daqqaq asserted, "The defect of the sincerity of each one said to be sincere is his own awareness of his sincerity. If

God wishes to purify his sincerity, He strips him of being aware of his sincerity, and he becomes sincere [by God, *mukhlas*], not sincere [on his own part, *mukhlis*]." Sahl said, "Only the sincere one *[mukhlis]* knows hypocrisy intimately." Abu Sa'id al-Kharraz declared, "The hypocrisy of the gnostics is better than the sincerity of the *murids.*"

Dhu'n-Nun stated, "Sincerity is what is protected from corruption by the enemy." Abu 'Uthman noted, "Sincerity is forgetting thought of creation through constant attention to the bounteous favor of the Creator." Hudhayfa al-Mar'ashi commented, "Sincerity means that the servant's actions are the same, outward and inward." It is said, "Sincerity is that by means of which God is desired and truthfulness is sought." It is also said, "Sincerity means blinding oneself to awareness of good deeds." As-Sari observed, "One who adorns himself in the view of men with something that is not his falls from the regard of God Most High." Al-Fudayl remarked, "To stop performing good works for the sake of men is hypocrisy, and to perform them for the sake of men is polytheism. Sincerity is that God cure you of both."

Al-Junayd said, "Sincerity is a secret between God and the servant. Even the recording angel knows nothing of it to write it [in the register of one's deeds]. The devil does not know of it to corrupt it, nor is passion aware of it that it might influence it." Ruwaym explained, "Sincerity in good deeds is that the one performing the deed wants compensation for it neither in the world nor in the hereafter, nor does he seek goodly treatment from the two angels who question the dead." It was asked of Sahl b. 'Abdallah, "What is the hardest thing on the self?" He answered, "Sincerity, because it has no share in it." When asked about sincerity, one of the Sufis responded, "It means that you call upon no one other than God to be a witness to your doings."

One of the Sufis related, "I went to Sahl b. 'Abdallah in his house on Friday before the prayer. There was a snake in the house, so I hesitated at the door. He exclaimed, 'Come in! No one attains the essential reality of faith while he remains fearful of anything on earth.' Then he asked, 'Would you like to attend the Friday congregational prayer?' I replied, 'There is a journey of one whole day and night from here to the mosque before us.' He took my hand, and after a moment there was the mosque. We went in and prayed; then we came out. Sahl stood there, watching the people, and said, 'Many are the people of *"La ilaha illa'llah"* [professing monotheism], but rare are the sincere.'"

Makhul declared, "Any servant who is sincere for forty days will experience wisdom springing forth from his heart and upon his tongue." Yusuf b. al-Husayn commented, "The dearest thing on earth is sincerity. How many times have I struggled to rid my heart of hypocrisy, only to have it reappear in another guise!" Abu Sulayman said, "If the servant is sincere, the abundance of temptations and hypocrisy will cease."

27

Truthfulness

ಎ Sidq

God Most High says, "O you who believe, fear God and be with the truthful ones" (9:119).

On the authority of 'Abdallah b. Mas'ud, the Prophet (may God's blessing and peace be upon him) stated, "If a servant remains continuously truthful and is intent on truthfulness, it will be written with God that he is veracious, and if he remains continously deceitful and is intent on deceit, it will be written with God that he is deceitful."

Truthfulness is the supporting pillar of this way. By it comes perfection on the path, and through it comes its order. It comes after the degree of prophethood, as God Most High says, "[Those who obey God and the Messenger] are in the company of those God has blessed—the prophets and the veracious" (4:69).

The word *sadiq* (truthful one) is derived from truthfulness. The word *siddiq* (exceedingly truthful, veracious) is the intensified form of it, being he who is pervaded by truthfulness. This is the case with other words of intensified meaning such as *sikkir* and *khimmir* (drunkard, filled with wine). The lowest degree of truthfulness is that one's inner being and outward actions are in harmony. The *sadiq* is one who is truthful in word. The *siddiq* is one who is truthful in all his words, deeds, and inward states.

Ahmad b. Khidruya instructed, "Let one who wishes God to be with him adhere to truthfulness, for God Most High has said, 'Surely God is with the truthful ones'" (2:153). Al-Junayd declared, "The truthful one is changed forty times in one day, but the hypocrite stays in one state for forty years." Abu Sulayman ad-Darani remarked, "If the truthful one wished to describe what is in his heart, his tongue would not say it." It is said, "Truthfulness means asserting the truth [even] in times of peril." Al-Qannad stated, "Truthfulness *[sidq]* is preventing the jawbone *[shidq]* from [uttering] what is forbidden." 'Abd al-Wahid b. Zayd commented, "Truthfulness is loyalty to God [may He be exalted] in actions." Sahl b. 'Abdallah said, "A servant who is deceptive to himself or to others will never gain a whiff of the fragrance of truthfulness." Abu Sa'id al-Qarshi noted, "The truthful one is he who is ready to die and he who would not be ashamed if his secret were disclosed. God Most High says, 'Wish for death if you are truthful'" (2:94). The master Abu 'Ali ad-Daqqaq (may God grant him mercy) related, "Abu 'Ali ath-Thaqafi was lecturing one day when 'Abdallah b. Munazil told him, 'O Abu 'Ali, prepare yourself for death, for there is no escape from it.' Abu 'Ali responded, 'And you, O 'Abdallah, prepare yourself for death, for there is no escape from it,' whereupon

'Abdallah lay down, stretched out his arm, put down his head, and announced, 'I die now.' Abu 'Ali was struck speechless by this because he could not match what 'Abdallah had done, for Abu 'Ali still held attachments to the world, but 'Abdallah was stripped bare of them."

The sheikh Abu 'Abd ar-Rahman as-Sulami (may God grant him mercy) reported, "Abu'l-Abbas ad-Dinawari was speaking before a gathering when an old woman among them gave a shout. Abu'l-'Abbas retorted, 'Die!' She rose up, took a few steps, turned to address him, and said, 'I have died.' Then she fell down, dead."

Al-Wasiti observed, "Sincerity is firm belief in God's unity along with intention." It is said, "'Abd al-Wahid b. Zayd looked at a youth among his companions whose body had wasted away and asked, 'Son, have you been prolonging your fast too much?' He replied, 'Neither have I been prolonging the meal nor breaking the fast.' Then he inquired, 'Have you been prolonging the time you rise at night [for prayer]?' He answered, 'No, nor have I been prolonging sleep.' So he asked: 'What has made you so thin?' The youth replied: 'A lasting passion.' 'Abd al-Wahid exclaimed, 'Be silent! What audacity!' The youth stood, took two steps, cried, 'O my God, if I am truthful, then take me,' and fell down, dead."

It is told that Abu 'Amr az-Zajjaji related, "My mother died, and I inherited a house from her. I sold it for fifty dinars and went on the pilgrimage. When I reached Babylon, a canal digger asked me, 'What do you have with you?' I told myself, 'Truthfulness is best' and replied, 'Fifty dinars.' He demanded, 'Hand them over.' So I gave him the bag. He counted them, and there were indeed fifty dinars. He said, 'Take them back; your truthfulness has touched me.' Then he got down from his horse and commanded, 'Take my horse.' I insisted, 'I do not want to!' He said, 'You have no choice' and pressed me to ride it. When I mounted at last, he declared, 'I will follow you.' After a year he caught up to me, and he stayed with me until he died."

Ibrahim al-Khawwas explained, "You can tell the truthful ones only by their performance of religious acts, both mandatory and voluntary." Al-Junayd commented, "The essence of truthfulness means that you tell the truth in situations in which only a lie would save you." It is said, "Three things are never lacking in the truthful one: sweetness [of manner], awesomeness [of presence], and kindliness." It is also said, "God [may He be exalted] revealed to David [peace be upon him], 'O David, whoever accepts what I say as truth in his inner being, I will confirm his veracity in the world among men.'"

Ibrahim b. Dawha reported, "I entered the desert with Ibrahim b. Sitanba, who told me, 'Cast off your attachments [to the world]!' I threw away everything I had with me except one dinar. Then he said, 'O Ibrahim, do not burden my mind! Cast off your attachments!' So I threw away the dinar. Again he commanded, 'O Ibrahim, cast off your attachments!' Then I remembered that I had some [spare] sandal thongs with me, and I threw them away. Whenever I needed a new thong on that journey, one appeared for me. Ibrahim b. Sitanba declared, 'This is the way of one who deals with God truthfully.'"

Dhu'n-Nun al-Misri (may God grant him mercy)

stated, "Truthfulness is the sword of God. Whenever it meets with something, it cuts it apart." Sahl b. 'Abdallah observed, "The beginning of deception on the part of truthful ones comes when they converse with their souls." When asked about truthfulness, Fath al-Mawsili thrust his hand into the blacksmith's bellows, brought out a glowing piece of iron, put it in the palm of his hand, and asserted, "This is truthfulness."

Yusuf b. Asbat said, "I would rather spend one night dealing with God Most High in truthfulness than fight with my sword in God's cause." Abu 'Ali ad-Daqqaq remarked, "Truthfulness is that you be with people just as you perceive yourself to be or that you perceive yourself to be just as you are."

When al-Harith al-Muhasibi was asked about the signs of truthfulness, he answered, "The truthful one is he who would not be concerned if the welfare of his heart demanded that all his fame among men should vanish. He does not want even one jot of his good works to be known by men, nor does he care if men were to know his wrongdoings. Any desire to be held in the good opinion of men is not a characteristic of the truthful."

One of the Sufis noted, "If a man does not fulfill the one perpetual religious obligation, his performance of religious obligations at the times assigned will not be accepted from him." Someone asked, "What is the one perpetual religious obligation?" He responded, "Truthfulness."

It is said, "If you seek God in truthfulness, He will give you a mirror in which you will behold all the wonders of this world and the next." It is said, "You must be truthful when you fear it will harm you, for it will benefit you. Do not be deceptive when you think it will benefit you, for certainly it will harm you." It is also said, "Everything is something, but the friendship of a liar is nothing." And it is said, "The mark of the liar is his eagerness to take an oath before it is demanded of him." Ibn Sirin declared, "The scope of speech is so wide that there is no need to lie." It is said, "An honest merchant is never destitute."

28

Shame

❧ Haya'

God Most High says, "Does he not know that God sees?" (96:14).

On the authority of Ibn 'Umar (may God be pleased with him), the Messenger of God (may God's blessing and peace be upon him) is reported to have stated, "Shame is a part of faith." On the authority of Ibn Mas'ud (may God be pleased with him), the Prophet of God is said to have told his companions one day, "Be fully ashamed before God." They replied, "But we are ashamed, O Prophet of God, and thanks be to Him!" He declared, "This is not true shame. Let one who wishes to be ashamed properly before God guard his mind and what it holds in consciousness, let him guard his stomach and what it contains, and let him remember death and the trial [of the grave]. Let the one who desires the Hereafter abandon the adornments of the worldly life. One who does all this has shame before God."

Makhlad relates that his father told him, "One of the

sages has instructed, 'Keep shame alive in you by keeping the company of one before whom others are ashamed.'" Ibn 'Ata' asserted, "The greatest part of knowledge is awe and shame. If these two go, nothing good remains in the heart." Dhu'n-Nun al-Misri said, "Shame means that you hold awe in your heart, being fearfully aware of the wicked things you committed before your Lord Most High in the past." He also noted, "Love makes one speak, shame silences, and fear makes one uneasy." Abu 'Uthman observed, "One who speaks on shame and yet is not ashamed of what he says before God is deceived by degrees." Abu Bakr b. Ishkib relates that al-Hasan b. al-Haddad came to 'Abdallah b. Munazil, who asked him where he was coming from. He replied, "From the gathering of Abu'l-Qasim the preacher." 'Abdallah asked him, "What did he speak about?" He answered, "Shame." 'Abdallah commented, "It is amazing that one who has never been ashamed before God could speak about shame!" As-Sari said, "Shame and intimacy come to one's heart. If they find there abstinence and renunciation, they settle down. If not, they keep on their journey." Al-Jurayri reported, "In the first generation people were concerned with the religion until the religion became weak. In the second generation people were concerned with loyalty until that was gone. In the third generation people were concerned with chivalry until chivalry disappeared. Then in the fourth generation people were concerned with shame until shame disappeared. Now the people act out of desire [for reward] and fear [of punishment]."

It is said with regard to His saying, "She [Potiphar's

wife] desired him, and he [Joseph] would have desired her had he not seen the proof of his Lord" (12:24), that the "proof" here is that she threw a cloth over an idol in the corner of the house. When Joseph asked her what she was doing, she replied, "I am ashamed in front of him," to which Joseph retorted, "I have more cause to be ashamed before God Most High." It is said with regard to His saying, "One of the women came to him [Moses], walking with shame" (28:25), that she was ashamed before him because she was offering him hospitality and was ashamed that Moses might not accept. So shame is the quality of the host. That is the type of shame that comes from generosity.

Abu Sulayman ad-Darani stated, "God Most High says, 'O my servant, as long as you are ashamed before Me, I will cause men to forget your faults, I will make the regions of the earth forget your sins, I will wipe out your shortcomings from the book of destiny, and I will not call you to account on the Day of Reckoning.'"

Someone asked a man who was seen praying outside a mosque, "Why do you not go inside and pray?" He replied, "I am ashamed to enter God's house when I have disobeyed Him." One of the signs of the man possessing shame is that he is never seen in a situation he is ashamed of.

One of the Sufis related, "One night we went out and passed by a tangled thicket. There was a man sleeping there, and his horse was grazing at his head. Rousing him, we inquired, 'Are you not afraid to sleep in this horrid place filled with wild beasts?' He raised his head and answered, 'I am ashamed before Him to fear anything other than Him.' He put his head down and fell back to sleep."

God Most High revealed to Jesus (peace be upon him), "Warn your own self. If it heeds the warning, then warn men. If not, then be ashamed before Me to warn men."

It is said that there are different kinds of shame. One is shame [arising from] transgressions, as was the case with Adam (peace be upon him) when he was asked, "Do you intend to escape from Us?" He replied, "No, I am ashamed before You." Another is shame of inadequacy, as was the case with the angels who exclaimed, "May You be exalted! We have not worshiped You as You deserve to be worshiped." There is shame that bears witness to God's splendor, as was the case with Israfil (peace be upon him), who wrapped himself in his wings out of shame before God. There is shame [coming from] generosity, as was the case with the Prophet (may God's blessing and peace be upon him) when he was ashamed before his community to tell them to leave him, and God (Glorious and Majestic) said [to the Muslims in Medina], "Do not stay to talk with the Prophet on familiar terms [after eating at his house]" (33:53). Another type is shame [coming from] modesty, as was the case with 'Ali (may God be pleased with him) when he asked al-Miqdad b. al-Aswad to ask the Messenger of God about the ruling of the feminine discharge with regard to Fatima (may God be pleased with her). There is shame [coming from] regarding something as too lowly to be cause for concern, as was the case with Moses (peace be upon him) when he remarked, "I need something of this world, and I am ashamed to ask You, O Lord," and God told him, "Ask Me, even for the salt for your dough, the fodder for your

sheep." Finally, there is shame [coming from] beneficence, this being the shame of the Lord. He gives a
sealed book to the servant after he has passed over the
bridge in the Hereafter. Inside the book is written, "You
committed such and such [sins]." God says, "I am
ashamed to show it to you, so go; I have already
forgiven you." Yahya b. Mu'adh said in commenting on
this, "Glory be to the One against Whom the servant
sins and Who is then ashamed before him!"

Al-Fudayl b. 'Iyad explained, "Five of the signs of
wretchedness in a man are hardness in the heart,
severity in the eyes, paucity of shame, desire for this
world, and limitless expectation for worldly gain." In
one of the divinely revealed books God says, "My
servant has not treated Me with justice. He prays to Me,
and I am ashamed to answer him. But he disobeys Me
without being ashamed before Me." Yahya b. Mu'adh
declared, "For the man who is ashamed before God
when he is obedient, God is ashamed [to punish him]
after he has sinned."

Know that shame causes, as it were, a melting, for it
is said that shame is the melting of man's inner organs
when he is aware of the Lord's gaze upon him. It is said,
"Shame is the heart's contracting in order to exalt the
majesty of the Lord." It is also said, "When a man sits
before a gathering of people, warning and admonish-
ing them, his two angels call out to him, 'Warn yourself
as you warn your brother. If you do not, then be
ashamed before your Lord, for He sees you.'"

When Al-Junayd was asked about shame, he replied,
"The state called 'shame' is born of knowing that
blessings from God persist despite one's negligence."

Al-Wasiti commented, "He who violates the limits [set by God] or who breaks an oath has never tasted the sting of shame." He also said, "The sweat streams forth from the one who feels shame. It is a blessing placed within him. As long as anything remains of his lower self, he will be kept away from shame."

The master Abu 'Ali ad-Daqqaq (may God grant him mercy) observed, "Shame means abandoning all pretensions before God." Abu Bakr al-Warraq related, "Sometimes I pray two rounds of prayer to God Most High and come away from it feeling shameful like a thief coming away from a robbery."

29

Freedom

ও Hurriya

God Most High says, "They gave to them in preference over themselves even though poverty was their lot" (59:9). This means, "They [the Medinans] gave generously to them [the Meccans] because the Medinans were free of attachment to [the earthly goods] that the Meccans received and thus were able to give to them freely."

On the authority of Ibn 'Abbas, the Messenger of God (may God's blessing and peace be upon him) is reported to have declared, "Whatever suffices his person is enough for any of you. All are traveling to four cubits [of the grave] in the end, and all things will return to their ultimate conclusion."

Freedom means that the servant is free of the bondage to creatures; the authority of created things holds no power over him. The sign of enduring in freedom is that one no longer prefers one thing over another in his heart, so that all worldly contingencies are equal to him.

Haritha (may God be pleased with him) told the Messenger of God (may God's blessing and peace be upon him), "I have shunned this world. The earth's rocks and its gold are one to me." The master Abu 'Ali ad-Daqqaq (may God grant him mercy) observed, "He who comes into this world free from it departs to the next world free from it." In another way of telling, "He who [lives] in the world free of the world will be free from the Hereafter."

Know that the essence of freedom is found in complete servitude, for if one's servitude is sincerely for God, then one's freedom will be complete, cleared of bondage to other-than-God. As for those who imagine that there is a time when one may cast off the bridle of servitude and turn away from the restraints implied by God's commands and prohibitions, while being of sound mind, that is apostasy. God Most High says to His Prophet (may God's blessing and peace be upon him), "Serve your Lord until [the day] of certainty comes to you" (15:99). The commentators agree that "certainty" here means "time of death."

When the Sufis speak on freedom, they mean that the servant is not under bondage to any created thing, neither the contingencies of worldly life nor those of the Hereafter; he will be uniquely devoted to God the Unique. Nothing enslaves him, whether it be the temporal things of this world, seeking satisfaction of desire, wishes, requests, intention, needs, or wealth.

Ash-Shibli was asked, "Do you not know that He is merciful?" He replied, "Certainly. But because I have known His mercy, I have never asked Him to be merciful to me." The station of freedom is found only rarely among men. Abu'l-'Abbas as-Sayyari used to say, "If words other than verses of the Qur'an could be used in the prayer, this line would be used:

I wish all the time for the impossible—
that my eyes might see the face of a free
man."

The sheikhs have spoken much on freedom. Al-Husayn b. Mansur stated, "Whoever desires freedom, let him be constant in servitude." When al-Junayd was presented with the case of a man whose worldly goods were equivalent to the moisture in a date stone, he said, "The indentured servant is a slave as long as he owes one dirham." He also remarked, "You will never attain true freedom as long as there remains one bit of the inner truth of servitude to Him that you have not reached."

Bishr al-Hafi commented, "Let one who desires a taste of freedom and deliverance from bondage purify the secret between himself and God Most High." Al-Husayn b. Mansur explained, "If the servant fulfills the stations of servitude completely, he becomes free of the hardships of servitude." So he is marked with servitude but without trouble or strenuous effort. This is the station of prophets and the veracious. That is to say, he is himself borne by that station; his heart experiences no strenuous effort, even though he is still subject to the ordinances of divine law. Mansur al-Faqih recited:

There remains not one free man,
Nor are any among the jinn free;
The free of both species have passed away
and so the sweetness of life has turned
bitter.

204

Know that the greatest kind of freedom comes from serving the poor. Abu 'Ali ad-Daqqaq (may God grant him mercy) said that God instructed David (upon whom be peace), "If you encounter one who seeks Me, serve him." The Prophet (may God's blessing and peace be upon him) noted, "The master of a people is their servant."

Yahya b. Mu'adh declared, "Male and female slaves serve the sons of this world; the free and righteous serve the sons of the Hereafter." Ibrahim b. Adham said, "The noble free man removes himself from the world before he is taken from it." He also advised, "Keep the company of none but a noble free man; he will listen and he will not speak."

30

Remembrance

❧ Dhikr

God Most High says, "O you who believe, make remembrance of God abundantly" (33:41).

On the authority of Abu'd-Darda' (may God be pleased with him), the Messenger of God (may God's blessing and peace be upon him) is said to have asked, "Should I tell you of the best of your good works, the purest of them in your Lord's sight, the highest of them in your ranks, that which is better than giving gold and silver in charity and fighting your enemies and striking their necks?" The companions inquired, "What is that, O Messenger of God?" He replied, "Remembrance of God." On the authority of Anas, the Messenger of God stated, "The Hour of Judgment will not come upon one saying 'Allah, Allah.'" [From another chain of transmission,] Anas b. Malik related that the Messenger of God declared, "The Hour will not come until 'Allah, Allah' is no longer said on earth."

Remembrance is a powerful support on the path to God (Glorious and Majestic) Indeed, it is the very foundation of this [Sufi] path. No one reaches God save by continual remembrance of Him. There are two kinds of remembrance: that of the tongue and that of the heart. The servant attains perpetual remembrance of the heart by making vocal remembrance. It is remembrance of the heart, however, that yields true effect. When a person makes remembrance with his tongue and his heart [simultaneously], he attains perfection in his wayfaring.

The master Abu 'Ali ad-Daqqaq (May God grant him mercy) commented, "Remembrance is the charter of sainthood. One who is granted success in remembrance is given the charter, and one who is deprived of remembrance is dismissed."

It is said that, at the beginning of ash-Shibli's wayfaring, he would walk down the road every day carrying a bundle of switches on his back. Whenever forgetfulness came into his heart, he would beat himself with a switch until it broke. Sometimes the bundle would run out before evening. Then he would pound his hands and feet on a wall [when forgetfulness came into his heart]. It is said, "Remembrance of the heart is the sword of the seekers, with which they slay the enemy and guard themselves from any harm aimed at them." If the servant takes refuge with God Most High in his heart, when suffering shadows his heart, all that he abhors will depart from him instantly.

When Al-Wasiti was asked about remembrance, he explained, "It means leaving the sphere of forgetfulness and going to the expanse of witnessing victory over fear, and intense love for Him." Dhu'n-Nun al-Misri asserted, "One who truly remembers God forgets everything apart from His remembrance. God protects him from all things, and he is compensated for all things [he has forsaken]."

A group of wayfarers complained to Abu 'Uthman, "We make vocal remembrance of God Most High, but we experience no sweetness in our hearts." He advised, "Give thanks to God Most High for adorning [at least] your limbs with obedience."

A well-known tradition relates that the Messenger of God (may God's blessing and peace be upon him) instructed, "Pause and graze in the meadows of Paradise when you pass them." Someone asked, "What are the meadows of Paradise?" He answered, "The circles of men making remembrance of God." Jabir b. 'Abdallah related, "The Messenger of God [may God's blessing and peace be upon him] came to us and commanded, 'O people, graze in the meadows of Paradise.' We asked, 'What are the meadows of Paradise?' He replied, 'The gatherings formed for making remembrance of God. Go forth, morning and evening, in remembrance of God. Let he who desires to know his standing with God look at the rank he accords God. The rank God Most High grants to His servant corresponds to the rank His servant accords Him.'"

Ash-Shibli inquired, "Has God not said, 'I am the companion of the one who sits and makes remembrance of Me'? What benefit have you gained in sitting with God [may He be exalted]?" He recited in his gathering:

> *I remember You not because I forgot You one instant;*

The least significant part of remembrance is
that made by my tongue.
Without ecstasy I would almost have died
from love,
My heart rising within me, beating,
When ecstasy showed You present with me,
I witnessed You present everywhere.
Then I addressed one present without speak-
ing,
And I beheld one known without seeing.

Among the qualities unique to remembrance is that it is not limited to appointed times. Indeed, the servant is commanded to make remembrance of God, whether as a duty or as a recommendation, at all times. The daily prayers, however, even though they are the noblest act of devotion, are not permitted at certain times. Remembrance of the heart is continual, in all conditions. God Most High commends "Those who make remembrance of God standing, sitting, and lying on their sides" (3:191). The *imam* Abu Bakr b. Furak (may God grant him mercy) stated, "'Standing' means establishing the true remembrance, and 'sitting' means refraining from false pretensions in it."

The sheikh Abu 'Abd ar-Rahman asked the master Abu 'Ali ad-Daqqaq, "Is remembrance or meditation better?" He retorted, "What do you say?" He answered, "In my opinion remembrance is better than meditation because God [may He be exalted] described Himself as making remembrance but not as meditating. Whatever is a characteristic of God is better than something that is peculiar to men." The master Abu 'Ali (may God grant him mercy) approved of this view.

Al-Kattani remarked, "If it were not an obligation for me, I would not make remembrance of Him—how disgraceful that one like me would make remembrance of God without cleansing his mouth with one thousand accepted penances for making remembrance of Him!" I heard the master Abu 'Ali (may God grant him mercy) recite to one of the Sufis:

> *Never do I make remembrance of You but my*
> *heart,*
> *My inward being, and my spirit rebuke me.*
> *It is as if an unseen observer from You calls*
> *out to me:*
> *"Beware," he says, "Woe unto you. Beware*
> *of remembrance!"*

One of the qualities unique to remembrance is that He placed men's remembrance of Him on a level with His remembrance of men. He commands, "Make remembrance of Me, and I will make remembrance of you" (2:147). A tradition states that Gabriel (peace be upon him) told the Messenger of God (may God's blessing and peace be upon him) that God Most High said, "I have given your community something I have not given to any other community." The Messenger of God asked Gabriel, "What is that?" He replied, "It is God's words, 'Make remembrance of Me, and I will make remembrance of you.' He has not said this to any other community." It is said, "The angel of death consults the one making remembrance before seizing his spirit."

It is recorded in a certain book that Moses (peace be upon him) asked, "O my Lord, where do You dwell?"

God Most High revealed to him, "In the heart of My believing servant." This refers to the dwelling of the remembrance of God in the heart, for God is exalted above every kind of in-dwelling and incarnation. This "dwelling" is only fixing remembrance and making it firm.

When Dhu'n-Nun was asked about remembrance, he explained, "It means the absence of the one making remembrance from his remembrance." Then he re-cited:

> *I make abundant remembrance of You not*
> *because I have forgotten You;*
> *That is simply what flows from my tongue.*

Sahl b. 'Abdallah observed, "Not a day passes but that the Exalted cries out, 'O My servant, you treat Me unjustly. I remember you, but you forget Me. I invite you to Myself, but you go to others. I take away afflictions from you, but you continue to sin. O son of Adam, what will you have to say on the morrow when you meet Me?'" Abu Sulayman ad-Darani stated, "There are plains in Paradise where the angels plant trees when one begins to make remembrance of God. Sometimes one of the angels stops his work, and the others ask him, 'Why have you stopped?' He says, 'My companion has slacked off.'" Al-Hasan al-Basri instructed, "Seek sweet-ness in three things: prayer, making remembrance of God, and reciting the Qur'an. It is to be found there or not at all. If you find no sweetness in these, then know that the gate is shut."

Hamid al-Aswad related, "When I was with Ibrahim al-Khawwas on a journey, we came to a place filled with snakes. He set down his pot, and sat, and I too sat. When night came and the air was chill, the snakes came out. I cried to the sheikh, who said, 'Remember God.' I did so, and the snakes withdrew. Then they returned. I cried out to him again, and he instructed me in the same way. This continued until morning. When we awoke, he stood up and walked on, and I walked on with him. Suddenly a huge snake fell out of his bedroll. It had been coiled around him all night. I asked him, 'Did you not feel the snake?' He replied, 'No. It has been a long time since I have slept as well as last night.'"

Abu 'Uthman declared, "One cannot taste the intimacy of remembrance without having suffered the desolation of forgetfulness." As-Sari asserted, "It is written in one of the divinely revealed books, 'If remembrance of Me overwhelms My servant, he loves Me, and I love him.'" He also said, "God revealed to David [peace be upon him], 'Rejoice in Me and take delight in My remembrance.'" Ath-Thawri noted, "There is a punishment for all things. The punishment for the gnostic is to be cut off from His remembrance."

It is written in the Christian Scriptures, "Remember Me when you are provoked to anger, and I will remember you when I am provoked to anger. Be content with My help for you, for it is better than your help for yourself." A monk was asked, "Are you fasting?" He answered, "I am fasting with His remembrance. If I remember other-than-God, my fast is broken." It is said, "When His remembrance takes possession of the heart and a demon approaches, the demon will writhe on the ground just as a man does when demons approach him. When this happens, all the demons gather around this demon and ask, 'What has happened to him?' One of them says, 'A human being has afflicted him.'" Sahl stated, "I know no more abhorrent sin than forgetfulness of the Lord Most High." It is said that the angels do not carry a man's inward remembrance of God to the heavens, for they are not even aware of it. It is a secret between the servant and God (Glorious and Majestic).

One of the Sufis related, "I was told of a man who made remembrance in the jungle. I went to him. When he was sitting there, a lion pounced on him and tore off a piece of his flesh. We both fainted. When he came to, I asked him about this. He told me, 'The lion is sent by God. Whenever I am lax in my remembrance of Him, the lion comes and takes a bite out of me, just as you have seen.'" Al-Jurayri reported, "We had, among our companions, a man who was always making remembrance, saying, 'Allah, Allah.' One day a branch fell on his head. His skull was split open, and the blood gushed out on the ground, forming the words 'Allah, Allah.'"

31

Chivalry

৯ Futuwa

God Most High says, "They were young men *[fitya]* who believed in their Lord, and We increased them in guidance" (18:13).

The root of chivalry is that one always be attentive to the cares of others. The Prophet (may God's blessing and peace be upon him) stated, "God Most High attends to the needs of a servant as long as the servant attends to the needs of his Muslim brother." [The same tradition is repeated on the authority of Zayd b. Thabit.]

The master Abu 'Ali ad-Daqqaq commented, "The perfection of the quality of chivalry belongs to the Messenger of God alone, for on the Day of Resurrection all men will say, 'Me, Me' while he [may God's blessing and peace be upon him] will say, 'My people, My people.'" Al-Junayd observed, "Chivalry is found in Syria, eloquence in Iraq, and truthfulness in Khorasan." Al-Fadl declared, "Chivalry means forgiving the stumblings of one's fellow man." It is said, "Chivalry means that one does not count oneself superior to others." Abu

Bakr al-Warraq asserted, "The chivalrous man is one who has no enemies." Muhammad b. 'Ali at-Tirmidhi explained, "Chivalry means that you are an enemy against your own self for God." It is said, "The chivalrous man is not an enemy to anyone."

An-Nasrabadhi remarked, "The companions of the cave [18:13] are called *fitya* because they believed in their Lord without any intermediary." It is said, "The chivalrous man is he who smashes idols, for God Most High says, 'We heard a youth *[fatan]* denounce the idols. He is called Abraham' (21:60), and 'He smashed the idols to pieces' (21:58). The idol of every man is his own self. So one who opposes his passions is truly chivalrous."

Al-Harith al-Muhasibi stated, "Chivalry requires that you be just with others and that you not demand justice from them." 'Umar b. 'Uthman al-Makki said, "Chivalry is [possessing] good moral character." When Al-Junayd was asked about chivalry, he replied, "It means that you have no aversion to the poor and that you do not avoid the rich." An-Nasrabadhi commented, "Nobility *[muruwa]* is a part of chivalry. It means to turn away from this world and the Hereafter, proudly disdaining them both." Muhammad b. 'Ali at-Tirmidhi noted, "Chivalry means that the permanent and the transitory are the same to you." Ahmad b. Hanbal's son related, "My father was asked, 'What is chivalry?' He replied, 'It means abandoning what you desire for what you fear.'"

It was asked of one of the Sufis, "What is chivalry?" He answered, "It means that you do not care whether the guest at your table is a saint or an unbeliever." I heard one of the scholars report, "A Magian invited

Abraham [peace be upon him] to be his guest. Abraham responded, 'I will accept your invitation on one condition—that you embrace Islam.' The Magian walked away. Then God Most High revealed to Abraham, 'For fifty years We have fed him despite his state of unbelief. [What would the harm be in] accepting a meal from him without demanding that he change his religion?' Abraham followed the Magian until he reached him and apologized to him. When he asked Abraham why he had apologized, Abraham told him the story, and the Magian embraced Islam."

Al-Junayd observed, "Chivalry means withholding offense and offering magnanimity." Sahl b. 'Abdallah explained, "Chivalry means following the Sunna." It is said, "Chivalry means being faithful and not transgressing the divinely set limits." It is also said, "Chivalry is a virtuous deed you perform without seeing yourself in the act." And it is said, "Chivalry means that you do not turn away when a man in need draws near you;" "chivalry means that you do not hide from those who seek you;" "chivalry means that you neither hoard your property nor make excuses [when asked to give of it];" "it means being generous with whatever you have been given and concealing your hardships;" "chivalry means that, if you invite ten guests, you would not be affected if nine or eleven were to come instead;" "chivalry means giving up preference [for one thing over another]."

Ahmad b. Khidruya told his wife, Umm 'Ali, "I want to host a feast to which I will invite a clever scoundrel known in his quarter as 'leader of the young toughs.'" His wife objected, "This is not right, inviting one of the young toughs to your house." He retorted, "It must be done." She remarked, "If you go ahead and do this, then slaughter goats and cows and donkeys, and set out the meat from that man's door to your house." He asked, "I understand what you mean by the goats and cows, but what do you mean about the donkey?" She replied, "You invite a young tough to our house; the least you can do is let it be a joyful occasion for the dogs of the neighborhood!"

This story is told of a gathering that some of the Sufis, including a Shirazi Sheikh, attended. When the *sama'* (session of invocation and music) began, the guests fell asleep. The Shirazi Sheikh asked the host, "Why have they fallen asleep?" He answered, "I do not know. I took great care to ensure that all the food was what is permitted; however, I did not ask about the eggplant." The next morning they went to find out about the eggplant from the vendor, who told them, "I did not have any eggplants [when the servants came to buy them], so I stole them from the land of such-and-such a man and sold them." They brought the vendor to the owner of the land to make amends. He exclaimed, "You bother me over a matter of [only] a thousand eggplants? I give him this plot of land and two oxen, a donkey, and the plows so he need not do such a thing again."

It is said that a man was married to a woman who broke out in smallpox before the night of consummation. The man proclaimed to people, "My eyes are diseased; I have become blind!" The woman was brought in the wedding procession to his house. After twenty years she died. The man suddenly opened his eyes. When someone asked him what had happened, he explained, "I never was blind. I feigned blindness so she would not be grieved [about her skin condition]." Someone told him, "You have surpassed all others in chivalry!"

Dhu'n-Nun al Misri instructed, "Let he who desires refined manners take the example of the Baghdadi water carriers." Someone asked him, "How is that?" He replied, "When I was brought before the caliph on charges of heresy, I saw a water carrier wearing a turban, dressed in fine Egyptian cloth, carrying fine earthenware pitchers. I said to someone, 'This must be the sultan's cupbearer.' He told me, 'No, this is the cupbearer of the common people.' I took a cup, drank from it, and ordered my companions, 'Give him a dinar.' He refused to take the money, saying, 'You are a prisoner. It would not be chivalrous to take anything from you.'"

One of our friends (may God grant him mercy) declared, "There is no place in chivalry for taking profit from one's friend." He was a young chivalrous man named Ahmad b. Sahl, the merchant, and I bought a linen cloak from him. He charged me only what he had paid for it, so I asked him, "Will you not take some profit?" He responded, "As for the price of the cloak, I will take it from you, and not impose an obligation on you. But I will not take a profit because there is no place in chivalry for taking profit from one's friend."

A man who made claims to chivalry came from Nishapur to Nasa, where a man invited him to be his guest along with a group of chivalrous men. When they had finished the meal, a slave girl came to pour water for them to wash their hands. The man from Nishapur drew in his hand, remarking, "It is not allowed, by the rules of chivalry, for a girl to pour water for men!" But another man present said, "I have been coming to this house for years, not knowing whether a man or a woman poured the water for our hands."

Mansur al-Maghribi related, "Someone wanted to test Nuh al-'Ayyar an-Nisaburi. He sold Nuh a slave girl dressed as a young man, with the expressed condition that it was a young man. She had a radiantly beautiful face. Nuh bought her thinking she was a young man. She stayed with him many months. Someone asked her, "Does he know that you are a girl?" She replied, "No, he has never touched me, thinking I am a young man."

It is said that a chivalrous man was ordered to turn over a young slave boy of his to the sultan, but he refused. He was given one thousand lashings, but he still would not surrender the boy. That night it was freezing cold. During the night, he had a nocturnal emission. When he woke, he took the bath of ablution with icy water. Someone told him, "You risk your life doing that!" He retorted, "I was ashamed before God Most High that I would suffer one thousand lashes for the sake of a creature, and not endure a cold bath for His sake."

A band of chivalrous young men went to visit a man known for his chivalry. The man called for the servant boy to bring the dining cloth. He did not bring it, so the man called for him again and again. The guests looked at one another, observing, "This is not right, in the rules of chivalry, that a man should employ a boy who refuses time and again to spread the dining cloth." The man asked the boy, "Why have you taken so long with the cloth?" He explained, "There was an ant on it. It is not proper in chivalry to present the cloth to chivalrous ones when there is an ant on it, nor is it right to throw the ant off the cloth. So I waited until it crawled off on its own." They told the boy, "You have shown great perception. You are the kind of boy to serve the chivalrous ones."

It is said that there was once a pilgrim who spent the night in Medina. He thought his satchel was stolen. He saw Ja'far as-Sadiq and grabbed him, demanding, "Are you the thief who stole my satchel?" Ja'far asked, "What was in it?" The man replied, "One thousand dinars!" Ja'far took him into his house and weighed out one thousand dinars for him. The man returned to where he was lodging, went into his room, and saw his satchel that he thought had been stolen. He went to Ja'far to apologize, and return the money to him. But Ja'far refused to take back the money, saying, "I never reclaim something I have given away." The man asked someone, "Who is that man?" He answered, "Ja'far as-Sadiq."

It is said, "Shaqiq al-Balkhi asked Ja'far b. Muhammad [as-Sadiq] about chivalry. He inquired, 'What is your opinion?' Shaqiq answered, 'If we are given something, we give thanks, and if we are denied something, we are patient.' Ja'far observed, 'Our dogs in Medina do as much.' Shaqiq asked, 'O descendant of the Messenger's daughter, then what is chivalry in your view?' He said, 'If we are given something, we give it to someone else, and if we are denied something, we give thanks.'"

Al-Jurayri related, "Sheikh Abu'l-'Abbas b. Masruq invited us one night to his house. We met one of our friends on the way and told him, 'Come along with us, for we are to be guests of the sheikh.' He objected, 'But he has not invited me.' We assured him, 'We will ask permission for you just as the Messenger of God [may God's blessing and peace be upon him] did for 'A'isha [may God be pleased with her].' We took him with us, and when he came to the sheikh's door, we told the sheikh what he had said and what we had said. The sheikh said, 'You have given me a place in your heart by coming to my house without invitation. May such-and-such befall me unless you take a place in the room on top of my cheek.' Thus he begged, and placed his face on the floor. The man was brought forward, and he put his foot on the sheikh's cheek in a way that caused him no pain. The sheikh drew his face along the floor until he reached his own seat."

Know that among the requirements of chivalry is to conceal the faults of friends, especially their misfortunes in which their enemies would take delight. I heard Abu 'Abd ar-Rahman as-Sulami tell an-Nasrabadhi many times, "'Ali, the singer, drinks by night and attends your gathering by day." An-Nasrabadhi paid no attention to this until it happened that one day he was walking in the company of one who had mentioned to him 'Ali's shortcoming. They found 'Ali lying face down, clearly drunk. An-Nasrabadhi started to wash his mouth. The man accompanying him asked, "How often have we said something about this to the sheikh without his listening? Here is 'Ali in the very condition we described!" An-Nasrabadhi looked at him and told the one rebuking 'Ali, "Carry him on your shoulders and take him to his house." He found himself obliged to comply.

Al-Murta'ish reported, "We went as a group with Abu Hafs to call upon a sick man we used to visit in his illness. Abu Hafs asked the sick man, 'Would you like to recover?' He answered, 'Yes.' So Abu Hafs ordered his companions, 'Take on his burden.' Then the sick man stood up and came away with us, and all of us became bedridden and were visited by others in our sickness."

32

Visionary Insight

❧ Firasa

God Most High says, "Certainly in that are indications for those who read the signs" (15:75). It is said that "by those who read the signs" is meant "the ones possessing insight."

On the authority of Abu Sa'id al-Khudri, the Messenger of God (may God's blessing and peace be upon him) warned, "Beware of the insight of the believer, for he sees with the light of God [may He be glorified]."

Visionary insight is a phenomenon that comes suddenly upon the heart, negating whatever is contrary to it; it thus dominates the heart. "Insight" *(firasa)* is cognate with the word "prey" *(farisa)* of a wild animal. The soul cannot oppose to insight that which it [customarily] regards as correct and possible. Insight is in accord with the strength of belief: whoever has strong belief is also strong in insight.

Abu Sa'id al-Kharraz commented, "One who sees with the light of insight sees with the light of God; the very substance of his knowledge comes from God, unmixed with either negligence or forgetfulness. Indeed, the decree of God flows through the tongue of the servant." By his saying "he sees with the light of God" is meant "by a light with which God [may He be exalted] has favored him." Al-Wasiti stated, "Insight consists of radiant lights in the heart, enabling gnosis to carry secrets in the unseen realms from one hidden realm to another, such that one may see things in the way that God displays them to him, so that he may speak about the innermost part of creation."

It is told that Abu'l-Hasan ad-Daylami related, "I went to Antakya because I heard of a black man who spoke of hidden things. I stayed there until he came down from the mountain Lukam. He had with him some licit goods he was selling. I was hungry, for it had been two days since I had eaten anything. So I asked him, 'How much is this?' I led him to believe that I would buy what he had. He instructed, 'Sit down over there, so that if I sell it, I will give you money with which you can buy something.' So I left him and went to another to make him think that I was bargaining with him. Then I went back to him and demanded, 'If you intend to sell this, then tell me the price.' He replied, 'You have gone hungry two days. Sit down. If I sell it, then I will give you money so you can buy something.' So I sat, and when he sold it, he gave me some money and walked away. I followed him and he turned to me saying, 'If need presents itself to you, then ask for it from God. If, however, your [lower] self has something to gain from the fulfillment of that need, you will be denied its fulfillment."

Al-Kattani declared, "Insight is having certainty manifested and viewing the unseen. It is one of the stations of belief." It is said that ash-Shafi'i and Muhammad b. al-Hasan (may God have mercy on them) were in the Sacred Mosque when a man came in. Muhammad b. al-Hasan remarked, "I have an insight that he is a carpenter," and ash-Shafi'i said, "I have an insight that he is a blacksmith." When they asked him, he replied, "I was a blacksmith at one time; now I am a carpenter."

Abu Sa'id al-Kharraz stated, "The one who is able to deduce the truth is he who is always attentive to the unseen. Nothing is hidden or kept from his view. He is the one indicated in God's saying 'The ones who are able to discover the truth would know of the matter'" (4:83).

He who reads the signs knows them [intuitively] and knows, too, what is in the depths of hearts by means of deduction and indication. God Most High says, "Certainly in that are indications for those who read the signs" (15:75), that is, for the ones who know the signs that He reveals concerning the two groups, His friends and His enemies.

The ones possessing insight see by the light of God Most High, this consisting of radiant lights that shine in their hearts and disclose the true meanings. This is among the properties of belief. More endowed in this matter are those learned in God. God Most High says, "Be ones learned in God" (3:79), that is, scholars and wise men whose characters are molded on the traits of God in observance and practice. They have no need to relate what others have said, or to pay them attention and be concerned by them.

It is related, "Abu'l-Qasim al-Munadi was sick. He was a great man among the sheikhs of Nishapur. So Abu'l-Hasan al-Bushanji and al-Hasan al-Haddad went to visit him, and on the way they bought an apple for him for half a dirham on credit. When they sat down, Abu'l-Qasim asked, 'What is this darkness surrounding you?' They went away and asked, 'What have we done wrong?' They thought, and then they suggested, 'Perhaps it is that we have not paid for the apple.' So they went to the vendor, gave him the money, and returned to Abu'l-Qasim. When he saw them, he observed, 'This is strange. Is man able to come out of darkness this quickly? Tell me what you have been doing.' When they told him this story, he affirmed, 'Yes, each of you depended upon his friend to give the money, and the man was shy of asking for it. So the conclusion of the sale was left undone. I was the reason, and only I saw that in you.' This same Abu'l-Qasim used to go into the market every day to sell off some goods. When an amount sufficient to his needs, from one-sixth to one-half of a dirham, came to him, he would leave the market and return to his main occupation [of worship] and watching over his heart."

Al-Husayn b. Mansur commented, "When God wishes to conquer a heart, He entrusts it with secrets, which the heart then perceives and proclaims."

When one of the Sufis was asked about insight, he answered, "It means that there are spirits that revolve about in the celestial realm and watch over the inner meanings of the unseen matters. They speak of the secrets of creation with words of direct witnessing, not with words of speculation or supposition."

It is said that Zakariya ash-Shakhtani had an affair with a woman before he converted to the Sufi path. After he had become one of Abu 'Uthman al-Hiri's foremost disciples, he was standing before him one day and thinking of this woman. Abu 'Uthman lifted his head and looked at him, inquiring, "Are you not ashamed?"

At the beginning of my connection with the master Abu 'Ali ad-Daqqaq (may God grant him mercy), a gathering was convened for me in the mosque al-Mutarriz. One time I asked permission for some time to go to Nasa, and he allowed me to go. As I was walking with him on the way to his gathering one day, it occurred to me, "I wish he would teach my sessions in my place while I am gone." He turned to me and announced, "I will teach in your place in the gatherings while you are gone." I walked on a little. Then it occurred to me that he was not in good health, and it would trouble him to teach for me two days a week. I wished that he would reduce the sessions to only once per week. He turned to me and said, "If I am not able to teach two days a week for you, I will do it only one time per week." As I walked on a little, a third thing occurred to me. He turned to me and spoke of the matter exactly.

The sheikh Abu 'Abd ar-Rahman as-Sulami (may God have mercy on him) reported that he heard his grandfather Abu 'Amr b. Nujayd say, "Shah al-Kirmani possessed a piercing insight in which he was never mistaken. He would remark, 'Insight will always be correct for one who lowers his gaze from illicit things, restrains his soul from passionate longings, cultivates his inner being with constant vigilant awareness and his outer being with conformity to the Sunna, and accustoms himself to eating [only] the licit.'"

Abu'l-Hasan an-Nuri was asked, "Where did the insight of the ones possessing it come from?" He replied, "From these words of God Most High: 'And I have breathed into him of My spirit' (15:29). So for one whose portion of that light is greater, his witnessing is more sound, and his judgment in insight is more trustworthy. Do you not see how the breathing of the spirit into him [Adam] was the cause of [the angels'] prostration to him, in His saying, 'When I have created him in due proportion and breathed into him of My spirit, then fall down before him in prostration' (15:29)?"

This opinion of Abu'l-Hasan an-Nuri contains some obscurity and ambiguity. He mentions the breathing [by God] of the spirit [into Adam] not to sanction those who subscribe to the pre-existence of spirits, as it might seem to the hearts of the weak ones. To whatever may correctly be applied the concepts of breathing, union and separation, that is also receptive to influence and change which are, in turn, qualities of createdness. God (may He be exalted) favored the believers with abilities of vision and lights by which they are able to perceive things by insight, these being, in truth, gnosis. This is the sense of the saying of the Prophet (may God's blessing and peace be upon him), "For he [the believer] sees with the light of God," that is, by the knowledge and discernment with which God has favored him and by which He has given him unique standing, distinct from all others. These faculties of knowledge and discernment can be called "lights" without resorting

228

any innovative speculation. It is also not far-fetched to speak of [the bestowal] of those lights as the "breathing" [spoken of in the verse in question], although [in context] creation is what is intended.

Al-Husayn b. Mansur declared, "The one possessing insight hits his target with the first [arrow] he looses. He never turns to interpretation, speculation, or supposition." It is said, "The insight of the seekers is speculation that brings about certainty, and the insight of the gnostics is a certainty that brings about inner realization."

Ahmad b. 'Asim al-Antaki instructed, "If you keep the company of the truthful, be truthful with them, for they are spies of the hearts. They come into your hearts and leave without your becoming aware." Abu Ja'far al-Haddad commented, "Insight is the first flash of intuition that comes to you, not accompanied by an opposing notion. If an opposing notion comes to counter it, then know that [the first notion] is only a stray thought and the chattering of the mind."

It is related that Abu 'Abdallah ar-Razi an-Nisaburi reported, "Ibn al-Anbari tailored a woolen garment for me. I saw ash-Shibli wearing a fine hat that went very well with the wool of my cloak. I wished secretly that I could have both the cloak and the hat. When ash-Shibli came away from his gathering, he turned to me. I followed him, for it was his custom to turn in my direction when he wanted me to come with him. When he went into his house, I followed him. He ordered me, 'Take off the cloak.' So I took it off. He folded it, tossed his hat on top of it, called for a fire to be made, and burned both of them."

Abu Hafs an-Nisaburi asserted, "It is wrong for anyone to claim to possess insight. It is, rather, proper to beware of another's insight because the Prophet [may God's blessing and peace be upon him] warned, 'Beware of the insight of the believer.' He did not say, 'Make use of the faculty of insight.' How might it be right for anyone to claim to have insight when he is supposed to be wary of it?"

Abu'l-'Abbas b. Masruq related, "When I went to see an old man who was one of our companions, I found him living in shabby surroundings. I asked myself, 'How does this old man make a living?' He told me, 'O Ibn al-'Abbas, drop these worldly notions. God possesses hidden kindnesses.'" Az-Zabidi reported, "I was in a mosque in Baghdad with a group of Sufis; we had not received anything for days. I came to al-Khawwas to ask him for something. When his eyes fell upon me, he inquired, 'This need that brings you here, does God know of it or not?' I replied, 'Of course He knows of it.' He commanded, 'Then hold your peace and do not display your need before created beings.' I went away, and before long we were given an amount beyond our need."

It is said, "Sahl b. 'Abdallah was in the mosque one day when a dove fell from the air from heat and exhaustion. Sahl announced, 'Shah al-Kirmani has just died, if God Most High willed it.' The people who were there wrote that down, and it was just as he said."

It is said, "Abu 'Abdallah at-Turughandi, who was a great man of the time, traveled to Tus. When he reached Kharw, he instructed his companion, 'Buy some bread.' He bought enough for the two of them, but Abu

'Abdallah told him, 'Buy more than that.' His companion deliberately bought enough for ten men. It was as if he thought little of the sheikh's words. When they had climbed the mountain, they came upon a group of people who had been tied up by thieves. Having had no food for some time, they asked for some. The sheikh said, 'Lay out the dinner cloth for them.'"

I was once with the master Imam Abu 'Ali (may God grant him mercy) when those present began to talk about how Sheikh Abu 'Abd ar-Rahman as-Sulami (may God grant him mercy) rose up during the *sama'* (session of invocation and music) like the common dervishes who were attending. The master Abu 'Ali exclaimed, "A man of his stature in a state like that! Perhaps remaining seated and still would be more suitable for him." Then he told me, in that same gathering, "Go to as-Sulami. You will find him sitting in his library. On top of the books is a small square red volume containing poems by al-Husayn b. Mansur. Take this book without saying anything to him and bring it to me." It was noontime. When I went to him, he was in his library, and the book was where Abu 'Ali had mentioned. When I sat down, Sheikh Abu 'Abd ar-Rahman as-Sulami began to speak, "There once was a man who censured one of the scholars for his actions in the *sama'*. This same man was seen one day, alone in his house, whirling around like the ones who display their ecstasy. When someone asked him why he did this, he replied, 'I encountered a troubling problem. Suddenly its solution was revealed to me. My joy was such that I could not control myself and I began whirling around.' They said of this man, 'A man of his stature acting like the common dervishes!'" When I saw what the master Abu 'Ali had ordered me to do and that all was in the manner he had described, I realized what Sheikh Abu 'Abd ar-Rahman was saying. I was perplexed; I asked myself, "What should I do, being between them this way?" Then I thought for myself on the matter and decided there was no alternative save truthfulness. I stated, "The master Abu 'Ali described a certain volume to me and told me to take it without asking your permission. I fear you [and do not want to deceive you], but I cannot oppose him. What do you think I should do?" He took down the six-part volume of al-Husayn's talks in which there was also a book by himself that he named *As-Sayhur fi Naqd ad-Duhur* and said, "Take this to him and tell him, 'I looked at this, and I copied some lines from it into my writings.'" So I departed.

Al-Hasan al-Haddad related, "I was in the company of Abu'l-Qasim al-Munadi and a group of Sufis who were his guests when he told me to go out and bring them some food. I was delighted to be given his bidding to provide for the Sufis and bring them food, although he knew me to be exceedingly poor. I took a large basket and went out. At the road of Sayyar, I saw a splendidly dressed sheikh, whom I greeted, saying, 'There is a group of Sufis gathered nearby. Might you have something you could give them?' He ordered his servant to bring out his store of food and took out some bread, meat, and grapes for me. When I reached Abu'l-Qasim al-Munadi's house, he called out from inside the door, 'Take that back to where you got it.' I returned and apologized to the sheikh, declaring, 'I could not find those Sufis. It seems they have departed.' I returned the food to him and went to the market. I was able to get some food, which I brought to Abu'l-Qasim's house. He commanded, 'Come inside.' When I told him all that had happened, he remarked, 'Yes, that Ibn Sayyar is a worldly man attached to the rulers. When you go to get food for the Sufis, come by it this way, not that.'"

Abu'l-Husayn al-Qarafi reported, "I visited Abu'l-Khayr at-Tinati, and when I bade him farewell, he walked with me to the door of the mosque and said, 'O Abu'l-Husayn, I know you do not carry provisions with you, but take these two apples.' I accepted them, putting them in my pocket, and went on my way. Nothing came my way for three days, so finally I took out one of the apples and ate it. Then I thought I would eat the second one also, and there they both were, [the two apples] in my pocket. I continued to eat them, and they continued to reappear until I reached the gates of Mosul. I commented to myself, 'These apples have ruined my state of trust in God, since they have become like provisions for me.' So I took them out of my pocket for the last time and looked around [to see what to do with them]. There was a poor man wrapped in a cloak crying, 'Oh, I wish I had an apple.' I gave them to him. When I considered the matter, it came to me that the sheikh had sent the apples to this man, and I was merely the bearer of his kindness. I went to find the poor man, but he was gone."

Abu 'Umar b. 'Alwan related, "There was a young man in the company of al-Junayd who used to read people's thoughts. Al-Junayd was informed of this, and he asked the youth, 'What is this they say of you?' He instructed al-Junayd, 'Think of something.' Al-Junayd announced, 'I have done so.' The youth said, 'You thought such and such.' Al-Junayd exclaimed, 'No.' The youth asked him to think of two more things, and al-Junayd replied each time that the youth was wrong. The boy observed, 'This is strange. You are trustworthy, and I am sure of my heart.' Al-Junayd admitted, 'You were right all three times, but I wanted to test whether your heart would change or not.'"

Abu 'Abdallah ar-Razi reported, "Ibn ar-Raqqi became ill. Medicine was brought to him in a cup, and he took it. Then he asserted, 'A grave incident has happened in the kingdom [the Hijaz] today. I will neither eat nor drink until I know what it is.' The news came after some days that the Carmathians had entered Mecca that day, committing great slaughter." Abu 'Uthman al-Maghribi said, "Someone told al-Katib this story and he remarked, 'This is strange.' I told him, 'This is not at all strange.' He asked, 'And what are the events of Mecca today?' I stated, 'The followers of Talha and the partisans of al-Hasan are fighting. The leader of the Banu Talha is a black man wearing a red turban. There is a cloud covering the sanctuary in Mecca today.' So Abu 'Ali wrote to Mecca and found that it was as I had told him."

It is related about Anas b. Malik (may God be pleased with him) that he reported, "I came to 'Uthman b. 'Affan [may God be pleased with him] after I had seen a woman on the road. I had gazed for a long time at her great beauty. 'Uthman observed, 'One of you has come to me today bearing clear traces of adultery in his eyes.'

I asked him, 'Can there be revelation after the Messenger of God!' He announced, 'No, but there is perspicacity, discernment, and true insight.'" Abu Sa'id al-Kharraz remarked, "I went into the Sacred Mosque, where I saw a dervish wearing two cloaks, begging from people. I said to myself, 'Men like him are a burden on people.' He looked at me and declared, 'Know that God knows all that is in your minds, so beware of Him' (2:235). After I asked his forgiveness in my heart, he retorted, 'He is the One Who accepts repentance from His servants' (42:25)."

Ibrahim al-Khawwas said, "One day when I was in the great mosque in Baghdad, there was a group of Sufis there. A bright young man came to us, sweet smelling, with beautiful hair and face. I told my companions, 'It has occurred to me that he is a Jew.' All of them disapproved of my saying that. Both the young man and I left. Then he went back to them and asked, 'What did the sheikh say about me?' They were too ashamed to tell him, but he pleaded with them until finally they revealed, 'He says that you are a Jew.' After that the young man came to me, bowed over my hand, and embraced Islam. When someone asked him why he had done this, he said, 'We read in our books that the veracious one's insight is never wrong. So I said, "I will test the Muslims." I searched among them and decided, "If there be a veracious one among them, he will be a Sufi, for they speak the words of God [may He be exalted]." I concealed my identity and deceived them. When this sheikh found me out and had an insight as to who I was, I knew that he was veracious.' That same young man became one of the greatest of the Sufis."

Muhammad b. Da'ud related, "We were with al-Jurayri once when he inquired, 'Is there a man among you whom God [may He be exalted] would tell when He means to bring about a fateful event in the land before it comes about?' We replied, 'No.' He declared, 'Weep for the hearts that experience nothing from God Most High.'"

Abu Musa ad-Daylami stated, "When I asked 'Abd ar-Rahman b. Yahya about trust in God, he explained, 'It means that if you were to thrust your hand up to the wrist into a snake's mouth, you would fear nothing but God Most High.' Then I went to Abu Yazid to ask him about trust in God. I knocked at his door, from behind which he answered, 'Are the words of 'Abd ar-Rahman not enough for you?' I requested, 'Open the door.' He responded, 'You have not come to visit me [you have come with a question], and the answer has come to you from behind the door.' He would not open the door, so I went away and waited one year. Then I went to him again, and he exclaimed, 'Welcome. Now you have come to me as a visitor.' I stayed with him for a month, and he would tell me all that came into my heart. When he bade me farewell, I begged, 'Please give me one more beneficial word from you.' He revealed, 'My mother told me that when she was pregnant with me, whenever licit food was presented to her, her hand reached for it. But if there was something dubious in the food, her hand recoiled from it.'"

Ibrahim al-Khawwas reported, "I went into the desert, where I experienced many trials. When I made it [safely] to Mecca, I was somewhat proud [of my arrival in safety]. An old woman called out to me, 'O Ibrahim,

I was with you in the desert, but I did not speak to you lest I disturb your inner state. Now throw out those evil thoughts.'"

It is told that although al-Farghani used to go every year for the pilgrimage, he would pass through Nishapur without going to see Abu 'Uthman al-Hiri. He explained, "I went one time to see him and gave him my greetings, but he did not return them. I asked him, 'A Muslim comes to another Muslim and extends his greetings without receiving them in return?!' Abu 'Uthman answered, '[What do you say of] one who makes the pilgrimage, leaving his mother, not treating her with reverence?' At that, I returned to Farghana and stayed there with my mother until she died. Then I went to Abu 'Uthman, and when I entered, he received me and bade me sit down." After that, al-Farghani stayed with him constantly. He asked to be in charge of Abu 'Uthman's horse, which remained his job until Abu 'Uthman died.

Khayr an-Nassaj related, "I was sitting in my house one day when it occurred to me that al-Junayd was at the door, but I denied my heart. It came to me a second and a third time, so finally I went to the door, and there was al-Junayd. He asked, 'Why did you not come the first time?'"

Muhammad b. al-Husayn al-Bistami reported, "When I went to see Abu 'Uthman al-Maghribi, I told myself, 'Perhaps he would have liked me to bring him a gift.' Abu 'Uthman declared, 'People are not satisfied that I accept things from them; they go so far as to want me to ask.'"

One of the Sufis related, "I was in Baghdad. It occurred to me that al-Murta'ish would come to me with fifteen dirhams so I could buy a food satchel, rope, and sandals that I might go into the desert. Later there was a knock at the door, and I opened it. There stood al-Murta'ish with a cloth purse. He ordered, 'Take this.' I exclaimed, 'O my master, I do not want it.' He asked, 'Then why did you trouble me? How much did you want?' I answered, 'Fifteen dirhams.' He retorted, 'Here it is, fifteen dirhams.'"

One of the Sufis said that God's words, "Or one who was dead whom we gave new life and a light with which he can walk among men, can he be like one who is in the depths of darkness from which he will never emerge?" (6:122) mean, "One whose intellect had died and so God gave him new life by the light of insight and whom God gave the light of manifestation and witnessing, he is not like one who walks among the people of negligence in his negligence."

It is said, "If a man's insight is sound, he ascends to the station of witnessing."

Abu'l-'Abbas b. Masruq reported, "An old man who would speak on Sufism in an excellent way came to us. He spoke with a pleasant manner and had excellent opinions. In one of his talks, he instructed us, 'Tell me whatever occurs to you.' It occurred to me that he was a Jew. It was a strong premonition that persisted, so I mentioned it to al-Jurayri. That caused him distress, but I asserted, 'I have no choice but to tell the man of this.' I remarked to him, 'You told us to tell you whatever occurred to us. It has occurred to me that you are a Jew.' He bowed his head for a time; then he raised it up, confirming, 'You have spoken the truth, [but] I [now] bear witness that there is no god but God and that

Muhammad is His Messenger.' Then he explained, 'I tried all the different religious paths, and I used to say, "If these people [the Muslims] have something [of the truth], then it is with these Sufis." So I mingled with you in order to test you. You are right.' He became a fine Muslim."

It is related that as-Sari used to urge al-Junayd to preach to people. Al-Junayd admitted, "I had dread in my heart of speaking before people, doubting that I was worthy of it. One Thursday night I saw the Prophet [may God's blessing and peace be upon him] in a dream. He instructed me, 'Preach to the people.' I woke up, went to as-Sari's door before he had woken up, and knocked on the door. He inquired, 'You did not believe me until it was told to you [by the Prophet]?'" That morning he sat before the people in the mosque, and it spread among many that al-Junayd was preaching. A young Christian man in disguise came to al-Junayd and asked, "Tell me, O sheikh, what is the meaning of the Messenger of God's words, 'Beware of the insight of the believer, for he sees with the light of God?'" Al-Junayd bowed his head, then raised it, saying, "Embrace Islam. The time for your Islam has come." And the young man became a Muslim.

33

Moral Character

❧ Khuluq

God Most High says, "Verily you [Muhammad] are upon a noble character" (68:4).

On the authority of Anas, it is related that someone asked, "O Messenger of God, who among the believers has the greatest faith?" He replied, "The ones of finest character." It is clear, then, that fine moral character is the most excellent virtue of the servant and the one by which his inner nature is known. Man is veiled by his body, revealed by his character.

The master Abu 'Ali ad-Daqqaq (may God grant him mercy) declared, "God Most High favored His Prophet [may God's blessing and peace be upon him] with many excellent qualities, but He never praised him for any of his qualities as He praised him for his character, for He says, 'Verily you are upon a noble character.'"

Al-Wasiti stated, "God described him as being upon a noble character because he sacrificed this world and the hereafter, being content with God Most High." He also said, "Noble character means that one neither disputes with others nor is disputed by them because he possesses complete inner knowledge of God Most High."

Al-Husayn b. Mansur explained, "The meaning of noble character is that the harshness of men does not affect you once you have become attentive to God." Abu Sa'id al-Kharraz noted, "Noble character means that you have no aspiration other than God Most High." Al-Kattani asserted, "Sufism is moral character. Whoever surpasses you in moral character has surpassed you in Sufism." It is told of Ibn 'Umar (may God be pleased with him) that he instructed, "If you hear me say to a slave, 'May God curse you,' then be witness to his release from slavery."

Al-Fudayl observed, "If a man acted with good moral character in all ways except that he mistreated one of his chickens, he could not be counted as one of moral character." It is said that when Ibn 'Umar saw one of his slaves performing the prayer well, he would set the slave free. The slaves all came to know this, and they began to perform the prayer well only to make a show for him. He would still set them free. When someone criticized him for this, he retorted, 'Whenever one would deceive us for God's sake, we would allow ourselves to be deceived for His sake.'"

Al-Harith al-Muhasibi commented, "It is our loss if we lack three things: handsome appearance combined with modesty, words well spoken combined with reliability, strong brotherliness combined with fidelity." 'Abdallah b. Muhammad ar-Razi remarked, "Moral character consists of thinking little of whatever comes from you to God and regarding as great whatever

comes to you from Him." Al-Ahnaf was asked, "Who
taught you moral character?" He answered, "Qays b.
'Asim al-Munaqqari." That person asked, "What was his
character like?" He related, "One time he was sitting in
his house when a slave girl came in with a flaming
skewer of meat. It fell from her hands and dropped on
one of his sons, who died. The slave girl was distraught.
He told her, 'Do not worry. You are free, for God's sake
[with no financial obligation].'"

Shah al-Kirmani stated, "A sign of moral character is
that you do not cause harm to others, and you bear the
harms they cause you."

The Messenger of God (may God's blessing and
peace be upon him) said, "You will not be able to give
happiness by means of your wealth, so do it by means
of a cheerful expression and good character."

Dhu'n-Nun al-Misri was asked, "Who are the people
with the most worries?" He replied, "The ones with the
worst characters." Wahb asserted, "If a servant assumes
the manners of moral character for forty days, God will
make moral character an innate quality for him."
Interpreting God's words, "And your garments you
must purify" (74:4), al-Hasan al-Basri explained that He
means, "And your character you must beautify."

It is said that a certain ascetic owned a ewe. When he
found her with one of her legs chopped off, he asked,
"Who has done this?" One of his slaves admitted, "I did
it." Asked why he had chopped off her leg, the slave
answered, "To make you show sadness over her." He
observed, "That has not come about. But I am pained
by your action. Go, for you are free." Ibrahim b. Adham
was asked, "Have you ever taken delight in this world?"

He affirmed, "Yes, twice. One day I was sitting and a man came and urinated on me. The second time I was sitting and a man came and slapped me."

It is said that Uways al-Qarani would be pelted with stones by some boys whenever they saw him. So he would tell them, "If you must do this, then use small stones so you will not bruise my legs and prevent me from standing to do my prayers." A man was once following after al-Ahnaf b. Qays, insulting him. When al-Ahnaf came close to his own neighborhood, he stopped and advised, "O young man, if you have any more to say, say it now before one of the neighborhood bullies hears you and answers you in kind."

Hatim al-Asamm was asked, "Should a man bear injuries from all men?" He averred, "Yes, except from himself." It is told that the Commander of the Believers, 'Ali b. Abi Talib (may God be pleased with him) once called to one of his slaves, but the slave did not answer. He called again and again, and still there was no answer. When 'Ali went to him and found him reclining on the floor, he inquired, "Did you not hear me, O slave?" He replied, "Yes." 'Ali asked, "Then why did you not answer me?" The slave explained, "I feel safe from your punishment, so I was lazy." 'Ali told him, "Go. You are free for the sake of God [with no financial obligation]."

It is said that when Ma'ruf al-Karkhi went down to the Tigris to make ablutions, he laid down his copy of the Qur'an and his cloak. A woman came along and stole them. Ma'ruf followed her, declaring, "O sister, I am Ma'ruf, and I do not blame you for this. Do you have a son who can read the Qur'an?" She answered, "No."

He asked, "Or a husband?" She said, "No." He instructed, "Then give me the Qur'an back and keep the cloak." Thieves broke into Sheikh Abu 'Abd ar-Rahman as-Sulami's house by force and stole everything. One of our companions heard the sheikh relate, "I passed through the market one day and saw my cloak being auctioned, but I turned away without paying the matter any attention."

Al-Jurayri reported, "I returned from Mecca [may God protect it], and the first thing I did was visit al-Junayd so he would not worry about me. I gave him my greetings and went home. The next day when I prayed the morning prayer in the mosque, I saw him standing in a row behind me. I remarked, 'I only came to you yesterday so you would not worry.' He observed, 'That was your generosity. This [taking a place in front of me] is your right.'"

When Abu Hafs was asked about moral character, he stated, "It consists of what God [Glorious and Majestic] chose for His Prophet [may God's blessing and peace be upon him] when He commanded, 'Hold to forgiveness and command what is right!'" (7:199). It is said, "Moral character means that you be close to people but a stranger to their affairs." It is said, "Moral character lies in accepting harsh treatment from men and the decree of God with neither sorrow nor anxiety." It is said that Abu Dharr was letting his camels drink at a cistern when a man suddenly rushed up to it. The cistern broke apart. Abu Dharr sat down; then he lay down. When someone asked him why he had done this, he replied, "The Messenger of God [may God's blessing and peace be upon him] told us that when a man is angered, he should sit down until the anger subsides. If it does not subside, then he should lie down."

It is written in the Christian Scriptures, "My servant, remember me when you are angered; I will remember you when I am angered." One of Malik b. Dinar's wives said to him, "O you hypocrite!" He retorted, "O woman, you have found that name of mine which the people of Basra had lost." Luqman told his son, "There are three kinds of people who can be recognized only at three times: a forbearing man at the time of anger, a coura-geous man at the time of war, and a brother at the time he is needed." Moses (peace be upon him) said, "O my God, I ask You to turn away things falsely said of me." God Most High revealed to him, "I have not done this for Myself. How could I do it for you?"

Yahya b. Ziyad al-Harithi owned a very bad slave. Someone asked him, "Why do you keep this slave?" He answered, "That I might learn forbearance."

It is said that His words "He has showered his blessings on you both without and within" (31:20) have the sense of "without" as God's ordering of man's physical consititution, and "within" as His purifying of man's character. Al-Fudayl commented, "I would rather have a sinning rogue of good character as a friend than a religious man of bad character." It is said, "Good moral character means bearing adversity with a good-natured spirit."

It is told that Ibrahim b. Adham went out into one of the great deserts. A soldier whom he met there asked, "Where is the nearest center of population?" Ibrahim pointed to the graveyard. The soldier beat him and broke his skull. When he finally let him go, someone told the soldier, "That was Ibrahim b. Adham, the

ascetic of Khorasan." The soldier went to beg his
pardon. Ibrahim noted, "While you were beating me,
I asked God Most High to bring you to Paradise." The
soldier inquired, "But why?" He said, "I knew that I
would be rewarded for taking the beating. I did not
want my fate to be good at your expense and yours be
bad on my account."

It is related that a man invited Abu 'Uthman al-Hiri to
be his guest. When Abu 'Uthman appeared at the man's
door, the man told him, "O Master, this is not a good
time for you to come inside. I am very sorry; please go
away." When Abu 'Uthman went another time to the
man's house, the man came and again said, "O Master,
I am very sorry." He begged Abu 'Uthman's pardon and
instructed, "Come at such-and-such a time." Abu 'Uthman
went away. When he returned again, the man said the
same thing. This happened again and again. Finally the
man explained, "O Master, I only wanted to test you."
He began to beg his pardon and praise him. Abu
'Uthman remarked, "Do not praise me for a quality
belonging to dogs. When a dog is called, he comes.
When he is driven away, he leaves." It is said that Abu
'Uthman was crossing a street in midday when someone on a roof dumped a bucket of ashes on his head.
His companions became furious and began to yell at
the one who had dumped the ashes. Abu 'Uthman
ordered, "Do not say anything. One who deserves the
Fire but is covered only with ashes has no right to be
angry."

It is said that a Sufi wanderer was staying as a guest
with Ja'far b. Hanzala, who offered him every possible
service. The man affirmed, "Yes, you would be quite a
man but for the fact that you are a Jew." Ja'far asserted,

"My religion does not affect how I serve your needs. Pray for a cure for your soul and for guidance for me."

It is said that 'Abdallah the tailor had a Magian customer for whom he sewed clothes. The man would pay him with counterfeit dirhams, and 'Abdallah would accept them. One day the Magian came from his tavern to pick up some clothing and tried to pay for it with counterfeit dirhams, but 'Abdallah's apprentice refused to take them. He finally paid him with real money. When 'Abdallah returned, he asked "Where are the Magian's shirts?" The apprentice told him what had happened. 'Abdallah explained, "You have done a terrible thing. For some time now he has done business with me in this way, and I was patient. I used to toss the counterfeit dirhams in the well so he would not cheat others with them."

It is said, "Bad moral character constricts the heart because it allows no room there for anything other than its own desires, and it becomes like a small space just large enough for its owner." It is said, "Moral character means that you do not care who stands next to you in line [for prayer]." It is also said, "A sign of a man's bad character is that he fixes his eyes on the bad character of others."

The Messenger of God (may God's blessings and peace be upon him) was asked, "What is the meaning of inauspiciousness?" He answered, "Bad moral character." On the authority of Abu Hurayra (may God be pleased with him) someone stated, "O Messenger of God, call [the wrath of] God down upon the polytheists!" He replied, "I was sent as a mercy; I was not sent as a punishment."

34

Bountifulness and Generosity

✣ Jud wa sakha'

God Most High says, "They gave to them in preference over themselves even though poverty was their lot" (59:9).

On the authority of 'A'isha (may God be pleased with her), the Messenger of God (may God's blessing and peace be upon him) commented, "The generous are near to God Most High, near to men, near to Paradise, and far from Hell. The miser is far from God Most High, far from men, far from Paradise, and near to Hell. The generous, ignorant man is more beloved to God than the miserly worshipper."

There is no difference between bountifulness and generosity in the usage of the Sufis. God (may He be exalted) is not described by the terms "generous" and "magnanimous" because there is no precedent [in the Qur'an or the Sunna] for doing so. The essence of bountifulness is that in sacrificing something, one feels no hardship.

Among the Sufis, generosity is the first step. Bountifulness follows, and then selfless giving [in preference to oneself]. One who gives away a portion and keeps a portion displays generosity. One who gives away a greater amount but retains something for himself displays bountifulness. One who is in a state of hardship but gives selflessly of his meager means displays selfless giving.

Asma' b. Kharija declared, "I do not like to turn away anyone who approaches me with a request. If he is noble, I allow him to retain his nobility, and if he is lowly, he allows me to retain my dignity." It is said that Muwarriq al-'Ijli used to be clever in his ways of showing kindness to his nearest companions. He would leave one thousand dirhams with them and say, "Keep these for me until I come back." Later he would write to them: "The money is yours."

When a man from Manbij met someone from Medina, he asked about him, "Where is he from?" He was told the man was from Medina. He said to him, "A man from your city named Hakam b. 'Abd al-Mutallib came to us once and made us rich." The man from Medina inquired, "How can this be? He came to you with nothing but the wool cloak on his back!" The man from Manbij replied, "He didn't make us rich with money. He taught us generosity. And so we gave to one another until we were no longer in need."

The master Abu 'Ali ad-Daqqaq related, "When Ghulam al-Khalil slandered the Sufis before the caliph, the caliph ordered them to be beheaded. Al-Junayd was protected by his esteemed position in jurisprudence. He used to offer opinions according to the school of Abu Thawr. As for ash-Shahham, ar-Raqqam, an-Nuri, and the rest, they were arrested, and the mat was spread for their beheading. An-Nuri stepped forward and the executioner asked him, 'Do you realize what is about to happen to you?' He affirmed, 'Yes.' The executioner inquired, 'Then what makes you so eager for it?' He answered, 'I would rather my friends live an extra moment.' The executioner was perplexed by this and sent the story to the caliph, who turned them over to a judge to examine their case. The judge posed several legal questions to Abu'l-Husayn an-Nuri, who answered every one and then stated, 'And furthermore, God has belonging to Him servants who, when they stand, stand by means of God, and when they speak, speak by means of God.' He continued to speak and his words made the judge weep. The judge sent word to the caliph, 'If these men are heretics, there is not a single Muslim on the face of the earth.'"

It is said that 'Ali b. al-Fudayl used to buy all his goods from the neighborhood vendors. Someone remarked, "You would save money if you would go to the main market." He replied, "These vendors have come to our neighborhood hoping to provide service to us."

A man sent a slave girl to Jabala when he had his companions with him. He commented, "It would be very bad if I were to accept her while you are present. I do not want to single out one of you to have her when all of you have a right to her and to my respect. The girl cannot be divided among you." (There were eighty of them.) Finally he ordered a slave girl or a male slave to be brought for each of them.

It is said that, being thirsty on the road one day, 'Ubaydallah b. Abi Bakra asked for water at the house of a woman. She filled a cup for him and stood behind the door, explaining, "Turn away from the door and send one of your slaves to get the cup from me—for I am an Arab woman [wishing to be modest], and my servant died some days ago." So 'Ubaydallah drank the water and told his slave, "Take her ten thousand dirhams." She exclaimed, "God forbid, do you ridicule me?" So he said, "Take her twenty thousand dirhams." She said, "Ask God Most High for good health." He then directed, "Take her thirty thousand dirhams." At that she slammed the door, exclaiming, "Shame on you." But he brought her the thirty thousand dirhams, which she accepted. By nightfall her suitors had multiplied.

It is said, "Bountifulness is acting on the first inclination [to give]." I heard one of the companions of Abu'l-Hasan al-Bushanji (may God have mercy on him) relate, "Abu'l-Hasan al-Bushanji was in the latrine. He called one of his pupils, commanding, 'Take this shirt off of me and present it to so-and-so.' Someone asked him, 'Can you not wait until you have finished in there?' He replied, 'I do not trust my self not to change my intention to oppose it by [giving] that shirt.'"

Qays b. Sa'd b. 'Ubada was asked, "Have you ever known anyone more generous than yourself?" He averred, "Yes. We stopped in the desert at the dwelling of a woman. Her husband came home, and she told him, 'You have guests.' So he brought a camel, slaughtered it, and announced, 'This is for you.' The next day he came with another camel, slaughtered it, and declared, 'This is for you.' We objected, 'But we have eaten only a little of the one you slaughtered for us yesterday.' He replied, 'I do not feed my guests stale meat.' We stayed with him two or three more days while it rained, and he continued to do the same. When we were about to depart, we left one hundred dinars for him in his house and told his wife, 'Apologize to him for us.' Then we traveled on. At midday the man came up behind us, shouting, 'Stop, you vile band! You want to pay me for my hospitality?' Then he pressed us [to take back the money], declaring, 'Either you take it, or I will stab you with my spear!' So we took it and went on our way." Then he recited:

> If you take away the reward for what I have
> given,
> Then let indignity be a fair prize for the
> winner.

I heard Sheikh Abu 'Abd ar-Rahman as-Sulami (may God grant him mercy) relate, "Abu 'Abdallah ar-Rudhbari went to the home of one of his companions. No one was at home and the door to the house was locked. He stated, 'This man is a Sufi, and he locks his door? Break open the lock.' So they broke the lock. He ordered them to take all the goods found on the grounds and in the house, carry them to the market, sell them, and take wages for their work from the money received. Then he and his companions waited in the house. When the owner came in he was speechless. His wife came in afterwards, wearing an outer garment. She threw off the cloak, declaring, 'O friends, this is also part of our worldly property, so sell it, too.' Her husband asked her, 'Why do you choose to suffer like this?' She replied, 'Keep quiet! How can we grudge anything from one such as this sheikh, who honors us by treating us with such familiarity and who disposes of our affairs?'"

Bishr b. al-Harith stated, "Paying attention to a stingy man hardens the heart." It is said that Qays b. Sa'd b. 'Ubada became ill. His friends were not coming to see him, so he inquired about them. Someone related, "They are ashamed because of the debts they owe to you." He cried, "May God curse money that prevents brothers from visiting [one another]!" He sent a messenger to proclaim that whoever owed him a debt was free from it. That night the threshold to his house was broken by the weight of all who came to visit him.

It was said to 'Abdallah b. Ja'far: "You give freely if you are asked, but you grudge even a small amount if you are opposed." He responded, "I give my money freely, but I am grudging with my intellect."

It is said that 'Abdallah b. Ja'far went out to one of his country estates. He stopped at a date palm orchard in which there was a black slave working. When the slave brought out his food, a dog came inside the walls and went up to the slave. So the slave threw him a piece of bread, and the dog ate it. Then he threw a second and a third piece to the dog, and he ate them as well. 'Abdallah b. Ja'far, who was watching this, asked the slave, "O slave, how much food do you receive each day?" He replied, "Just what you have seen." 'Abdallah b. Ja'far inquired, "Then why do you give it to the dog instead of yourself?" The slave explained, "There are no dogs living here. This one has come, hungry, a great distance, so I would hate to turn him away." He was asked, "How will you manage today?" The slave responded, "I will spend my day hungry." 'Abdallah b. Ja'far declared, "And I have been reproached for being [overly] generous! This man is more generous than I." So he purchased the orchard, the slave, and the tools, then freed the slave and gave the orchard to him.

It is said that a man went to his friend one day and knocked on his door. When the friend came out, he asked, "Why have you come?" The man answered, "Because of a debt of four hundred dirhams that is weighing on me." So his friend went inside, weighed out four hundred dirhams, and brought them to him. Then he went inside, weeping. His wife asked him, "Why did you not make excuses to him when [you knew that] giving him the money would cause you hardship?" He replied, "[That is not why I am weeping.] I weep only because I did not see his plight before he was compelled to reveal it to me."

Mutarrif b. ash-Shikhkhir instructed, "Whenever one of you needs something from me, let him deliver it in a message, for I hate to see the humiliation of need in a man's face."

It is said that a man wanted to cause harm to 'Abdallah b. al-'Abbas. So the man brought together the prominent men of the city and told them that Ibn al-'Abbas had invited them to his home for dinner that very day. They went to his home, and the grounds were filled with them. Ibn al-'Abbas asked, "What is this?" Someone told him the story. He immediately ordered someone to buy fruits, bread, and cooked dishes. All was done in due order. When the food was all eaten, he asked his advisors, "Is it possible for me to provide this much every day?" They answered, "Yes." He declared, "Then let all of these men be my guests every day."

I heard Sheikh Abu 'Abd ar-Rahman as-Sulami (may God grant him mercy) relate, "When master Abu Sahl as-Su'luki was making his ablutions in his courtyard one day, a man came in and begged him for charity. He had nothing with him and said, 'Wait until I am finished.' The man waited. When Abu Sahl was finished, he told the man, 'Take this scent bottle and go.' The man took it and went. Abu Sahl waited until he was certain the other was far away; then he cried out, 'A man has broken in and taken a scent bottle!' They pursued him, but did not catch up with him. Abu Sahl did this only because his household used to reproach him for his extreme generosity."

I also heard Sheikh Abu 'Abd ar-Rahman as-Sulami relate, "The master Abu Sahl gave his robe to a man in the winter. Because he had no other, he used to wear a woman's robe when he went out to teach. A delegation of famous scholars composed of representatives from every field came from Fars. It included leading jurists, theologians, and grammarians. The head of the army, Abu'l-Hasan, sent to Abu Sahl, ordering him to ride out to meet them. He put on an outer garment over the woman's robe and rode away. The head of the army asserted, 'He is mocking me before the whole city, riding [in public] in the robe of a woman!' But Abu Sahl then debated with the entire delegation, and his arguments proved superior to theirs in every field."

I also heard Sheikh Abu 'Abd ar-Rahman as-Sulami

report, "The master Abu Sahl never gave alms to anyone by his own hand. He would cast it on the ground for the other to take up, and declare, 'This world is of so little worth that I do not [want to] see, because of it, my hand over the hand of another!' However, the Prophet [may God's blessing and peace be upon him] has stated, 'The upper hand is better than the lower.'"

It is said that Abu Marthad (may God grant him mercy) was the foremost of the generous ones, for which one of the poets praised him. He said [to the poet], "I do not have anything to give you, but report me to the judge and charge that I owe you ten thousand dirhams so that I can confess to it. Then have me arrested, for my family will not leave me in prison." The poet did as he was told. Before nightfall he was paid ten thousand dirhams, and Abu Marthad was released from prison.

A man asked al-Hasan b. 'Ali b. Abi Talib (may God be pleased with him) for some charity, so he gave him fifty thousand dirhams and five hundred dinars. He ordered, "Bring a porter to carry it for you." So the man brought a porter. Al-Hasan then gave him his shawl, saying, "The porter's wages also come from me."

When a woman asked al-Layth b. Sa'd for a bowl of honey, he ordered a whole skin full of honey to be brought to her. Someone critized him for this, and he replied, "She asked according to her need, and I gave according to my ability."

One of the Sufis related, "I prayed the morning prayer in the mosque of al-Ash'ath in Kufa because I was looking for one of my creditors. After I completed the prayer, someone placed a suit of clothes and a pair of sandals before each one there, including myself. I inquired, 'What is this?' They answered, 'Al-Ash'ath has returned from Mecca, and he ordered this to be done for all the congregation of his mosque.' I explained, 'But I only came looking for one of my creditors; I am an outsider.' They declared, 'It is for all who are present.'"

It is said that when the time for ash-Shafi'i's death (may God be pleased with him) drew near, he instructed, "Tell so-and-so to wash my body [after my death]." But the man was not there. When he did come, he was told of this request. So he called for ash-Shafi'i's account book, where he found that ash-Shafi'i had a debt of seventy thousand dirhams. This man settled the debt and commented, "This is my cleansing of him."

It is said that when ash-Shafi'i returned to Mecca from San'a, he had with him ten thousand dinars. Someone told him, "You [should] buy some property with this money." Thereupon ash-Shafi'i set up a tent outside Mecca where he poured out the dinars. He would give a handful to everyone who came to him. When noontime arrived, he stood up and shook out his robe: nothing was left.

It is said that as-Sari went out on the festival day, and a man of great standing met him. As-Sari gave him only a cursory greeting. Someone remarked, "But this is a man of great standing!" He replied, "I know who he is, but it is related that 'When two Muslims meet, one hundred parts of mercy are divided between them: ninety to the more cheerful of the two.' I wanted him to have the greater portion."

It is said that the Commander of the Believers, 'Ali b.

Abi Talib (may God be pleased with him), was weeping one day. Someone asked him, "What makes you weep?" He responded, "No guest has come to me for seven days, and I fear that God Most High has scorned me."

It is related that Anas b. Malik (may God be pleased with him) stated, "The poor tax due on a home is that a room be set aside in it for guests."

It is said concerning the words of God Most High, "Has the story of the honored guests of Abraham reached you?" (51:24), [that they are called "honored"] because Abraham served them himself. It is also said [that they are called this] because the guest of an honorable man is himself honorable.

Ibrahim b. al-Junayd related, "There are four [acts] the noble man should not disdain, even if he be a prince: standing up from his place for his father, serving his guest, serving a scholar from whom he has learned, and asking about what he does not know."

Ibn 'Abbas (may God be pleased with him) commented with regard to the words of God Most High, "There is no blame on you whether you eat in company or separately" (24:61), that it means, "They would feel anguished that one of them would eat alone, so God made that permissible for them."

It is said that 'Abdallah b. 'Amir b. Kurayz was once host to a man. He was exceedingly generous in his hospitality. When the man wished to depart, 'Abdallah's slaves refused to help him. When asked about this, 'Abdallah b. 'Amir answered, "They will not assist one who leaves us." Al-Mutanabbi composed the following on this story:

> *If you leave a people who could prevent you*
> *from parting,*
> *Then they are the ones who depart.*

Abdallah b. al-Mubarak said, "Generously restraining the soul from *(sakha' 'an)* [desire] for men's possessions is better than generosity *(sakha')* of the soul in giving away [one's own possessions]."

One of the Sufis reported, "I went to Bishr b. al-Harith on a very cold day. He had taken off some of his robes, and he was shivering. I told him, 'O Abu Nasr, people put on extra garments on days such as this. Why are you wearing so few?' He replied, 'I remembered the poor and their state, and I have nothing to give them. So I wanted to suffer the cold as they do.'"

Ad-Daqqaq declared, "Generosity is not the rich giving to the poor. Generosity is [in reality] the poor giving to the rich."

35

Jealousy

❧ Ghayra

God Most High says, "Say, My Lord has forbidden only shameful deeds whether apparent or hidden" (7:33).

On the authority of 'Abdallah b. Mas'ud, the Messenger of God (may God's blessings and peace be upon him) is said to have declared, "There is no one more jealous than God Most High. One of the signs of His jealousy is that He forbade shameful deeds whether apparent or hidden." On the authority of Abu Hurayra, the Messenger of God stated, "God is jealous and the believer is jealous. God's jealousy is a quality that is aroused when the believing servant commits what God has forbidden."

Jealousy is dislike that another partake [in something one possesses]. When God (may He be exalted) is described with the attribute of jealousy, it means that the possibility of another's sharing in the right of God alone to the obedience of His servant brings Him displeasure.

It is related that when the verse "When you recite the

Qur'an, We place an impenetrable veil between you
and those who do not believe in the hereafter" (17:45)
was recited in as-Sari's presence, he asked his companions, "Do you know what this veil is? It is the veil of
jealously. There is none so jealous as God Most High."
By his saying "It is the veil of jealousy," as-Sari intends
that God has not allowed the unbelievers access to the
veracity of the religion. The master Abu 'Ali ad-Daqqaq
(may God grant him mercy) used to say, "God has tied
the weight of banishment to the feet of those who are
lax in their worship of Him. He singles them out for
distance from Him and makes them fall back from the
station of nearness. Because of this, they are incom-
plete in their worship of Him." They recite:

> *I am a devoted lover to the one I love but*
> *What recourse do I have against the evil*
> *plots of masters?*

They also say on this matter, "A sick man receives no
visitors, and a desiring one is not desired."

Al-'Abbas az-Zawzani observed, "I was blessed with
soundness in the beginning of my wayfaring. I would
know what remained between me and my goal. One
night I saw myself in my dream, tumbling down a
mountain whose peak I had wanted to reach. I was
grieved at this. Then sleep came over me again, and I
heard a voice explaining, 'O 'Abbas, God did not wish
you to reach the goal you were seeking. However, He
has brought wisdom to your tongue.' I woke up, and
indeed, I had been given the inspiration of words of
wisdom."

The master Abu 'Ali ad-Daqqaq (may God grant him

mercy) related, "There once was a sheikh who experienced states and moments with God. He was absent for a time, and He was not seen among the dervishes. He came back after that in a lower state than what he had enjoyed previously. When they asked him what had happened, he replied, 'Ah, a veil has fallen.'" The master used to remark when something occurred during the session that occupied the hearts of those present, "This is God's jealousy. He does not want them to experience the serenity of this moment." They recite on this matter:

> She was of a mind to come to us but then she
> gazed
> In the mirror, and her comely face detained
> her.

One of the Sufis was asked, "Do you wish to see Him?" He answered, "No." They inquired, "Why is this?" He responded, "Such sublime beauty is exalted beyond the gaze of one like me." On this they recite:

> I envy my eyes' gazing upon you
> So much that I lower them when I look at
> you.
> Seeing you display your beauteous features
> that
> Cause me such agitation makes me jealous
> of you, for you.

Ash-Shibli was asked, "When do you rest [from jealousy]?" He answered, "When I find no other man making remembrance of Him."

The master Abu 'Ali ad-Daqqaq (may God grant him

mercy) has commented on words the Prophet (may God's blessing and peace be upon him) spoke when he had just concluded a transaction with a Bedouin for the purchase of a horse. The Bedouin demanded to cancel the sale, so the Prophet canceled it. Then the Bedouin said, "May God Most High give you long life. Who are you?" The Prophet replied, "A man of the Quraysh." One of the Companions present demanded, "What rudeness could be greater than not recognizing your Prophet?" Abu 'Ali said, "The Prophet replied, 'A man of the Quraysh' out of jealousy. If the case were otherwise, he would have answered anyone who asked him who he was. Then God [may he be exalted] made that Companion disclose his identity to the Bedouin by asking, 'What rudeness could be greater than not recognizing your Prophet?'"

Some comment, "Jealousy is an attribute of those at the beginning of the path. The one who has realized the unity of God does not experience jealousy. He cannot be said to have choice in matters, nor does he have control over what occurs in the land. It is God [may He be exalted] Who is most capable to determine all things." Abu 'Uthman al-Maghribi stated, "Jealousy belongs to the seekers, not to those who have attained inner truths." Ash-Shibli explained, "There are two kinds of jealousy: human jealousy for one another and divine jealousy for their hearts." He also asserted, "Divine jealousy is for the breaths of men, lest they be wasted on other-than-God."

There are indeed two kinds of jealousy: God's jealousy for the servant, meaning that He denies and grudges him to mankind, and the servant's jealousy for

God, meaning his refusal to devote his states or breaths to other-than-God Most High. It should not be said, "I am jealous of God;" rather, "I am jealous for the sake of God." Jealousy of God Most High is idiocy and might lead to straying from the religion. But jealousy for the sake of God engenders purer devotion in performing good works and in observing His rights over men.

Know that it is God's way with His saints that if they find contentment in other-than-God, heed other-than-God, or permit other-than-God to settle in their hearts, that will bring them agitation [of the heart]. He is so jealous for their hearts that He restores them to Himself, empty of all else that brought them contentment, all else they heeded, and all else they allowed to settle therein. This was the case with Adam (peace be upon him). When he accustomed himself to the idea of staying eternally in Eden, he was exiled from it. This was also the case with Abraham (peace be upon him). When he took delight in his son Ishmael, God ordered him to sacrifice Ishmael so that he would cast him out of his heart. But "When they had both surrendered themselves to God and he had laid him prostrate on his forehead [for sacrifice]" (37:103) and Abraham had purified his inmost being of his attachment to his son, He commanded him to make a substitute sacrifice [of a lamb] instead of Ishmael.

Muhammad b. Hassan related, "Once when I was wandering in the mountains of Lebanon, a young man came upon me. He was burned by the sandstorms and wind. When he saw me, he turned away and fled. I followed him, saying, 'Give me a word of counsel.' He responded, 'Beware, for He is jealous. He hates to find anything other than Himself in the heart of His servant.'" An-Nasrabadhi observed, "God Most High is jealous. One of the signs of His jealousy is that He has made no path to Himself other than Himself."

It is said that God (may He be exalted) revealed to one of His prophets, "So-and-so had need of Me and I, too, have need of him. If he satisfies My need, I will satisfy his need." That prophet (peace be upon him) asked, "O my God, how can You have need of anything?" God answered, "That man has found contentment in other-than-Me. If he empties his heart of that, I will satisfy his need." It is said, "Abu Yazid al-Bistami saw a band of houris in his sleep. He gazed upon them lovingly. After that night his state with God faded for some days. Then again he saw them in his sleep, but he did not look at them, exclaiming, 'You are distracting me!'"

It is said that Rabi'a al-'Adawiya fell ill one time and someone asked her the cause of her illness. She replied, "Because I turned my heart to Paradise, He chastised me. Now He is content with me. I will not do it again." It is related that as-Sari reported, "I was looking for one of my friends one time. I crossed over some mountains and came upon a crowd of people, all of whom were diseased, blind, or ailing. When I asked them what they were doing, they responded, 'We have been told that here lives a man who comes out [of the cave] once a year. If he prays for people, they are cured.' So I waited until he came out. He prayed for those people and they were cured. I followed him, came close to him, and asked, 'What is the treatment for my inward disease?' He instructed, 'O Sari, go away from me lest God Most

High, Who is jealous, see you asking for comfort from other-than-Him. This would lower your standing in His sight.'"

Another aspect of jealousy is that some are unable to tolerate men making remembrance of Him negligently; this is hard for them. I heard the master Abu 'Ali ad-Daqqaq comment on the time a Bedouin came into the Prophet's mosque and urinated. The Companions rushed to throw him outside. Abu 'Ali (may God grant him mercy) remarked, "The Bedouin behaved with bad manners, and the Companions were ashamed and very upset when they looked upon what he had done. This is the case also with the servant. If he knows God's power and glory, it is upsetting for him to hear someone make remembrance of Him vainly or to know of someone who performs religious duties without truly worshiping Him with reverence."

It is related that a son of Abu Bakr ash-Shibli, named Abu'l-Hasan, died. In mourning for him, his mother cut off all her hair. Ash-Shibli went to the bathhouse and shaved off his beard. Everyone who came to offer him their condolences asked, "What have you done, O Abu Bakr?" He would say, "I have followed my wife's example." One of them inquired, "Tell me, O Abu Bakr, [the real reason] why you have done this." He replied, "I knew that people would come to console me using God's name vainly by saying, 'May God recompense you!' I sacrificed my beard [to atone] for their vain mention of God Most High."

When An-Nuri heard a man making the call to prayer, he exclaimed, "Lies and poison of death!" Upon hearing a dog bark, he declared, "Here I am at your service!"

Someone commented, "This is heresy. He says to a believer who makes the testimony of God's unity, 'Lies and poison of death,' and he calls out 'Here I am at your service' to a barking dog!" When asked about this, An-Nuri asserted, "That man's mention of God was pure vanity. As for the dog, God Most High has said, '[The seven heavens and the earth and all beings therein] there is naught but celebrates His praise [but you do not understand their praise]'" (17:44).

One time ash-Shibli made the call to prayer. When he finished the two testimonies ["I bear witness that there is no god but God, I bear witness that Muhammad is the Messenger of God"], he stated, "If You had not ordered me to do so, I would not mention another along with You." A man once heard another man cry, "May God be exalted!" He responded, "I wish you would consider Him too exalted for this [using His name vainly]."

Abu'l-Hasan al-Khazafani (may God grant him mercy) stated, "[I say] 'There is no god but God' from my heart. [I say] 'Muhammad is the Messenger of God' from the earlobe [because I have been told to do so]." One who looks only to the surface of this expression imagines that he has belittled the religious law. But this is not the case, because to esteem other-than-God while being aware of His power is itself a form of belittling.

36

Sainthood

❧ Wilaya

God Most High says, "Behold! There is no fear on the saints of God, nor do they grieve" (10:62).

On the authority of 'A'isha (may God be pleased with her), the Prophet (may God's blessing and peace be upon him) stated, "God Most High says, 'Whoever harms a saint has called forth My battle against him. A servant best draws near to Me by performing the obligations I have enjoined on him. He continues to draw near to Me by means of supererogatory acts of worship until I love him. I hesitate in doing nothing as I hesitate in taking the spirit of My believing servant, for he abhors death, and I abhor offending him, but there is no escape from it.'"

The word *wali* (saint) has two meanings. One of them derives from the paradigm *fa'il* with a passive meaning. That is, God (may He be exalted) takes possession *(yatawalla)* of the saint's affairs. As God Most High says, "And He takes possession of the righteous" (7:196). He does not give him charge over himself even for an instant. God takes over caring for him. The second meaning derives from the paradigm *fā'il* with an intensified active sense. This applies to the one who actively undertakes worship of God and obedience to Him such that his acts of worship constantly succeed each other without any intervening rebelliousness. Both meanings must be present for the saint to be a true saint; his fulfillment of God's rights over him must be performed fully while God's constant guarding and preserving of him, in good times and bad, must also be present.

One of the qualifications of the saint is that God protect him [from the repeated commission of major sins], just as one of the qualifications of the prophet is that he be preserved [from all sins]. Anyone who acts in a manner objectionable to the divine law is deluded and deceived. The master Abu 'Ali ad-Daqqaq (may God grant him mercy) related, "Abu Yazid al-Bistami set out to find a man others had described as a saint. When Abu Yazid came to the man's mosque, he sat down and waited for him to come out. The man came out after having spat in the mosque. Abu Yazid left without greeting him, asserting, 'This is a man who cannot be trusted with maintaining correct behavior as stated in the divine law. How could he be a reliable keeper of God's secrets?'"

There is disagreement among the Sufis as to whether it is permissible for one to realize whether he is a saint or not. Some of them comment, "It is not permissible. The saint looks upon himself with contempt. If a miraculous deed takes place through him, he fears that it might be [a form of divine] guile, and he is always afraid that his outcome might be contrary to his current state." These Sufis contend that fidelity to sainthood until the very end [of one's life] is a part of sainthood. Many tales have been told on this matter about the sheikhs. The Sufi sheikhs who concur on this point are beyond reckoning. If I were to engage in mentioning all they have said, I would have to go beyond the limits of the summary nature of this book. Among the sheikhs I have met who concur on this point is the *imam* Abu Bakr b. Furak (may God grant him mercy). However, some of the Sufis claim, "It is permissible that the saint know he is a saint, and fidelity to sainthood until the end [of one's life] is not a condition for attaining sainthood in the present."

If such fidelity were a condition for attaining sainthood [in the present], then it is conceivable that a saint would be favored with a particular miraculous deed by which God would be notifying him of the surety of his final end. Now, belief in the possibility of the saint's miraculous deeds is obligatory. Even if [the state of] the saint is mingled with fear for his final outcome, his reverence, glorification, and exaltation of God in the present are more complete and firm [and hence predominate]. A small amount of glorification and reverence quickens the heart more effectively than does an abundance of terrific fear. When the Prophet (may God's blessing and peace be upon him) said, "Ten of my companions will be in Paradise," then those ten most certainly believed the Messenger of God and knew the surety of their final end. This did not lessen their state in the present.

A correct understanding of prophethood requires a

grasp of the nature of miracles; a corollary of this is knowledge of the nature of the saints' miraculous deeds. It is therefore impossible for the saint, when he observes a miraculous deed taking place through him, not to distinguish it from a miracle of the kind performed by prophets. If he beholds something such as this, the saint knows that he is on the path of truth. Therefore, it is permissible for him to know that his final end will be this state [of sainthood]. Being granted this knowledge is in itself one of his miraculous deeds. The doctrine of the saints' miraculous deeds is true, as many of the Sufi tales attest. I mention some of them in the chapter on miraculous deeds.* Among the sheikhs I have met who concur on this point is the master Abu 'Ali ad-Daqqaq (may God grant him mercy).

It is said that Ibrahim b. Adham asked a man, "Would you like to be a saint of God?" He said, "Yes." Ibrahim replied, "Then desire not the things of this world or of the next. Empty yourself for God Most High. Turn your face to Him so that He may turn to you and make you His saint." Yahya b. Mu'adh thus described the saints: "They are servants clothed with intimacy with God Most High after suffering and who embrace rest after striving when they arrive at the station of sainthood."

Abu Yazid stated, "The saints of God are His brides, and none looks upon brides save those of their family. They are veiled in seclusion in His presence by intimacy. No one sees them, neither in this world nor the next." I heard Abu Bakr as-Saydalani, who was a righteous man, relate, "I used to repair the gravestone

---

* "*Karamat al-awliya*'", a chapter beyond the states and stations portion here translated.

at the grave of Abu Bakr at-Tamastani one time in the cemetary of al-Hira and engraved his name upon it, many times. Every time the stone was dug out and stolen, although the other graves were untouched. Perplexed about this, I asked Abu 'Ali ad-Daqqaq (may God grant him mercy), who explained, 'That sheikh preferred anonymity in this world, but you wanted to give him a gravestone that would promote his memory. God (may He be exalted) determined that his grave remain as concealed as he preferred himself to be in this life.'" Abu 'Uthman observed, "The saint might be known far and wide, but he is not tempted by this." An-Nasrabadhi commented, "The saints make no demands; they are [outwardly] weak and unknown." He also said, "The farthest step of the saints is the very first step of the prophets."

Sahl b. 'Abdallah remarked, "The saint's actions are perpetually in accord with the divine law." Yahya b. Mu'adh declared, "The saint does nothing for the sake of men's approval, nor is he hypocritical." How few are the friends of one whose character is such! Abu 'Ali al-Juzjani stated, "The saint passes away in his state and abides in the witnessing of God [may He exalted]. God takes over his affairs so that, by that direction, lights come upon him without interruption. He knows nothing of himself, nor does he take comfort from other-than-God."

Abu Yazid reported, "The allotted portions of the saints derive from four divine names. Each party of the saints acts according to one of those names: the First, the Last, the Outward, and the Inward. When a saint passes away from them after being clothed in them, he is perfected. One whose state derives from God's name 'the Outward' beholds the wonders of His might. One whose state derives from God's name 'the Inward' beholds the divine lights [that shine in] the inner aspects of things. One whose state derives from His name 'the First' is occupied with the past. One whose state derives from His name 'the Last' is linked with the future. Each is given manifestation of these names according to his capacity except [the saint] whom God has taken over and sustained for Himself." These words of Abu Yazid indicate that the elect of God's servants rise above these divisions, not being occupied [only] with the future, nor thinking [only] of what has preceded the present, nor being taken up with whatever befalls them. Such is the case with those who have attained inner realities; they are effaced of the qualities of created beings. As God Most High says, "You thought them to be awake when they were asleep" (18:17).

Yahya b. Mu'adh declared, "The saint is a fragrant plant placed in the earth by God. The truthful take in his fragrance, and it comes into their hearts so that they long for their Master. Then they increase their worship according to their different natures." Al-Wasiti was asked, "How is the saint nourished in his sainthood?" He replied, "In the beginning, he is nourished by his worship. In his maturity, he is nourished by God's veiling him in His imperceptibility. Then He lures him back to his former qualities and attributes; and finally, He causes him to taste the nourishment of being subsisted by Him at all times." It is said, "There are three signs of the saint: He is occupied with God. He flees to God. He is concerned only with God."

Al-Kharraz said, "When God wishes to befriend one of His servants, He opens for him the gate of His remembrance. When he experiences the sweetness of remembrance, He opens for him the gate of nearness. Then He raises him to the gatherings of His intimacy. Then He settles him upon the throne of unity. Then He lifts the veil from him and leads him into the abode of unicity and reveals for him the divine splendor and majesty. When his eyes fall upon the divine splendor and majesty, naught of himself remains. Thereupon the servant is entirely extinguished for a time. After this he comes under God's exalted protection, free from any pretensions of his self."

Abu Turab an-Nakhshabi stated, "Whenever any man's heart becomes habituated to turning away from God, the event is noticed by the saints of God Most High."

It is said, "One of the attributes of the saint is that he has no fear, for fear is anticipating some disagreeable event that might come or expecting that something beloved might pass away in the future. The saint is concerned only with the present moment. He has no future to fear." Just as he has no fear, the saint also has no hope, for hope is expecting something good to occur or something disagreeable to be taken away. That, too, is beyond the present moment. The saint also feels no grief because grief is a hardship of the heart. How could one who feels the glow of contentedness and the pleasures of being in harmony with the divine law grieve? God Most High says, "Behold! There is no fear upon the saints of God nor do they grieve" (10:62).

37

Supplicatory Prayer

❧ Du'a

God Most High says, "Call upon your Lord in prayer, humbly and in secret" (7:55). He (Glorious and Majestic) says, "Your Lord says, 'Call upon Me, I will answer you'"(40:60).

On the authority of Anas b. Malik (may God be pleased with him), the Messenger of God (may God's blessing and peace be Upon him) is reported to have said, "Supplicatory prayer is the essence of worship."

Supplicatory prayer is the answer for every need. It is the resting place for those in want, a shelter for those disturbed, a relief for those with desires. God Most High brought low a people who abandoned prayer, observing, "They drew in their hands" (9:67). It is said that this means, "They did not raise their open hands to Us to ask through prayer."

Sahl b. 'Abdallah related, "God Most High brought forth creation and said, 'Entrust Me with your secrets. If you do not do this, then look toward Me. If you do not do this, then listen to Me. If you do not do this, then wait at My door. If you do none of this, [at least] tell me of your needs.'" Sahl also said, "The prayer most likely to be answered is the prayer of the moment," by which he meant the one the supplicant is forced to make because of his pressing need for what he prays for.

Abu 'Abdallah al-Makanisi said, "I was with al-Junayd when a woman came to him requesting, 'Pray to God on my behalf to return my son to me, for he is lost.' He told her, 'Go, and have patience.' So she left. Then she returned and asked him again. Al-Junayd said, 'Go, and have patience.' She left and returned again. This happened many times; each time al-Junayd told her to have patience. She exclaimed at last, 'My patience is exhausted. I cannot bear it any longer. Pray for me!' Al-Junayd replied, 'If this is true, then go now, for your son has come back.' She left, and she found her son. She returned to thank al-Junayd. Someone asked al-Junayd, 'How did you know [that the son had come back]?' He explained, 'God Most High says, "Who is the One Who answers the one in distress when he calls upon Him and Who removes evil?"'" (27:62).

People dispute whether praying or keeping silent and being content is better. Among them are some who say, "Supplicatory prayer is in itself an act of worship because the Prophet [may God's blessing and peace be upon him] has declared, 'Supplicatory prayer is the essence of worship.' It is better to perform anything that is an act of workship than to omit it. In addition, it is a right due to God. Even if He does not answer the servant's prayer and the servant receives no advantage by the prayer, he has [at least] granted his Lord's right because prayer is the outward expression of the neediness of servitude." Abu Hazim al-A'raj said, "Not being able to pray is more distressing to me than being unanswered in my prayers."

There are others who assert, "Silence and being inactive under the flow of the divine decree are better than prayer. Being content with whatever God has chosen for us is more proper than praying [for some alteration to His choice]." For this reason al-Wasiti said, "Choosing what has been determined for you in preeternity is better for you than opposing the present state of affairs." The Prophet (may God's blessing and peace be upon him) stated, "God Most High said, 'I give more to the one who is so occupied with My remembrance that he does not ask things of Me than I give to the supplicants.'"

There is a third group, who say, "The servant must pray with his tongue while, at the same time, being content in his heart, thus combining the two possibilities."

The most fitting stance to be taken on this matter is to say that times [and circumstances] vary. In some states, supplicatory prayer is better and the most correct course to take; in other states, maintaining silence is better. This can be known only at the moment because knowledge of the moment can be reached only at the moment. If one finds his heart inclining toward prayer, then prayer is best. If he finds his heart inclining toward silence, then silence is best.

It is also correct to say that it is not proper for the servant to be heedless of witnessing his Lord Most High when he is in the state of supplicatory prayer. He must also pay close attention to his state. If he experienecs increased expansion in his state from prayer, then prayer is best for him. If he experiences something such as constraint and his heart becomes constricted at the time of making prayer, then it is best for him to give up making prayer at that time. If he experiences neither of these, then continuing with the prayer or leaving it are equal at that point. If his main concern is with the religious sciences, then supplicatory prayer is best, for it is an act of worship. If his main concern is with gnosis, [spiritual] states and silence, then refraining from supplicatory prayer is best. In matters that concern the fate of the Muslim community or that relate to one's duty to God, making prayer is better than not making it, but in matters concerning the needs of the self, silence is better.

A tradition relates, "When a servant whom God loves prays to Him, He says, 'O Gabriel, delay answering the need of My servant, for I love hearing his voice.' When a servant whom God dislikes prays to Him, God says, 'O Gabriel, answer My servant's need, for I dislike hearing his voice.'" It is related that Yahya b. Sa'id al-Qattan (may God grant him mercy) saw God (may He be exalted) in his sleep and exclaimed, "O my God, how many times I have prayed to you and You have not answered me!" He said, "O Yahya, this is because I love hearing your voice."

The Prophet (may God's blessing and peace be upon him) explained, "By the One in Whose hand is my soul, when he with whom God is angry prays to Him, He refuses him. Then he prays to Him again, and He refuses him again. Again he prays to Him and He refuses him. Then God Most High tells His angels, 'My servant refuses to pray to other-than-Me, so I have answered him.'"

Anas b. Malik (may God be pleased with him) related, "There was a man during the time of the Prophet (may God's blessing and peace be upon him) who traded between Syria and Medina. He used to go alone on his journeys, without accompanying the caravans, out of his trust in God [Glorious and Majestic]. One time when he was going from Syria to Medina, a thief came up to him on a horse and cried to the merchant, 'Stop! Stop!' The merchant stopped and told him, 'Take my goods and get out of my way!' The thief replied, 'The goods are easily taken. I want you.' The merchant asked him, 'What do you want with me? Take the goods and get out of my way!' The thief repeated what he had said before. The merchant retorted, 'Wait until I make ablution and pray to my Lord.' He said, 'Go ahead and do what you must.' So the merchant rose, made his ablution, and prayed four cycles of prayer. Then he raised his hands to the heavens and prayed, 'O Loving One, O Loving One, O Lord of the Glorious Throne, O One from Whom all begins and to Whom all returns, O One Who does what You wish, I ask You by the light of Your countenance that fills the corners of Your Throne, I ask You by Your power by which You command Your creation, and by Your mercy that encompasses all things, there is no god but You, O Helper, come to my aid!' He said this three times. When he was finished with his prayer, a rider on a grey horse, wearing green garments and holding a lance made of light, suddenly appeared. When the thief saw the rider, he left the merchant and started toward the rider. When he came near, the rider charged him and landed a blow on him that threw him from his horse. Then he came up to the merchant and demanded, 'Get up and kill him!' The merchant responded, 'Who are you? I have never killed anyone and would take no pleasure in killing him.' The rider then went back to the thief and killed him, returned to the merchant, and declared, 'I am an angel from the third heaven. When you made your first prayer, we heard a noise at the gates of the heavens. We said, "Something evil has happened." When you made your second prayer, the gates opened and sparks of fire shot out. When you made your third prayer, Gabriel [peace be upon him] descended to our heaven, crying, "Who will come to the aid of this one in distress?" I prayed to my Lord to allow me to kill that thief. Know, O servant of God, that God will relieve and help one who makes this prayer of yours in any moment of distress, calamity, or desperation.' The merchant went on after that in safety until he reached Medina and came to the Prophet, to whom the merchant told the story of his journey and of the prayer he had made. The Prophet told him, 'God has inspired you with His most beautiful names to which, when invoked by them, He responds. When asked for something by them, He bestows it.'"

One of the requirements for correct behavior in making supplicatory prayer is to have presence of heart. It must not be heedlessly made. It has been related that the Prophet (may God's blessing and peace be upon him) said, "God Most High will not answer the prayer of the servant whose heart is heedless." Another requirement for correct behavior in making supplicatory prayer is that one's food be lawfully obtained. The Prophet asserted, "If your livelihood is made in a rightful way, your prayer will be answered." It has been said, "Supplicatory prayer is the key to that which one needs, and the ridges of the key are lawfully obtained food."

Yahya b. Mu'adh used to say, "O my God, I am such a sinner; how can I pray to You? You are so generous; how can I not pray to You?"

It is said that Moses (peace be upon him) passed by a man who was humbly praying to God. Moses declared, "O my God, if his need were in my hands, I would answer his prayer." God Most High revealed to him, "I am more compassionate toward him than you are. He is praying to Me, but his heart is taken up with his sheep. I will not answer the prayer of a servant of Mine whose heart is taken up with other-than-Me." When Moses told the man of this, he turned his heart with all attention to God Most High, and his affairs were settled.

Someone asked Ja'far as-Sadiq, "Why is it that we pray, but we are never given an answer?" He replied, "This is because you pray to One of Whom you have no knowledge."

I heard the master Abu 'Ali ad-Daqqaq (may God grant him mercy) relate, "Ya'qub b. al-Layth was stricken with a disease that confounded the doctors. They told him, 'There is a righteous man in your land called Sahl b. 'Abdallah. If he were to pray for you, God [may He be exalted] might answer his prayer.' So he summoned Sahl and instructed, 'Pray to God for me.' Sahl asked, 'How could my prayer for you be answered while you hold people unjustly in your prison?' So Ya'qub b. al-Layth released all his prisoners. Sahl prayed, 'O God, just as you have shown him the disgrace of disobedience to You, show him the glory of obedience to You and take away his suffering.' Ya'qub b. al-Layth was cured. He tried to give Sahl riches and property, but Sahl refused. Someone told Sahl, 'If you would only accept it, you could give it to the poor.' Some time later Sahl was looking at the pebbles in the desert; they were transformed into precious jewels. He asked his companions, 'What need does one who is given such bounty have of the wealth of Ya'qub b. al-Layth?'"

It is said that Salih al-Murri would often assert, "Whoever is persistent in knocking at the door is on the verge of having it opened for him." Rabi'a asked him, "How long are you going to say this? When was the door closed so that one had to ask to have it opened?" Salih replied, "An aged man was ignorant of the truth and a woman knew it!"

As-Sari related, "I attended the gathering of Ma'ruf al-Karkhi one time. A man went up to him and requested, 'O Abu Mahfuz, pray to God on my behalf to return my satchel to me. It was stolen and it contained one thousand dinars.' Ma'ruf fell silent. The man repeated his request. Ma'ruf remained silent. The man repeated his request another time. Then Ma'ruf responded, 'What should I say? "Return to him what You have withheld from Your prophets and pure saints?"' but the man persisted, 'Pray on my behalf to God.' Ma'ruf prayed, 'O God, choose what is best for him.'"

It is related that al-Layth said, "I saw 'Uqba b. Nafi' one time and he was blind. Then I saw him again and he could see. I asked him, 'How was your sight

returned?' He answered, '[A voice] called out to me in my sleep, "Say, 'O Near One, O One Who answers, O Hearer of my prayer, O Kind One in what He wishes, restore my sight for me.'" I repeated this and God [Glorious and Majestic] gave me back my sight.'"

The master Abu 'Ali ad-Daqqaq reported, "I had a painful disease in my eyes when I first returned from Marv to Nishapur. It had been some time since I had been able to sleep. One morning I fell into a light sleep and heard someone asking me, 'Is God not sufficient for His servant?' (39:36). I woke up and found that the inflammation had gone from my eyes and the pain stopped immediately. After that I was never afflicted with eye disease."

It is related that Muhammad b. Khuzayma said, "I was in Alexandria when Ahmad b. Hanbal died. I was filled with sadness. I saw Ahmad b. Hanbal in my sleep after that, and he was dancing about. I inquired, 'O Abu 'Abdallah, what sort of movement is this?' He replied, 'This is the manner of movement of the servants in the abode of peace.' I asked, 'What has God done with you?' He answered, 'He forgave me, placed a crown on my head, and gave me golden sandals to wear. God told me, "O Ahmad, all this is because you maintained the Qur'an to be My word." Then He said, "O Ahmad, pray to Me with the words you received from Sufyan ath-Thawri, which you used to say when you were on earth." So I prayed, "O Lord of everything, by Your power over everything, forgive me for everything and do not question me about anything." God then declared, "O Ahmad, this is Paradise. Enter!" And I entered.'"

It is said that there was once a young man who would clutch the draping that covers the Kaʻba and exclaim, "O my God, there is no one to be approached other than You, nor is there any mediator who might be bribed [to gain access to You]. If I obey You, it is because of Your bountiful grace, and all praise belongs to You. If I disobey You, it is because of my ignorance and conceit. You have a clear proof against me by means of Your evidence against me and by means of my lack of proof in Your presence unless You forgive me." Then he heard a voice call, "This young man is freed from Hell."

It is said, "The benefit of supplicatory prayer is in making a need known before God. If it is not made, the Lord will do as He wishes." It is also said, "The prayer of the common people is made by their words, the prayer of the ascetics is made by their actions, and the prayer of the gnostics is made by their states." And it is said, "The best prayer is the one kindled by sorrow."

One of the Sufis declared, "When you ask God Most High for something in prayer and it is granted you, then forthwith ask Him for Paradise. It might be that that day is the day you will be answered." It is said, "The tongues of the beginners are fluent in supplicatory prayer, but the tongues of those who have attained inner realities are reduced to silence."

When al-Wasiti was asked to make a prayer, he replied, "I am afraid that if I make a prayer, God will say to me, 'If you are asking Me for something that is already determined for you, then you have doubted Me. If you are asking Me for something that is not to come to you, then you have not praised Me as you

should. But if you are content, then in time I will bring about all things I have already determined for you.'"

It is related that 'Abdallah b. Munazil reported, "I have not made a prayer for fifty years, and I do not wish another to pray in my behalf." It is said, "Supplicatory prayer is a ladder for sinners." It is also said, "Prayer is an exchange of messages. As long as the two sides continue, all will be well." And it is said, "Sinners speak their prayers by their tears."

The master Abu 'Ali ad-Daqqaq (may God grant him mercy) remarked, "When the sinner weeps, he has started the exchange of communication with God [Glorious and Majestic]." On this they recite:

> *The young man's tears reveal what he hides within;*
> *His breaths make clear what his heart holds secret.*

One of the Sufis stated, "Making prayer means abandoning sins" It is said, "Supplicatory prayer is the lover's way of expressing his longing."

It is said, "Granting the servant the ability to pray is better for him than granting [his prayer]." Al-Kattani declared, "God Most High has given the believer the ability to ask for pardon only so that He may open the door to forgiveness." It is also said, "Making prayer causes you to be present with God, and being granted your prayer causes you to turn away. Standing at the door is better than making off with the reward." It is said, "Prayer means facing God directly [and speaking] with the tongue of shame." It is said, "A requirement for prayer is that one accept the outcome with contentment."

It is also said, "How can you wait for the answer to your prayer when you have blocked its path by committing sins?"

Someone asked one of the Sufis to pray on his behalf. The Sufi responded, "What greater distance could you create between yourself and God than by placing an intermediary between yourself and Him?"

'Abd ar-Rahman b. Ahmad said, "I heard my father relate that a woman came to Taqi b. Makhlad and told him, 'The Byzantines have taken my son prisoner. I have nothing other than my house, and I cannot sell that. If only you could lead me to one who could ransom him, for I know not which is night and which is day; I cannot sleep or rest.' He told her, 'All right. Go until I have looked into the matter, if God wills.' Then the sheikh bowed his head and moved his lips. We waited for some days. Then the woman came along with her son and began to call out to the sheikh, 'He has come back safely, and he has something to tell you.' The boy related, 'I was under the charge of a Byzantine prince along with a group of prisoners. The prince had a man who made us work every day. He would take us out into the desert for work and then return us, in chains. Once we were coming from our work after sunset with this man who watched over us. The chains suddenly were split and fell from my legs onto the ground.' The boy described the day and the hour this happened, and it was the same time that the woman had come to the sheikh and he had made his prayer. He continued, 'The guard pounced on me and exclaimed, "You have broken this chain!" I said, "No, it fell from my legs!" That man was in a quandry. He called his

companions, who brought the ironsmith. They shackled me again. But when I took a few steps, the chain fell from my legs once more. They were amazed and they called for their priests. The priests asked me, "Do you have a mother?" I affirmed, "Yes." They declared, "Her prayer has been answered. God has set you free. We cannot keep you in chains." Then they gave me food and provisions and sent me off with an escort who led me to the Muslims' territory.'"

38

Poverty

≈ Faqr

God Most High says, "[Alms are] for the poor who are in need for the cause of God, who cannot move about in the land [seeking livelihood]. The ignorant one thinks them wealthy because of their restraint [in asking]. You will know them by their mark: they do not beg from men in a demanding way. Whatever wealth you give, God is well aware of it" (2:273).

On the authority of Abu Hurayra, the Prophet (may God's blessing and peace be upon him) is reported to have said, "The poor will enter Paradise five hundred years before the rich. In the reckoning of Paradise this equals one half of a day." On the authority of 'Abdallah, the Messenger of God (may God's blessing and peace be upon him) is said to have observed, "The indigent one is not he who wanders about hoping to be thrown a mouthful or two, or a date or two." Someone asked, "Who then is the indigent one?" He replied, "He is one who cannot meet his essential needs and who is ashamed to beg from men, nor are they aware of him so that he might be given charity." This saying, "He is ashamed to beg from men," means that he is ashamed before God to beg from men, not that he is ashamed before men.

Poverty is the distinguishing trait of the saints, the adornment of the pure, and God's chosen quality for His elect—the righteous and the prophets. The poor are the elect of God (Glorious and Majestic) among His servants. They are the vessels among His creation for His secrets, by whom God safeguards creation and by whose blessedness nourishment is spread among men. The patient poor ones will be the companions of God Most High on the Day of Resurrection, as it is told in the tradition on the authority of 'Umar b. al-Khattab (may God be pleased with him), who said that the Messenger of God (may God's blessing and peace be upon him) said, "There is a key to everything, and the key to Paradise is love of the indigent. The patient poor are those who will be the companions of God Most High on the Day of Resurrection."

It is reported that a man brought ten thousand dirhams to Ibrahim b. Adham, but Ibrahim refused to take them from him, saying, "You want to blot out my name from the register of the poor with ten thousand dirhams! I will never take this!" Mu'adh an-Nasafi asserted, "God has never destroyed a people, whatever [evil] they commit, unless they hold the poor in contempt and humiliate them."

It is said that if the poor had no other virtue in the view of God than their wish and longing that provisions be abundant and cheap among the Muslims, this would be sufficient, for they need to buy the goods and the rich need to sell them. This is the case with the common people of those who are poor, so consider how it is with the elect among them.

When Yahya b. Mu'adh was asked about poverty, he replied, "Its inner truth is that the servant is independent of all except God, and its sign is the absence of all property." Ibrahim al-Qassar said, "Poverty is a garment, which, once attained, brings forth contentment."

A poor man came to the master Abu 'Ali ad-Daqqaq in the year 394 or 395 from Zuzan. He wore sackcloth and a hat made of sackcloth. One of the master's companions asked him in jest, "How much did you pay for this sackcloth?" He answered, "I paid for it with this world, and the afterlife was offered to me for it. But I will not sell it at that price."

The master Abu 'Ali ad-Daqqaq related, "A poor man once came to a gathering to beg for some charity, saying, 'I have gone hungry for three days.' One of the sheikhs there called out to him, 'You lie! Poverty is God's secret. He does not entrust His secret to one who displays it to whomever he wishes!'" Hamdun al-Qassar observed, "When Iblis and his legions gather together, they delight in nothing so much as a believer who has killed a believer, a man who dies in a state of unbelief, or a heart that harbors fear of poverty."

Al-Junayd said, "O you poor ones, you are made known by God, and honored on His account. But look to how your state will be when you are alone with Him." Al-Junayd was asked, "Which is the better state: being needy and dependent on God or being made wealthy by Him?" He replied, "If one's neediness is sound, then one's wealthiness with Him is sound. If one's wealthiness with Him is sound, then one's neediness and dependence on Him are also perfected. Do not ask, 'Which is the better state?' for they are two states neither of which is complete without the other."

Ruwaym declared, when asked about the sign of the poor one, "It is submitting the soul to God's ordinances." It is said that there are three signs of the poor one: He protects his inmost being. He performs his religious obligations. He conceals his poverty. Someone asked Abu Sa'id al-Kharraz, "Why does the beneficence of the rich not reach the poor ones?" He answered, "For three reasons: Their riches are ill gained, they are not enabled to give charity, and affliction of the poor is willed."

It is said that God (Glorious and Majestic) revealed to Moses (peace be upon him), "When you encounter the poor, ask after them just as you do with the rich. If you fail to do this, then throw all I have taught you in the dirt." It is related that Abu'd-Darda' asserted, "I would rather fall from the walls of a castle and be smashed to bits than sit together with the rich because I heard the Messenger of God [may God's blessing and peace be upon him] say, 'Beware of sitting together with the dead.' Someone asked him, 'Who are the dead?' He answered, 'The rich.'" Someone remarked to ar-Rabi' b. Khuthaym, "Prices are rising sky high!" He retorted, "We are not worthy of being made hungry by God. He does this only for His saints." Ibrahim b. Adham observed, "We asked for poverty, and wealth came to us. The rest of the people asked for wealth, and poverty came to them."

A man asked Yahya b. Mu'adh, "What is poverty?" He

said, "Fear of poverty." The man inquired, "Then what is wealth?" He replied, "Security with God Most High." Ibn al-Karanbi said, "The true poor one shuns wealth lest it come to him and corrupt his poverty, just as the rich one shuns poverty lest it come and corrupt his wealth." Abu Hafs was asked, "By what means does the poor one approach his Lord [Glorious and Majestic]?" He answered, "The poor one has nothing but his poverty with which to approach his Lord."

It is said that God Most High revealed to Moses (peace be upon him), "Would you like to be credited with an amount of good works equal to that of all mankind on the Day of Resurrection?" Moses replied, "Yes." God instructed, "Then visit the sick and make sure that the poor have clothing." Moses then set aside seven days in each month to go among the poor and inspect their clothing and visit the sick.

Sahl b. 'Abdallah declared, "There are five instances of nobility of soul: a poor man who pretends to be free of want, a hungry man who pretends to be satiated, a grieving man who pretends happiness, a man who has an enemy but pretends love for him, and a man who fasts by day and stays up the night [in prayer] without showing weakness." Bishr b. al-Harith said, "The best station is that of firm belief in patience through poverty until the grave." Dhu'n-Nun observed, "A sign of God's displeasure with a servant is that the servant fears poverty."

Ash-Shibli commented, "The very least sign of poverty is that if all the wealth of this world were given to one man and he spent it all in charity in one day, but then it occurred to him that he should have saved enough for one day's food, he would not be truthful in his poverty." The master Abu 'Ali ad-Daqqaq said, "People question whether poverty or wealth is preferable. In my opinion it is best that a man be given enough to sustain him and then maintain himself within those limits."

Abu Muhammad Yasin related, "I asked Ibn al Jalla' about poverty. He fell silent; then he withdrew and went away. He returned a short time later and said, 'I had four coins, and I was ashamed before God [Glorious and Majestic] to speak about poverty until I had gotten rid of them.' Then he began to speak about poverty." Ibrahim b. al-Muwallad said, "I asked Ibn al-Jalla', 'When does the poor one deserve the name?' He replied, 'When nothing of it remains for him.' I inquired, 'How is that?' He answered, 'When he possesses it, he does not have it [poverty]. And when he no longer possesses it, then he has it.'" It is said that a sound state of poverty is when the poor one is not satisfied with any aspect of his poverty other than the One of Whom he has need. 'Abdallah b. al-Mubarak observed, "Making oneself appear wealthy while in poverty is better than poverty."

Banan al-Misri related, "I was sitting in Mecca once, and there was a youth in front of me. A man came to him with a satchel filled with money and placed it before him. The youth said, 'I have no use for this.' The man retorted, 'Then distribute it among the poor.' In the evening I saw the youth in the valley begging for himself! I observed, 'It would have been better for you to have taken some money for yourself from that satchel.' He responded, 'I did not know that I would live to this moment.'"

Abu Hafs said, "The best means for the slave to reach his Master is by being constantly in need of Him in all states, adhering to the Sunna in all deeds, and seeking his nourishment in a lawful manner." Al-Murta'ish commented, "It is best that the poor one's aspiration not go beyond his steps."

Abu 'Ali ar-Rudhbari related, "There were four who were the models of [virtuous ways of poverty] in their time. One—Yusuf b. Asbat—would accept nothing from his brethren, nor from the ruler. He inherited seventy thousand dirhams from his brother but accepted none of it. He used to weave palm leaf mats with his own hands. The second—Abu Ishaq al-Fazari—would accept gifts from both his brethren and the ruler. He would spend what his brethren gave him on the poor whose poverty was hidden and who did not seek charity, and he would take what the ruler gave him to the deserving ones among the people of Tarsus. The third— 'Abdallah b. al-Mubarak—accepted gifts from his brethren but not from the ruler. He would take what his brethren gave him and then spend it [on others] together with a like amount. The fourth—Makhlad b. al-Husayn—would accept [gifts] from the ruler but not from his brethren. He used to say, 'The ruler does not hold one under obligation for gifts, but my brethren do.'"

The master Abu 'Ali ad-Daqqaq said, "There is a tradition that says, 'The one who humbles himself before a rich man on account of his wealth loses two thirds of his religion.' This is because a man consists of his heart, his tongue, and his outward person. If he humbles himself before a rich man with his outward person and his tongue, he loses two thirds of his religion. But if he humbles himself before him also with his heart, he loses his religion entirely."

It is said, "The very least that is required of a poor one in his poverty is four things: a knowledge that leads him, an abstemiousness that restrains him, a certainty that sustains him, and a remembrance that brings him intimacy." It is also said, "One who desires poverty because it is a noble state dies poor. One who desires poverty because it means he will not be occupied with other-than-God dies rich." Al-Muzayyin declared, "There used to be more paths leading to God than stars in the heavens. But none of them remain now except poverty, and it is the best of them all."

An-Nuri observed, "The mark of the poor one is contentedness when he has nothing and generosity when he has plenty." When asked about the inner truth of poverty, Ash-Shibli responded, "It is that the servant is not satisfied with anything less than God [Glorious and Majestic]." Mansur b. Khalaf al-Maghribi related, "Abu Sahl al-Khashshab al-Kabir told me, 'Poverty is poverty and humiliation' I replied, 'No. Rather say, "It is poverty and glory."' He said, 'Poverty and dust of the earth.' I retorted, 'No. Rather say, "It is poverty and the divine throne."'"

The master Abu 'Ali ad-Daqqaq commented on the tradition of the Prophet (may God's blessing and peace be upon him) "Poverty is near to being unbelief" by saying, "The harm that might come from a thing is in inverse proportion to its virtue and benefit. Whatever is most beneficial in itself has the most harmful quality as its opposite. Such is the case with 'faith.' Because it is the noblest quality, its opposite is 'unbelief.' Because the danger inherent in poverty is that it could become unbelief in God, we have proof that poverty is the noblest characteristic."

Al-Murta'ish said, "I heard al-Junayd instruct, 'When you meet a poor man, meet him with kindness, not with your learning. Kindness draws him close, and learning repels him.' I asked, 'O Abu'l-Qasim, does learning really repel the poor man?' He replied, 'Yes. If the poor man is truthful in his poverty, and you cast your learning upon him, it will melt just as lead melts in the fire.'" Muzaffar al-Qarmasini said, "The poor one is he who has no need of God." This expression is obscure in meaning when heard by one ignorant of the Sufis' aim. He merely indicates the cessation of making demands, the end of choice (by the poor one), and contentment with whatever God (may He be exalted) brings about.

Ibn Khafif stated, "Poverty means having no possessions and leaving behind the dictates of human attributes." Abu Hafs said, "Poverty is not complete for anyone until he prefers giving over receiving. Generosity is not that the one with wealth gives to the one with nothing; it is [in reality] that the one with nothing gives to the one with wealth."

Ibn al-Jalla' remarked, "If it were not for the [higher] noble purpose of being humble before God, it would be the way of the poor one to strut proudly when he walks." Yusuf b. Asbat said, "For forty years I have had only one shirt." One of the Sufis related, "I saw [in my dream] events such that the Day of Resurrection took place. It was said, 'Bring Malik b. Dinar and Muhammad

b. Wasi' into Paradise.' So I watched to see which one of them went in first, and it was Muhammad b. Wasi'. When I asked why he had preceded, it was explained to me, 'He owned only one shirt, but Malik owned two.'" Muhammad al-Musuhi said, "The poor one is the one who experiences no need himself for anything of the goods of the world." Sahl b. 'Abdallah was asked, "When can the poor one find rest?" He replied, "When he expects nothing other than the present moment for himself."

When there was talk about poverty and wealth in the presence of Yahya b. Mu'adh, he said, "Neither poverty nor wealth will carry any weight on the Day of Reckoning. Only patience and thankfulness will be weighed. Thus it will be said, 'He is thankful and he is patient.'"

It is told that God Most High revealed to one of the prophets (upon whom be peace), "If you wish to know whether I am pleased with you, look to whether the poor are pleased with you."

Abu Bakr az-Zaqqaq said, "One who has no fear of God along with his poverty consumes wholly unlawful food." It is related that the poor ones at the gatherings of Sufyan ath-Thawri were like princes. Abu Bakr b. Tahir stated, "Among the characteristics of the poor one is that he does not have a desire for (things of) this world. But if he does, and there is no doubt but that he will, then his desire will not go beyond what is sufficient for him."

One of the Sufis recited:

> They said, "Tomorrow is the festival day. What
>   will you wear?"
> I said, "The robe of honor given by One who
>   pours out love in generous droughts.
> Poverty and Patience, they are my garments
>   under which
> Is a heart for whom the Friend is all Fridays
>   and festivals combined."
> The most proper garment in which to meet the
>   Beloved
> On the day of visiting, is the garment He
>   has beloved.
> The whole of time is a season of morning for
>   me, if you are absent, O my hope,
> The festival is when I see and I hear you.

It is said that this poem is by Abu 'Ali ar-Rudhbari.

When asked about the true poor one, Abu Bakr al-Misri answered, "He is one who neither possesses [anything] nor wishes to possess." Dhu'n-Nun al-Misri said, "I prefer constant need for God Most High mixed with unease, over constant felicity mixed with pride."

Abu 'Abdallah al-Husri related, "Abu Ja'far al-Haddad worked for twenty years, making one dinar each day. He spent it on the poor while he would fast; then he would go around seeking charity after the sunset prayer in order to break his fast." An-Nuri observed, "The mark of the poor one is contentment when he has nothing and generosity and selfless giving when he has much."

Muhammad b. 'Ali al-Kattani said, "There was a young man with us in Mecca who wore old tattered rags. He never entered into conversation with us or sat with us. I felt great affection for him in my heart. Once I was given two hundred dirhams from a lawful source. I brought the money to him, put it down on the edge of his prayer mat, and told him, 'This has come to me from a lawful source. Spend it on yourself for what you need.' Looking at me with disdain, he revealed what had been unknown to me, 'I purchased this opportunity to sit with God Most High in unencumbered devotion for seventy-thousand dinars over and above my properties and estates. You want now to cheat me out of this for this money that you offer!' Then he stood up and threw down the money. I sat and gathered it up from the ground. I have never witnessed such dignity as his when he walked away, nor such humiliation as was mine as I gathered up the money."

Abu 'Abdallah b. Khafif remarked, "I have not been obliged to pay the poor-due at the end of Ramadan for forty years, while enjoying a great reception among the elect and the common people." Abu Ahmad as-Saghir said, "I asked Abu 'Abdallah b. Khafif, 'What would a dervish be called who was hungry for three days and went out and asked for [charity] enough to meet his needs?' He said, 'A beggar. Go, eat, and be quiet. If a dervish uses these means, all of you will be disgraced.'"

When ad-Duqqi was asked about bad conduct among the dervishes before God in their affairs, he said, "It consists in their descending from [seeking] inner truths to scholastic learning." Khayr an-Nassaj related, "I entered a mosque, and there was a dervish there.

When he saw me, he clung to me, pleading, 'O Sheikh, have compassion for me, for my suffering is great!' I inquired, 'How is that?' He answered, 'I have been deprived of being tried, and I am always in good health!' I watched him, and he was being given alms." Abu Bakr al-Warraq said, "Blessed is the poor one in this world and the Hereafter." When he was asked what he meant, he replied, "The ruler in this world does not demand taxes from him, and the All-Powerful One in the Hereafter will not call him to account."

39

Sufism

❧ Tasawwuf

Purity *(safa')* is an admirable attribute in every tongue, and its opposite, impurity, is blameworthy. Abu Hujayfa related, "The Messenger of God [may God's blessing and peace be upon him] came out to us one day, his face drained of color, and said, 'The earth's purity has vanished, and only impurity remains. Today death is a blessing for every Muslim.'"

The designation 'Sufi' has become the common one for this group. Thus it is said of a man that he is a *"sufi"* and of the group as a whole that they are *"sufiya."* The man who tries to become like one of them is called *"mutasawwif,"* and these people as a whole are called *"mutasawwifa."*

There is no etymology or analogy with another word in the Arabic language to be drawn from the name *sufi.* The most plausible interpretation is that it is much like a surname. There are those who say that it comes from 'wool' *(suf).* Thus *"tasawwuf"* is used for the wearing of wool, just as *"taqammus"* is used for wearing a shirt (*qamis*). That is one possibility. But in fact the Sufis are not distinguished by wearing wool. Others say that the Sufis are related to [the men who sat on the] bench (*suffa*) outside the mosque of the Messenger of God (may God's blessings and peace be upon him). But the adjective of *"suffa"* would not take the form *sufi*. Another groups says that it is derived from *safa'*, "purity." The derivation of *"sufi"* from *"safa"* is unlikely from a linguistic point of view. Others say that it is derived from *saff* "row" or "rank," because the Sufis are in the foremost rank by virtue of their hearts. This is correct in meaning, but *sufi* cannot be the adjective of *saff*. In conclusion, this group [the Sufis] are so well known that it is not necessary to find an analogy or derivation for their designation.

Everyone who speaks on the meaning of Sufism and who is called a Sufi speaks according to his own experience. To go into this matter at length would take me beyond my intention to be brief in this work. I will mention here some of the Sufis' words on the subject in order to give a hint of their meanings, if God Most High wills.

When Muhammad al-Jurayri was asked about Sufism, he explained, "It means taking up every sublime moral characteristic and leaving behind every lowly one." Al-Junayd said, "Sufism means that God causes you to die to yourself and gives you life in Him." Al-Husayn b. Mansur, when asked about the Sufi, commented, "He is solitary by nature. No one accepts him, and he accepts no one." Abu Hamza al-Baghdadi said, "The mark of the true Sufi is that he becomes poor after having been rich, he experiences abasement after having been held in high esteem, and he becomes unknown after having been famous. The mark of the false Sufi is that he becomes rich after having been poor, he becomes the object of high esteem after having been abased, and he becomes famous after having been unknown."

'Amr b. 'Uthman al-Makki was asked about Sufism, and he asserted, "It is that the servant acts according to whatever is most fitting to the moment." Muhammad b. 'Ali al-Qassab stated, "Sufism consists of noble characteristics shown at a noble time by a noble man among noble people." When asked about Sufism, Samnun said, "It means that you possess nothing and nothing possesses you." Ruwaym observed about Sufism, "It means giving up the self to be with God in whatever manner He wishes." Al-Junayd was asked about Sufism, and he declared, "It is that you be solely with God with no attachments." Ruwaym b. Ahmad al-Baghdadi said, "Sufism is founded on three traits: adhering to poverty and dependence on God, attaining the virtues of generosity and selfless giving, and abandoning resistance and choice." Ma'ruf al-Karkhi explained, "Sufism is holding to hidden realities and severing hope from all that is in the hands of men."

Hamdun al-Qassar said, "Befriend the Sufis, for they see reasons for excusing disagreeable acts and they are not impressed with good deeds to the point that they would think you great for performing them." When asked about the adherents of Sufism, Al-Kharraz responded, "They are a people who give until they experience expansion, who deprive themselves until

they lose everything. Then they are summoned by mysteries close unto them: [Say] 'Arise, weep over us.'"
Al-Junayd said, "Sufism is a war in which there is no peace." He also said, "The Sufis are members of a single household that none other than they can enter." He also explained, "Sufism is invocation [of God] together with inward concentration ecstasy together with attentive hearing, and action combined with following [the Sunna]."

Al-Junayd stated, "The Sufi is like the earth—every kind of abomination is thrown upon it, but naught but every kind of goodness grows from it." He also said, "The Sufi is like the earth—both the righteous man and the sinner walk upon it. He is like the clouds—they give shade to all things. He is like the raindrop—it waters all things." He also remarked, "If you see a Sufi caring for his outer appearance, then know that his inward being is corrupt."

Sahl b. 'Abdallah commented, "The Sufi is he who would not object if his blood were shed and his property taken." An-Nuri said, "A sign of the Sufi is that he is content when he has nothing and he gives selflessly when he has much." Al-Kattani asserted, "Sufism is good moral characteristics. Whoever surpasses you in good moral characteristics surpasses you in purity." Abu 'Ali ar-Rudhbari said, "Sufism is staying at the lover's door even when you are driven away." He also stated, "Sufism is the purity of nearness after the impurity of remoteness." It is said, "The most odious thing of all is the miserly Sufi." It is also said, "Sufism is an empty hand and a pure heart." Ash-Shibli observed, "Sufism is sitting with God, without care." Abu Mansur said, "The Sufi is one whose indication is from God Most High, for surely man indicates something of God." Ash-Shibli stated, "The Sufi is separated from mankind and united with God as He says [to Moses], 'I have attached you to Myself (20:41), cutting him off from all else. Then He said to him, 'You will never see Me'" (7:143). Ash-Shibli also said, "The Sufis are children in the lap of God," "Sufism is a flaming flash of lightning," and "Sufism is being protected from paying heed to creation." Ruwaym declared, "The Sufis remain full of goodness as long as they quarrel with one another. As soon as they make peace, there is no good in them."

Al-Jurayri said, "Sufism means maintaining a vigilant awareness over one's states and holding to correct behavior." Al-Muzayyin asserted, "Sufism is submission to God." Abu Turab an-Nakhshabi remarked, "The Sufi is not made impure by anything, and by him all things are made pure." It is said, "The search does not tire the Sufi, and worldly things do not annoy him." When Dhu'n-Nun al-Misri was asked about the Sufis, he answered, "They are a people who prefer God [Glorious and Majestic] over all things and whom God prefers over all things." Al-Wasiti (may God grant him mercy) said, "At first the Sufis were given clear indications; then these became only motions, and now naught remains but sorrow."

An-Nuri was asked about the Sufi, and he replied, "He is one who heard the audition and who preferred the [mandated] causes [of salvation]." Abu Nasr as-Sarraj related, "I asked al-Husri, 'Who, in your opinion, is the Sufi?' He responded, 'The earth does not carry him, nor do the heavens shade him.'" He refers here to the Sufi's effacement. It is said, "The Sufi is one who, when presented with two goodly states or two moral characteristics, takes the better of the two." Ash-Shibli was asked, "Why are the Sufis called by this name?" He said, "It is because of the traces of the self that remain within them. If this were not the case, there would be no name attached to them." Ibn al-Jalla' was asked, "Who is called a 'Sufi'?" He answered, "We do not know him by the conditions set in learning. But we know that he is one who is poor, stripped of worldly causes. He is with God without being tied to a place, but God [may He be exalted] does not bar him from knowing all places. This is the one called a 'Sufi.'" One of the Sufis declared, "Sufism means a loss of dignity and rank and a blackening of the face in this world and in the Hereafter." Abu Ya'qub al-Mazabili explained, "Sufism is a state in which all human attributes fade away." Abu'l-Hasan as-Sirwani said, "The Sufi is he who is concerned with inspired states, not with litanies and recitations."

The master Abu 'Ali ad-Daqqaq (may God grant him mercy) said, "The choicest thing that has been said on this matter is, 'This path is fit only for those persons whose spirits God has used to sweep the dunghills.'" For this reason Abu 'Ali stated one day, "If the dervish had nothing left but his spirit and he offered it to the dogs at this door, not one dog would pay it any attention." The master Abu Sahl as-Su'luki said, "Sufism is turning away from inward objections [to what God has decreed]."

Al-Husri commented, "The Sufi is not existent after his non-existence nor is he non-existent after his existence." This point is not readily understood. When he says, "He is not existent after his non-existence," he means that after his defects have passed away, they do not return. When he says, "Nor is he non-existent after his existence," he means that if he is entirely oriented to God, he does not decline to the rank of mankind at large, so that worldly events have no effect on him.

It is said, "The Sufi is effaced in the flashes he receives from God." It is said, "The Sufi is overpowered by the flow of lordship and veiled by the demeanor of servitude." It is also said, "The Sufi does not change. But if he were to change, he would not grieve." Al-Kharraz related, "I was in the Kairouan mosque on the day of congregational prayer, and I saw a man going among the rows of worshipers saying, 'Show me charity, for I was a Sufi, and now I have become weak and feeble.' So I offered him some alms, and he said to me, 'Leave me be; woe unto you! This is not what I seek.' And he would not take the alms."

40

Correct Behavior

🕊 Adab

God Most High says, "His [the Prophet's] sight did not swerve nor did it stray" (53:17). It is said that this means, "He upheld the correct behavior of being in the presence of God." God Most High says, "Protect yourselves and your families from a fire [whose fuel is men and stones]" (66:6). Ibn 'Abbas said in commenting on this verse that it means, "Instruct them and teach them correct behavior."

On the authority of 'A'isha (may God be pleased with her), the Prophet (may God's blessing and peace be upon him) is reported to have declared, "It is the child's right that his father give him a good name, have him provided with pure and plentiful milk, and educate him in correct behavior and conduct."

It is related that Sa'id b. al-Musayyib said, "Whoever has no knowledge of what claims God [Glorious and Majestic] has over his person and is not versed in His commands and prohibitions has no access to correct behavior." It is told that the Prophet (may God's blessing and peace be upon him) said, "God instructed me in correct behavior and made excellent my instruction."

The inner truth of correct behavior is that all good traits are combined. Thus the one with correct behavior *(adib)* is the one in whom all good traits are combined. From this comes the word *"ma'duba"* "a banquet" i.e., a gathering for food.

The master Abu 'Ali ad-Daqqaq (may God grant him mercy) said, "The servant reaches Paradise by obeying God. He reaches God by observing correct behavior in obeying Him." He also said, "I saw someone who was about to move his hand during prayer to pick his nose, but his hand was stopped." He refers, obviously, to himself here because it is impossible for one man to know that the hand of another man was stopped. The master Abu 'Ali ad-Daqqaq never would lean against anything when he was sitting. One day he was in a gathering, and I wanted to put a cushion behind his back because I saw that he had no support. [After I placed the cushion behind him] he moved away from the cushion slightly. I thought he was wary of the cushion because it had no cloth or rug covering it. But he explained, "I do not want any support." After that I reflected on his state and [realized] he never would lean against anything.

Al-Jalajili al-Basri commented, "Asserting divine unity requires faith. So one who has no faith cannot assert divine unity. Faith requires [obeying] the divine law. So one who does not obey the divine law has no faith, nor has he asserted the divine unity. Obeying the divine law requires correct behavior. So one who does not observe correct behavior cannot obey the divine law, have faith, nor assert divine unity."

Ibn 'Ata' said, "Correct behavior means that you are occupied with commendable things." Someone asked, "What do you mean by this?" He replied, "This means that you observe correct behavior with God both inwardly and outwardly. If you conduct yourself in this way, you will have correct behavior, even if your speech is not that of an Arab." Then he recited:

> *When she spoke, she displayed full eloquence.*
> *When she was silent, again she was elo-*
> *quent.*

'Abdallah al-Jurayri related, "For twenty years, during my solitary retreat, I have not stretched my legs once. Upholding correct behavior with God is the best course." The master Abu 'Ali ad-Daqqaq (may God grant him mercy) declared, "One who associates with kings and displays unseemly manners will be consigned by his folly to be killed." It is related that Ibn Sirin was asked, "What kind of correct behavior brings one nearest to God?" He answered, "Having direct knowledge of His Lordship, acting out of obedience to Him, and giving thanks to Him for well-being and having patience through suffering." Yahya b. Mu'adh said, "If the gnostic abandons the correct behavior with the object of his gnosis, then surely he will perish along with the doomed."

The master Abu 'Ali ad-Daqqaq (may God grant him mercy) declared, "Abandoning correct behavior results in expulsion. One who is ill-mannered in the courtyard will be sent back to the gate. One who is ill-mannered at the gate will be sent to watch over the animals." Someone said to al-Hasan al-Basri, "So much has been said concerning the various sciences of correct behavior. Which of them are most beneficial in the world and most effective for [gaining a goodly reward in] the Hereafter?" He replied, "Learning religion, moderation in the world, and knowledge of what constitutes your duty toward God [Glorious and Majestic]."

Yahya b. Mu'adh said, "One who is well versed in correct behavior toward God Most High will become one of those God loves." Sahl observed, "The Sufis are those who ask God's help in [carrying out] His commands and who steadfastly observe correct behavior toward Him." Ibn al-Mubarak said, "We stand more in need of a small amount of correct behavior than a great deal of knowledge." He also said. "We sought the knowledge of correct behavior after those who taught it had passed away." It is related, "There are three things that will never make one feel a stranger [in a place]: avoiding corrupt people, displaying correct behavior, and refraining from causing harm to others." Sheikh Abu 'Abdallah al-Maghribi (may God be pleased with him) said these lines on this matter:

> *Three things adorn the stranger when he is*
> *away from home:*
> *First, observing correct behavior;*
> *Second, having excellent character;*
> *Third, shunning corrupt people.*

When Abu Hafs arrived in Baghdad, al-Junayd told him, "You have instructed your companions in the manners of sultans!" Abu Hafs replied, "Displaying refined maners on the outside is a token of refined manners on the inside." 'Abdallah b. al-Mubarak said, "Observing correct behavior is to the gnostic what repentance is to the novice."

Mansur b. Khalaf al-Maghribi related, "Someone said to a Sufi, 'What poor manners you have!' He retorted, 'I do not have poor manners.' The man asked, 'Who taught you manners?' The Sufi said, 'The Sufis.'" Abu'n-Nasr at-Tusi as-Sarraj observed, "People can be divided into three categories with respect to correct behavior: The people of this world are concerned with refinement of and correct behavior in using Arabic, with style and memorization of the sciences, with names of dynasties, and with Arabic poetry. The people of religion are concerned with training the soul, instructing man's outer faculties, observing the limits set by God, and abandoning passions. The elect are concerned with cleansing the heart, guarding the secrets, being faithful to oaths, holding to the present moment, stopping attention to stray thoughts, and having correct behavior at times of requesting when in the divine presence, and in the stations of nearness."

It is related that Sahl b. 'Abdallah stated, "He who subdues his soul with correct behavior worships God sincerely." It is said, "Perfection in correct behavior is reached only by the prophets and the veracious." 'Abdallah b. al-Mubarak asserted, "People hold many views on what constitutes correct behavior. We say, 'It is knowledge of the soul.'"

Ash-Shibli said, "Lack of restraint in speaking with God [may He be exalted] is an abandonment of correct behavior." Dhu'n-Nun al-Misri commented, "The gnostic's manners are better than the manners of anyone else because he has been instructed in his manners by the object of his gnosis." One of the Sufis remarked, "God [may He be exalted] says, 'I have made correct behavior binding on the one I have brought to take on My names and attributes. I have made perdition binding on the one barred from the inner reality of My essence.' So choose whichever you wish: correct behavior or perdition."

It is said that Ibn 'Ata' stretched his leg out one day when he was with his companions and observed, "Forsaking correctness among the people of correct behavior is an act of correct behavior." This statement is supported by the tradition in which it is related that the Prophet (may God's blessing and peace be upon him) was with Abu Bakr and 'Umar one day when 'Uthman came in to see him. The Prophet covered up his thighs and said, "Should I not have shame before a man in whose presence the angels are ashamed before him?" The Prophet indicated by this that however praiseworthy he held 'Uthman's modesty to be, the state of intimacy between himself and Abu Bakr and 'Umar was better. Close to the import of this tale are the lines:

> *I act with restraint and modesty, but when*
> *I sit with those possessing loyalty and honor,*
> *I set free my soul to its spontaneous way of*
> *being*
> *And I speak openly, without reticence.*

Al-Junayd declared, "When one's love is sound, the stipulations of correct behavior fall away." But Abu

'Uthman said, "When one's love is sound, adhering to correct behavior is an urgent requirement for the lover."

An-Nuri asserted, "He who does not observe correct behavior in the present moment will meet with a loathsome state." Dhu'n-Nun al-Misri said, "If the beginner on the Sufi path turns away from correct behavior, he is sent back whence he came." The master Abu 'Ali ad-Daqqaq (may God grant him mercy) explained concerning the verse "Job cried to his Lord, 'I am stricken with pain and You are the Most Merciful of those who show mercy'" (21:83), "Job did not say, 'Show me mercy!' because he was maintaining the correct behavior of address." In the same way Jesus (peace be upon him) stated, "If You punish [those making false claims as to what I have said], they are Your servants," (5:121) and "Had I said such a thing [asking men to worship me] then You would know of it" (5:121). He did not assert, "I never said such a thing!" because of his watchful attention to maintaining correct behavior in God's presence. Al-Junayd related, "A righteous man came to me one Friday requesting, 'Send one of the dervishes along with me to bring me happiness by eating with me.' So I looked around, and there was a dervish I knew to be in need. I called to him and told him, 'Go with this sheikh and bring him happiness.' It was but a short while before the man came back to me and said, 'O Abu'l-Qasim, that dervish ate only one mouthful and then left me!' I replied, 'Perhaps you said something that offended him.' He retorted, 'I said nothing.' I turned and found that dervish sitting nearby and asked him, 'Why did you not let him be happy [with hosting you]?' He answered, 'O my master, I left Kufa and came all the way to Baghdad without having eaten anything. I did not want to appear ill-mannered in your presence because of my poverty [and have to ask you for food], but when you called on me [to go with that sheikh], I was happy that you recognized my need before I said anything. I went along with him, wishing for him the felicity of Paradise. When I sat at his table, he set out a dish, saying, "Eat this, for I love it more than ten thousand dirhams." When I heard this, I knew that his aspirations were low. So I was loathe to eat his food.' I responded, 'Did I not tell you that you were ill-mannered in not allowing his happiness?' He said, 'O Abu'l-Qasim, I repent!' I told him to go back to the sheikh and gladden his heart."

41

Gnosis

٪ Ma'rifa Bi'llah

God Most High says, "They have not estimated God as He deserves to be estimated" (6:91). It is written in commentaries on this verse that it means "They have not known God as He deserves to be known."

On the authority of 'A'isha (may God be pleased with her), the Prophet (may God's blessing and peace be upon him) is reported to have stated, "The support of a house is its foundation. The support of religion is direct knowledge of God, certainty, and intelligence that safeguards against error." At this 'A'isha asked, "May my father and mother be ransomed for you, what is intelligence that safeguards against error?" He replied, "Refraining from disobedience to God and being eager to obey Him."

In the usage of the scholars, *ma'rifa* is *'ilm* (knowledge). Thus in their opinion all *'ilm* is *ma'rifa*, all *ma'rifa* is *'ilm,* and everyone who is *'alim* (knowledgeable) with respect to God is an *'arif* (gnostic) and vice versa. But among the Sufis, *ma'rifa* is the attribute of one who knows God (may He be exalted) by His names and attributes and is truthful toward God by his deeds, who then purifies himself of base qualities and defects, who stands long at the door, and who withdraws his heart continually (from worldly matters). Then he enjoys a goodly nearness to God, who verifies him as true in all his states. The temptations of his soul stop, and he does not incline his heart to any thought that would incite him to other-than-God for, when he becomes a stranger to men and is free of the calamities of his soul, when he is purified of joy in, and concern for, other-than-God, when his intimate prayers with God Most High in secret are constant, when he is sure in every glance of Him of his return to Him, and when God inspires him by making him aware of His secrets concerning his destiny, he is, at that time, called a "gnostic" *('arif)* and his state is called "gnosis" *(ma'rifa)*. In short, the degree of gnosis he will reach is determined by the degree to which he is estranged from his self.

When the sheikhs spoke on gnosis, each spoke of his own experience and indicated what came to him at a given moment. The master Abu 'Ali ad-Daqqaq (may God grant him mercy) said, "One of the signs of gnosis is the attainment of awe. For one whose gnosis increases, awe of God increases." He also stated, "Gnosis brings about utter tranquility to the heart, just as knowledge brings about peacefulness. So for one whose gnosis increases, tranquility increases." Ash-Shibli commented, "For the gnostic there is no attachment, for the lover there is no grievance, for the servant there is no claim, for the one who fears God there is no rest, and for no one is there escape from God." When ash-Shibli was asked about gnosis, he answered, "The first of it is God Most High and its last has no end."

Abu Hafs said, "Since I have attained gnosis, neither truth nor falsehood has entered my heart." This expression of Abu Hafs is not easily understood. He indicates, most probably, that in the Sufi's view gnosis causes the servant to be absent from his self because he is overwhelmed by His remembrance and so does not see other-than-God (Glorious and Majestic), nor does he have recourse to other-than-Him. Just as the intelligent man has recourse to his heart and his reflective and retentive faculties concerning thoughts that come to his mind or states he encounters, the gnostic's recourse is to his Lord. If a person is occupied with his Lord alone, he has no recourse to his heart. Furthermore, how might the matter enter the heart of one who has no heart? There is a difference between the one who lives by means of his heart and the one who lives by means of his Lord. When asked about gnosis, Abu Yazid replied, "Kings, when they enter a country, corrupt it and make the noblest of its people its meanest" (27:34). This is the meaning Abu Hafs intends.

Abu Yazid observed, "Mankind has states, but the gnostic has none. His human traits are effaced, and his essence has passed away into the essence of another. His traits are gone because the traits of another have taken their place." Al-Wasiti said, "Gnosis is not sound while there remain in the servant satisfaction with God and need of Him." By this al-Wasiti intends that need and satisfaction are signs of sobriety in the servant and of the abiding of his traits, need and satisfaction being among his traits, but the gnostic is effaced in the object of his gnosis. How might his gnosis be sound, while he is consumed in His existence or immersed in witnessing Him, but has not totally attained existence and is still separated by awareness of whatever attributes he may have? For this reason al-Wasiti also said, "Whoever has direct knowledge of God is cut off; he is rendered mute and impotent." The Prophet (may God's blessing and peace be upon him) declared, "I cannot praise You enough." This refers to those whose goal is far away. As for those who are content with something more easily attainable, they have spoken about gnosis at greater or lesser length.

Ahmad b. 'Asim al-Antaki said, "The more one knows God, the more one fears Him." One of the Sufis stated, "Whoever knows God Most High is pained by his [own] existence, and the earth, for all its spaciousness, becomes confining for him." It is said, "Whoever knows God, living is joyous for him and life is pleasant for him; all things stand in awe of him, he fears nothing among created beings, and he becomes intimate with God Most High." It is said, "Whoever knows God, desire for things leaves him, and he is neither detached from them nor attach to them." It is also said, "Gnosis brings about shame and glorification of God, just as asserting the divine unity brings about satisfaction and submission to God."

Ruwaym commented, "Gnosis is the gnostic's mirror. When he gazes in it, his Master is shown." Dhu'n-Nun al-Misri related, "The spirits of all the prophets raced in the plain of gnosis, and the spirit of our Prophet [may God's blessing and peace be upon him] led them all [peace be upon them] to the meadow of union." He also said, "The conduct of the gnostic [toward others] is like the conduct of God Most High—he endures you and is forebearing with you because he imitates the characteristics of God." Ibn Yazdanyar was asked, "When does the gnostic witness God [may He be exalted]?" He answered, "When the Witness is manifested, the means of witnessing pass away, the senses depart, and sincerity dissolves."

Al-Husayn b. Mansur said, "When the servant reaches the station of gnosis, God makes even his stray thoughts a means of inspiration, and He guards his innermost being lest thoughts of other-than-Him occur there." He also observed, "The sign of the gnostic is that he is empty both of this world and of the Hereafter." Sahl b. 'Abdallah declared, "The utmost degree of gnosis is dismay and perplexity." Dhu'n-Nun al-Misri asserted, "The ones who know God the most are those whose bewilderment concerning Him is greatest."

A man told al-Junayd, "There are some among the gnostics who say, 'Abandonment of any kind of activity is a part of righteousness and piety.'" Al-Junayd replied, "These are the ones who propound suspension of [all] works, which is a serious error in my opinion. The thief and the adulterer have better states than they, for the gnostics obtain the works from God Most High and they return by means of them to God. If I were to live a thousand years, I would never reduce performing works of righteousness by one atom."

It was asked of AbuYazid, "By what means did you attain this gnosis?" He responded, "By a hungry stomach and a naked body." Abu Ya'qub an-Nahrajuri related, "I inquired of Abu Ya'qub as-Susi, 'Does the gnostic grieve over anything other than God [Glorious and Majestic]?' He retorted, 'And does he perceive anything other than Him over which he might grieve?' So I asked, 'Then with what eye does he see things?' He answered, 'With the eye of passing away and extinction.'"

Abu Yazid said, "The gnostic flies and the ascetic travels afoot." It is said, "The gnostic's eye weeps, but his heart laughs." Al-Junayd declared, "A man will not be a gnostic until he is like the earth—both the righteous and the sinner tread on it—and until he is like the clouds—they shade all things—and until he is like the rain—it waters all things, whether it loves them or not." Yahya b. Mu'adh stated, "The gnostic leaves the world without having fulfilled his aim in two things: weeping over himself and praising his Lord [Glorious and Majestic]."

Abu Zayd said, "They attain gnosis only by forfeiting what they have and remaining with what He has." Yusuf b. 'Ali asserted, "A man will not be a true gnostic until, if he were given Solomon's kingdom [peace be upon him], it would not take his attention away from God for one instant." Ibn 'Ata' explained, "Gnosis is built on three pillars: awe, shame, and intimacy." Dhu'n-Nun al-Misri was asked, "By what means do you know your Lord?" He replied, "I know my Lord by my Lord. If it were not for my Lord, I would not know my Lord." It is said, "The scholar is a source of imitation, and the gnostic is a source of guidance." Ash-Shibli observed, "The gnostic does not look to anything other than Him, does not speak by the speech of anything other than Him, and does not perceive any protector for himself other than God Most High."

It is said, "The gnostic gains intimacy with His remembrance, and flees in terror from His creation. He is in need of God, and God makes him independent of His creation. He is humble toward God, He ennobles him among His creation." Abu't-Tayyib as-Samarri stated, "Gnosis is the rising of the Truth [like the sun] over the innermost being by means of a continuous effusion of light."

It is said, "The gnostic is more than what he says, and the scholar is less than what he says." Abu Sulayman ad-Darani observed, "God Most High reveals for the gnostic in his bed what He does not reveal for another who stands in prayer." Al-Junayd declared, "God speaks out of the innermost being of the gnostic while he is silent." Dhu'n-Nun stated, "For everyone there is a [certain form] of punishment, and the punishment of the gnostic is being cut off from His remembrance." Ruwaym said, "The hypocrisy of the gnostic is better than the sincerity of the seekers." Abu Bakr al-Warraq commented, "The silence of the gnostic is most beneficial, and his speech is best and most pleasant." Dhu'n-Nun asserted, "Even though ascetics are kings in the Hereafter, in comparison to the gnostics, they are beggars."

When al-Junayd was asked about the gnostic, he replied, "The color of the water is the color of its container." That is, the nature of the gnostic is always determined by the nature of his state at a given moment. Abu Yazid was asked about the gnostic. He said, "He sees nothing other than God in his sleep and nothing other than God in his waking hours. He does not conform to other-than-God, and he does not look to other-than-God."

One of the sheikhs was asked, "By what means do you know God Most High?" He answered, "By a burst of light that flashes through the tongue of one who is taken away from normal modes of discernment and by a word that flows on the tongue of one who is destined to perish and be lost. This speaker points to a clear ecstasy and relates an obscure secret; he is himself by virtue of what he reveals, and other than himself by virtue of what he leaves obscure." Then the sheikh recited:

> *You spoke without speech. This is the true speech,*
> *"Speech belongs to You whether verbal or distinct from speech.*
> *You appeared when before You had been hidden.*
> *You made a lighting flash appear to me, making me speak."*

When asked about the sign of the gnostic, Abu Turab explained, "He is not made impure by anything, and all things are by him made pure." Abu 'Uthman al-Maghribi said, "The lights of knowledge shine for the gnostic, so he sees by knowledge wondrous things of the unseen." The master Abu 'Ali ad-Daqqaq declared, "The gnostic is drowned in the seas of inner reality. As one of the Sufis has said, 'Gnosis is like the surging waves—they raise up and they set down.'" Yahya b. Mu'adh was asked about the gnostic, and he replied,

"He is a man who is both with creation and separated from it." Another time he said, "First he was; then he separated." Dhu'n-Nun al-Misri observed, "There are three signs of the gnostic: the light of his gnosis does not block out the light of his abstemiousness; he does not believe in any inward knowledge that contradicts an outward ordinance; and the abundance of the blessings of God [Glorious and Majestic] upon him does not impel him to rend the veils that cover God's hidden sanctity."

It is said, "The one who speaks of gnosis in the presence of people attached to the Hereafter is not a gnostic, and he would be even less a gnostic if he were to speak about gnosis in the presence of people attached to this world." Abu Sa'id al-Kharraz stated, "Gnosis comes from an eye that weeps abundantly and from expending effort."

When asked about the words of Dhu'n-Nun al-Misri concerning the sign of the gnostic, "He was here but now he has gone," al-Junayd replied, "One state does not hold the gnostic back from another state and one station does not veil him from changing stations. Thus he is with the people of every place just as they are, he experiences whatever they experience, and he speaks their language so that they might benefit by his speech." Muhammad b. al-Fadl stated, "Gnosis is the heart's life with God." Abu Sa'id al-Kharraz was asked, "Does the gnostic end in a state wherein he never weeps?" He affirmed, "Yes. Weeping belongs to the time they are traveling to God. When they dismount and halt in the inner realities of nearness and experience the taste of attaining this favor, they no longer weep."

42

Love

❧ Mahabba

God Most High says, "O you who believe, whoever among you turns away from his religion, [know that in his stead] God will bring forth a people He loves and who love Him" (5:54).

On the authority of Abu Hurayra, the Messenger of God (may God's blessing and peace be upon him) said, "He who loves to meet God, God will love to meet him. And he who does not love to meet God, God will not love to meet him."

On the authority of Anas b. Malik, the Messenger of God (may God's blessing and peace be upon him) is said to have related that Gabriel (peace be upon him) told that his Lord (Glorious and Majestic) said, "Whoever harms one of My saints has called forth My battle against him. I hesitate in doing nothing as I hesitate to take the soul of My believing servant, for he abhors death, and I abhor harming him, but there is no escape from it. A servant best draws near to Me by performing the obligations I have enjoined on him. He continues to draw near to Me by means of supererogatory acts of worship until I love him. For him whom I love, I become his ear, his eye, his hand, and his support."

On the authority of Abu Hurayra, the Prophet (may God's blessing and peace be upon him) is said to have declared, "When God [Glorious and Majestic] loves one of His servants, He says to Gabriel, 'O Gabriel, I love this person, so you, too love him.' Gabriel then loves him, and he calls out to the other angels, 'God Most High loves this person, so you, too, love him.' Then the other angels love him and he is accepted by men on earth." Malik stated, "I believe that he [the Prophet] said something similar concerning God's dislike for a servant."

Love is a noble state that God has confirmed as a quality belonging to the servant, and He has made known His love for the servant. So God (Glorious and Majestic) is characterized as loving the servant, and the servant is characterized as loving God.

It is the scholars' opinion that love means volition or desire. But the Sufis mean something other than simple desire when they speak of love. Desire cannot be attributed to the Eternal unless, by using that term, one means desire for bringing man near to God and for honoring Him. We will go into this matter briefly in order to substantiate the Sufis' opinions, if God wills.

God's love for the servant is His desire to bestow blessings specifically on a given servant, just as His mercy for him is His more general desire to bestow blessings. So mercy carries a more specific meaning than desire, and love carries a more specific meaning than mercy. God's desire to extend rewards and blessings to the servant is called "mercy," and His desire to confer nearness and exalted states on him is called "love." God's desire is one attribute that takes on different names according to the different acts to which it is connected. If it is connected with punishment, it is called "wrath." If it is connected to universally bestowed blessings, it is called " mercy." If it is connected with particularly bestowed blessings, it is called "love."

Some people say, "God's love for the servant consists of His praising him and commending him in goodly terms." The meaning of God's love for the servant, according to this view, comes back to His speech, and His speech is eternal.

Other people say, "God's love for the servant consists of the attributes of His acting, being a specific manifestation of goodness by means of which the servant encounters God and a specific state to which He causes the servant to ascend." As one of them has explained, "God's mercy toward the servant consists of His conferring blessings upon him."

A party of the early generation of Muslims stated, "God's mercy is an attribute mentioned in hadith." They use the word, but they refrain from interpreting it.

In addition to the preceding possibilities for the meaning of God's love for the servant are the kinds of love experienced among mankind, such as: having affection for something, feeling an intimate liking for something, or feeling what a human lover feels for his beloved. But the Eternal God (may He be glorified) is exalted above all this.

As for the servant's love of God, it is a state experienced in his heart, too subtle for words. This state brings him to glorify God and to try to gain His pleasure. He has little patience in separation from Him, feels an urgent longing for him, finds no comfort in anything other than Him, and experiences intimacy in his heart by making continual remembrance of Him. The servant's love for God does not imply affection or enjoyment [in the human sense]. How could this be when the essence of God's eternal subsistence is exalted beyond all attainment, perception, and comprehension? Describing the lover as annihilated in the Beloved is more fitting than describing him as having enjoyment of Him. There is no clearer or more understandable description of love than love [itself]. One engages in lengthy discussion of the matter only when difficulties appear, but once obscurity and ambiguity depart, there is no need to plunge into the interpretation of words.

People have spoken much on love and speculated on its etymology. It is said, "Love *[hubb]* is a name for the purest kind of love and affection because the Arabs say of someone's pure white teeth, *'habab al-asnan.'*" It is said, *"Hubab* are the bubbles that form on the water's surface during a strong rainstorm, so 'love' *[mahabba]* is the bubbling up of the heart when it thirsts and is desperate to meet the beloved." It is also said, *"Habab al-ma'* is the topmost water level. Love is named *'mahabba'* because it is the foremost concern of the heart." It is said, "'Love' is so named because one says *'ahabba'* to describe the state of a camel when it kneels down and refuses to stand up again. Just so, the lover *muhibb* will not move his heart away from remembering his beloved *[mahbub].*" It is said, "'Love' *[hubb]* is taken from *'hibb'* meaning 'earring.' On this a poet has said:

> *Her snake-like tresses flicking their tongues*
> *spent the night*
> *Next to the earring listening to secrets.*

The earring is called *'bibb'* either because of its fixed position in the ear or because of the way it jangles about. Both senses are true of love also."

It is claimed, "'Love' comes from *'habb'* [seeds, singular *habba*], and *habbat al-qalb* [the seed of the heart] is that which sustains it. Thus 'love' [*hubb*] is so named because it is lodged in the *habbat al-qalb*." It is said, "The words for seeds and love [*habb* and *hubb*] are [only spelling variations of the same meaning,] like the words for 'lifespan' (*'amr* and *'umr*)." It is also said, "'Love' is taken from *'hibba,'* meaning the seeds of of wilderness. Love is called *'hubb'* because it is the seed of life, just as *'habb'* means the seeds of the plants." It is said, "'*Hubb*' are the four planks on which the water jug is set. Love is called *'hubb'* because it bears the burdens of glory and disgrace that come in the path of seeking the beloved." It is also said, "'Love' comes from *'hibb'* (water jar) because it holds water, and when it is full, there is no space for anything else. Just so, when the heart is full of love, there is no space in it for anything other than the beloved."

The sayings of the sheikhs on love are many. One of the Sufis declared, "Love is perpetual turning toward the Beloved with a heart distraught with love." It is said, "Love means preferring the Beloved to all that is familiar." It is said, "Love means that the lover conforms to the Beloved's wishes whether present with Him or absent away from Him." It is said, "Love is effacement by the lover of his attributes and the affirmation of the Beloved in His essence." It is said, "Love is the heart's agreement with the wishes of the Lord." It is also said, "Love means that a person is afraid lest he stop being reverent when he performs a service."

Abu Yazid al-Bistami commented, "Love is to think nothing of the great amount that comes from yourself and to regard as plentiful the small amount that comes from your Beloved." Sahl remarked, "Love means embracing obedience [to the Beloved] and parting from disobedience [to Him]." When al-Junayd was asked about love, he observed, "It means that the lover takes on the Beloved's attributes in place of his own." He points out here how the lover's heart is seized with remembrance of the Beloved until nothing remains there but remembrance of the Beloved's attributes, until the lover is heedless and unaware of his own attributes.

Abu 'Ali ar-Rudhbari stated, "Love is conformity [to the wishes of the Beloved]." Abu 'Abdallah al-Qurashi declared, "The inner reality of love means that you give all of yourself to the One you love until nothing remains of you for you." Ash-Shibli explained, "Love is called 'mahabba' because it obliterates everything but the Beloved from the heart." Ibn 'Ata' said, "Love means inviting unending reproach."

The master Abu 'Ali ad-Daqqaq (may God grant him mercy) asserted, "Love is a sweetness, but its inner reality is bewilderment." He also said, "Passionate love ['ishq] is exceeding all limits in *mahabba*. God [may He be exalted] cannot be described as exceeding limits, so He cannot be characterized as possessing passionate love for anything. If the love of all mankind were joined together in one man, this would not come close to the measure of love due to God. Let it not be said, 'This person has exceeded all limits in the love of God.' God cannot be described as having the quality of passionate love, nor can the servant be described as having it in his relation to God. Passionate love cannot be used [as a description of the relations between man and God] because there is no way for it to be related to God, either from Him toward the servant or from the servant to God."

Ash-Shibli remarked, "Love means that you are jealous for the Beloved lest one like yourself love Him." When asked about love, Ibn 'Ata' answered, "It is small saplings planted in the heart that bear fruit according to the ability of the intellect." An-Nasrabadhi commented, "One kind of love prevents bloodshed, and another kind causes it." Samnun observed, "The lovers of God have carried off nobility in this world and in the Hereafter, for the Prophet [may God's blessing and peace be upon him] has said, 'A person is with the one he loves, and they are with God Most High.'" Yahya b. Mu'adh declared, "The inner reality of love means that it will not decrease when one experiences hardships, nor will it increase when one is shown kindness." He also said, "One who claims to love God is a liar as long as he disregards His limits." Al-Junayd asserted, "If one's love is sound, the stipulations of correct behavior fall away." The Master Abu 'Ali ad-Daqqaq composed the following on this saying of al-Junayd:

> *If the affection among a people is pure,*
> *And love long lasting among them, the*
> *exchange of praise is odious.*

Al-Junayd also used to say, "You will never see a kindly father address his son with deference. While the rest of the people use courteous formulae in addressing the son, the father says, 'O so and so!'"

Al-Kattani said, "Love is preferring the Beloved [over oneself]." Bundar b. al-Husayn related, "Someone saw Majnun of the Banu 'Amir in his sleep and asked him, 'What has God done with you?' Majnun replied, 'He has forgiven me, and He has appointed me to be proof over the lovers.'" Abu Ya'qub as-Susi stated, "The inner reality of love is that the servant forget both his destined portion from God and his needs of Him [in this world]."

Al-Husayn b. Mansur observed, "The inner reality of love is that you remain always with your Beloved and strip off your own qualities." Someone told an-Nasrabadhi, "[They say] you have not experienced love." He answered, "They are correct. But I do have their sorrows, and in that I am inflamed." He also said, "Love is the avoidance of forgetfulness in all circumstances." Then he recited:

> *One whose passion is prolonged tastes a kind*
> *of forgetting,*
> *But I experience no taste of forgetfulness of*
> *Layla.*
> *The closest I came to union with her*
> *Consisted of wishes that did not come true,*
> *passing like lightning.*

Muhammad b. al-Fadl said, "Love means that all loves but love of the Lover fall away from the heart." Al-Junayd declared, "Love is intense striving [for the Beloved] with no attainment." It is said, "Love is a disturbance the Beloved places in the hearts." It is also said, "Love is a great tumult placed in the hearts by the One they desire." Ibn 'Ata' recited:

> *I planted a branch of desire for the people of love*
> > *And not one knew, before me, what desire was.*
> *It sprouted branches, and sensual longing ripened*
> > *And left me with a bitter taste from the sweet fruits.*
> *The desire of all the passionate lovers,*
> > *If they were to trace it, comes from that source.*

It is said, "The beginning of love is deception, and its end is murder."

The master Abu 'Ali ad-Daqqaq (may God grant him mercy) commented on the tradition of the Prophet (may God's blessing and peace be upon him) "Your love for something makes you blind and deaf" by saying, "It blinds one to the other out of jealously and to the Beloved out of awe." Then he recited:

> *If His overpowering greatness had not appeared to me,*
> > *I would have been sent back in the state of one who had never arrived.*

Al-Harith al-Muhasibi explained, "Love is to incline to a thing with your whole being, then to prefer it over your own soul, your spirit, or your property, then to be in harmonious accord with it, inwardly and outwardly, then to know that even after all this, you are still deficient in your love for it." As-Sari stated, "Love between two is not complete until one can say to the other, 'O, I.'" Ash-Shibli observed, "The lover is destroyed if he is silent, but the gnostic is destroyed if he is not." It is said, "Love is a fire in the heart that burns up all but the Beloved's wishes." It is also said, "Love is tremendous effort while the Lover does as He wishes." An-Nuri remarked, "Love means tearing down the veils and exposing the secrets."

Abu Ya'qub as-Susi said, "Love is true only when one has gone from being aware of love to being aware of the Beloved by forgetting the science of love." Al-Junayd related, "As-Sari gave me a slip of paper and said, 'This will be better for you than seven hundred pious stories or elevating traditions.' On it was written:

> *When I claimed I loved her, she said, 'You lie to me,'*
> *For what am I to do when I see your plump and fine limbs?*
> *There can be no love until the heart clings to the entrails*
> *And you wither until there is naught to answer the caller,*
> *And you are wasted away until no passion remains*
> *Other than the eye that weeps and that whispers to me your secret."*

334

Ibn Masruq commented, "I was present when Samnun was speaking on love and all the lamps in the mosque shattered." Ibrahim b. Fatik related, "I was listening to Samnun speak about love one time in the mosque when a small bird came and moved toward him. It came closer and closer until it sat on his hand. Then it pounded its beak on the floor until blood flowed out of its beak and it died."

Al-Junayd explained, "All love is for one purpose. If this purpose were to cease, love too would cease." It is said that a group of men came to visit ash-Shibli when he was confined to the lunatic asylum. He asked, "Who are you?" They replied, "We are men who love you, O Abu Bakr!" Then he started to pelt them with rocks, and they fled. He asserted, "If you really loved me, then be patient through my testing you." He recited:

> *O dear noble sir, love for you is lodged in my entrails.*
> *O you who lifts sleep from my eyelids, you know all that befalls me.*

Yahya b. Mu'adh wrote to Abu Yazid saying, "I am drunk from the long draught I drank from the cup of His love." Abu Yazid wrote back, "Someone else drank the seas of heavens and earth and his thirst is not quenched. His tongue is hanging out and he is pleading, 'Is there no more?'" They recite:

> *I am amazed at one who says, "I make re-membrance of my love."*
> *How might I forget and so have something to remember?*

> *I die, but when I remember You, I live.*
>> *If it were not for my hopes of You I would not live.*
> *I live by my desires, and I die out of longing.*
>> *How many times I have lived through hope for You, and how many times I have died!*
> *I drank cup after cup of love,*
>> *But the cup kept brimming over and my thirst remained.*

It is said that God Most High revealed to Jesus (peace be upon him), "If I look into someone's heart and I find no love there for this world or for the afterlife, I fill it up with My love."

I saw the following written by the master Abu 'Ali ad-Daqqaq: "One of the revealed books says, 'O My servant, You have a right to My love, so it is My right that you love Me!'"

'Abdallah b. al-Mubarak declared, "Whoever is granted a portion of love but not the same amount of fear has been deceived." It is said, "Love blots out all traces of yourself from you." And it is said, "Love is a drunken state; sobriety comes only by seeing the Beloved. But then the drunkenness that comes from seeing the Beloved is beyond description."

They recite:

> *The cup was passed around, and they became drunk,*
>> *But my intoxication comes from the cup-bearer.*

The master Abu 'Ali ad-Daqqaq would often recite:

> *I enjoy two states of drunkenness while my*
> *fellow drinkers have but one.*
> *It is only I among them who is favored so.*

Ibn 'Ata' said, "Love means inviting constant reproach."

The master Abu 'Ali had a slave named Fayruz whom he loved because she served him so long. He told me, "Fayruz insulted me one day, saying rude and nasty things to me. Abu'l-Hasan al-Qari' asked her, 'Why are you vexing the sheikh?' She answered, 'Because I love him.'" Yahya b. Mu'adh stated, "I would rather have a mustard seed's worth of love than seventy years of worship performed without love." It is said that a young man looked down at the people gathered on the festival day and recited:

> *Let he who would die a lover die like this.*
> *There is nothing good in love without death.*

Then he threw himself from the balcony and fell to the ground, dead.

It is related that a man from India had a passionate love for his slave girl. On the day she left him, he came out to bid her farewell. Tears fell from one of his eyes, but not from the other. For eighty-four years he held the eye that had remained dry shut to punish it for not weeping when his beloved left. Concerning this the Sufis recite:

> *My eye shed tears the morning we parted,*
> *But the miserly eye refused to weep.*

> *So I punished that miserly eye*
> *By closing it shut the day we bade each*
> *other farewell.*

One of the Sufis said, "One day when we were talking with Dhu'n-Nun al-Misri about love, he demanded, 'Leave off this talk lest others hear you and claim to [know] love.'" Then he recited:

> *Fear is fit for the evildoer when he moans, and*
> *sorrow,*
> *While love befits the pious and those utterly*
> *pure.*

Yahya b. Mu'adh remarked, "Anyone who spreads love among those who are strangers to it is an imposter in his claims." It is said that a man claimed he loved a certain boy. The boy said to him once, "How can you love me when my brother is finer and more beautiful than I?" The man raised up his head, looking around for the brother. They were on a roof, and the boy threw the man off it, saying, "Here is just reward for one who claims to love me and then looks for another!"

Samnun gave precedence to love over gnosis, but most of the Sufis give precedence to gnosis over love. In the view of those who have attained inner truths, love is being consumed in a state of sweetness, and gnosis is witnessing in a state of perplexity and effacement in awe.

Abu Bakr al-Kattani related, "The question of love was being discussed among the sheikhs in Mecca during the pilgrimage season. Al-Junayd was the youngest one present. They called on him one time, saying, 'O 'Iraqi, tell us what you have to say.' He bowed his head and wept; then he replied, 'Love is a servant who leaves his soul behind and attaches himself to making remembrance of his Lord, establishing himself in performing God's injunctions with constant awareness of Him in his heart. The lights of His essence inflame his heart and he partakes of the pure drink of the cup of His love. The Omnipotent One is revealed to him from behind the veils of His unseen realms, so when he speaks, he speaks by means of God and what he says is of God. When he moves, it is by means of God's command, and when he is still, then it is to be with God. He acts by means of God, he belongs to God, he is with God.' At this the sheikhs all wept, asserting, 'There is no more to say. May God strengthen you, O crown of the gnostics!'"

It is said that God Most High revealed to David (peace be upon him), "I have forbidden that love for Me come into men's hearts while love for other-than-Me has a place therein." Abu'l-'Abbas, the servant of al-Fudayl b. 'Iyad, related, "Al-Fudayl suffered one time from retention of urine. He raised his hands and prayed, 'Oh my God, by my love for You, release this from me.' No sooner did we rise to leave than he was cured."

I heard the master Abu 'Ali ad-Daqqaq say that love means preferring another to oneself, as was the case with Potiphar's wife when she renounced what she had done, explaining, "I asked an evil act of him while Joseph is a truthful man" (12:51). Earlier she had said [confronting her husband after she had tried to seduce Joseph], "What is the recompense for one who wished evil for your wife, save prison or harsh punishment?" (12:25). So at first she charged Joseph with the sin, but in the end she blamed herself for this treachery.

Abu Sa'id al-Kharraz reported, "I saw the Prophet [may God's blessing and peace be upon him] in my sleep and said to him, 'O Messenger of God, please forgive me. My love for God has filled me and left me no room for loving you.' He replied, 'Blessings be upon you. Whoever loves God loves me.'"

It is said that Rabi'a asked in her private prayer, "O my God, will You burn in the Fire a heart that holds love for You?" To this an invisible caller answered, "We will never do such a thing. Do not think so poorly of Us."

It is said, "The word 'love' *[hubb]* is composed of the two letters *ha'* and *ba'*, which indicates that the lover leaves behind his own spirit *[ruh]* and body *[badan]*." As the generally accepted opinion among the Sufis states, love is harmonious conformity [to the Beloved], and the hardest way in this is by the heart. Love itself ends separation, so that the lover is constantly with his Beloved. On this point is the tradition on the authority of Abu Musa al-Ash'ari that someone asked the Prophet (may God's blessing and peace be upon him), "Can a man love a certain people and not be joined with them?" The Prophet replied, "A man is with the one he loves."

Abu Hafs asserted, "Corrupt states arise mostly from the following: sinfulness of the gnostics, betrayal of the lovers [of God], and lying of the initiates."

Abu 'Uthman declared, "The sinfulness of the gnostics is making use of their speech, sight, and hearing in the service of worldly causes and gaining benefit from this. The betrayal of the lovers [of God] is choosing their own desires over the pleasure of God [Glorious and Majestic] in their affairs. The lying of the initiates is that they are more concerned with being aware of and attentive to men than they are to remembrance of God."

Abu ʿAli Mamshad b. Saʿid al-ʿUkbari related, "A male swallow tried to seduce a female swallow under the dome of Solomon [peace be upon him], but she refused him. He asked her, 'How is it that you refuse me when, if I wished, I could make this dome collapse on Solomon?' Solomon called for him to come and demanded, 'Whatever made you say such a thing?' The swallow answered, 'O Prophet of God, the things that lovers say cannot be held against them.' Solomon replied, 'You have spoken truly.'"

43

Longing

❧ Shawq

God Most High says, "For those who hope for the meeting with God, [let them know] the time is surely coming" (29:5).

'Ata' b. as-Sa'ib related that his father told him, "'Ammar b. Yasir led us in the prayer one time and made it very short. I remarked, 'You have been short in the prayer, Abu'l-Yaqzan.' He answered, 'There is no fault in this because I offered to God a supplication I heard from the Messenger of God [may God's blessing and peace be upon him].' When he got up to leave, one of the men followed him, asking about this supplication. He repeated it: 'O God, by Your knowledge of the Unseen and by Your power over all creation, give me life as long as You know that life holds goodness for me and end my life when You know that death holds goodness for me. O God, I ask You that I may be fearful of You in all matters, known and unknown. I ask You for [the ability to speak] just words when I am pleased and when I am angry. I ask You for moderation in wealth and in poverty. I ask You for unending tranquillity and happiness. I ask You for contentment with whatever is determined for me [in this world], and I ask You for a blessed life after death. I ask to be able to gaze upon Your sublime countenance. I ask You for longing to meet You without coming to harm or [being prey to] delusive temptations. O God, adorn us with the beauty of faith. O God, make us [both] guides and guided.'"

Longing is a state of commotion in the heart hoping for meeting the Beloved. [The depth of] longing is commensurate with the servant's love of God. The master Abu 'Ali ad-Daqqaq distinguished between longing *(shawq)* and ardent desire *(ishtiyaq)*: longing is assuaged by meeting God and looking upon Him, but ardent desire continues even after the meeting has taken place. Concerning this the Sufis recite:

> *The eye never turns away when seeing Him*
> *Without returning immediately to Him*
> *filled with desire.*

An-Nasrabadhi declared, "All people possess the station of longing, but not all of them possess the station of ardent desire. Whoever enters the state of ardent desire becomes so absorbed in it that no trace or impression of him remains."

It is said that Ahmad b. Hamid al-Aswad came to 'Abdallah b. Munazil one day and told him, "I dreamed that you will die after one year. Perhaps you should prepare for death." 'Abdallah b. Munazil replied, "You have given me quite a long time to live, a full year! I have always had a liking for this verse I heard from Abu 'Ali ath-Thaqafi:

> *Oh you who suffer from longing because of
> your long separation,
> Have patience. You might meet the One you
> love tomorrow."*

Abu 'Uthman stated, "The mark of longing is a peaceful love of death." Yahya b. Mu'adh observed, "The mark of longing is weaning the body of passions."

The master Abu 'Ali ad-Daqqaq related, "David [peace be upon him] went out alone into the desert one day, where God Most High revealed to him, 'O David, how is it that I find you here alone?' He responded, 'O God, my longing to meet You has consumed my heart, I cannot be with men!' So God Most High said to him, 'Go back to them. If you guide only one servant who has strayed back to Me, I will imprint your name on the Preserved Tablet as a great sage.'"

It is said that a young man belonging to the family of an old woman returned home after a journey. All the rest of the family was overjoyed, but the old woman cried. They asked her, "Why do you cry?" She answered, "This young man's homecoming reminds me of the day we will return to God Most High."

When Ibn 'Ata' was asked about longing he said, "Entrails burn, hearts blaze, and livers are cut into shreds." He was asked another time, "Is longing or love more exalted?" He replied, "Love, because longing is born of love." One of the Sufis declared, "Longing is a flame that is ignited in the entrails; it appears of separation [from God]. When reunion takes place, the flame dies out, and if witness of the Beloved predominates over one's innermost being, longing will not announce itself." One of the Sufis was asked, "Do you long for God?" He responded, "No. Longing is only for one who is absent, and He is present." The master Abu 'Ali ad-Daqqaq commented, concerning the words of God (Glorious and Majestic) "[Moses said] I hastened to You, O my Lord, to please You" (20:84), "He means, 'I hastened to You out of longing for You,' and he hid this by saying, 'to please You.'" Abu 'Ali (may God grant him mercy) also stated, "One of the signs of longing is the desire for death in times of good health and spirit. This was the case with Joseph [peace be upon him]. When he was thrown into the well, he did not say [to God], 'Let me die!' When he was put in prison, he did not say, 'Let me die!' But when his parents came to him and all his relations fell down before him in prostration, and he was granted dominion and blessings, he said, 'Let me die, as a Muslim (12:101).'" On this the Sufis recite the following:

> We live in perfect joy,
>   But only through you is joy perfected.
> The blemish remaining, O people of my love,
>   Is that you are absent and we are present.

And they also recite:

> Who can be gladdened by this festival
>   For I feel no happiness this day.
> My joy would be complete
>   Only if my loved ones were near to me.

Ibn Khafif observed, "Longing is the heart's delight that comes of ecstasy and of love for meeting [God] by being near [to Him]."

Abu Yazid said, "God has certain servants who, if He were not to allow them vision of Him, would cry out for deliverance from Paradise just as the denizens of Hell cry out for deliverance from the fire." Al-Husayn al-Ansari related, "I dreamed that the Day of Resurrection had come. There was someone standing beneath the Divine Throne. God [may He be exalted] asked, 'O My angels, who is this?' The angels replied, 'You know best.' He said, 'This is Ma'ruf al-Karkhi. He is drunk with love for Me; he will become sober only by meeting Me.'" Another telling of this same dream goes, "'This is Ma'ruf al-Karkhi. He left the world longing for God.' So God allowed him to gaze upon Him."

Faris asserted, "The hearts of those filled with longing are illumined with the light of God Most High. When their longing stirs within them, that light radiates throughout the heavens and earth, and God shows them to the angels, saying, 'These are the ones who long for Me. I call you to bear witness that I long for them even more than this.'"

The master Abu 'Ali ad-Daqqaq explained, concerning the words of the Prophet (may God's blessing and peace be upon him) "I ask You for longing to meet You," "Longing was composed of one hundred parts. The Prophet possessed ninety-nine of these, and one part was divided among mankind. He wanted that part also, for he was jealous lest a portion of longing be given to another."

It is said, "The people who enjoy nearness to God possess a more complete longing for Him than those who are veiled from Him." Thus it is said:

The worst of all things is desire on a day
When the tents draw near the tents.

It is also said, "The ones filled with longing feel naught but sweetness at the advent of death, because the joy of attaining [their Beloved] has been revealed to them as sweeter than honey." As-Sari stated, "Longing is the greatest station for the gnostic. When he attains longing, he becomes oblivious to everything that might turn him away from the object of his longing."

Concerning the words of God Most High "For those who hope for the meeting with God [let them know] the time is surely coming" (29:5), Abu 'Uthman al-Hiri observed, "This is said to comfort the ones filled with longing. It means 'I know that your longing for Me is overwhelming. I have appointed a time for your meeting with Me. You will soon come to the One for Whom you long.'" It is said that God Most High revealed to David (peace be upon him), "Say to the youth of the Children of Israel: 'Why do you concern yourselves with other-than-Me when I long for you? This is a grave injustice.'" It is said that He also revealed to David, "If those who have turned their backs on Me knew how I wait for them, bestow kindnesses on them, and long for them to quit their disobedience to Me, they would perish from longing for Me, and their joints would melt for love of Me. O David, this is My way with those who have turned their backs on Me—imagine what My way is with those who turn toward Me!" It is said that it is written in the Torah, "We aroused longing in you, but you have not longed for Us. We instilled fear in you, but you do not fear Us. We lament for you, but you do not lament." The master Abu 'Ali ad-Daqqaq related, "Shu'ayb wept one time until he went blind. God [Glorious and Majestic] gave him back his sight. He wept again until he went blind. God gave him back his sight. Again he wept until he went blind, and God gave him back his sight. Then God revealed to him, 'If your weeping is for Paradise, then rest assured that I have permitted you to enter it. If it is because of Hell, then rest assured that I have made you safe from it.' Shu'ayb replied, 'It is not for these reasons. It is because of my longing for You.' God revealed to him, 'Because of this, I appoint My prophet and interlocutor [Moses] to serve you for ten years.'" It is said, "Whoever longs for God, all things long for him." There is a tradition that states, "Paradise longs for three men: 'Ali, 'Ammar, and Salman." One of the sheikhs declared, "I go into the bazaar, and the goods long for me. But I am free of them all."

Malik b. Dinar stated, "I read in the Torah, 'We aroused longing in you, but you did not long for Us. We played the flute for you, but you did not dance.'"

Al-Junayd was asked, "What makes the lover weep when he meets the Beloved?" He answered, "This is only because of his great joy over Him and because of the ecstasy born of his great longing for Him. I have heard the story of two brothers who embraced [after a long separation]. One of them cried, 'Ah, what longing!' The other responded, 'Ah, what ecstasy!'"

INDEX